Communications
in Computer and Information Science 432

Didar Zowghi   Zhi Jin (Eds.)

Requirements Engineering

First Asia Pacific
Requirements Engineering Symposium, APRES 2014
Auckland, New Zealand, April 28-29, 2014
Proceedings

 Springer

Volume Editors

Didar Zowghi
University of Technology, Sydney (UTS)
Faculty of Engineering and Information Technology
Sydney, NSW, Australia
E-Mail: didar.zowghi@uts.edu.au

Zhi Jin
Peking University
Department of Computer Science
School of Electronics Engineering and Computer Science
Beijing, China
E-Mail: zhijin@pku.edu.cn

ISSN 1865-0929   e-ISSN 1865-0937
ISBN 978-3-662-43609-7   e-ISBN 978-3-662-43610-3
DOI 10.1007/978-3-662-43610-3
Springer Heidelberg New York Dordrecht London

Library of Congress Control Number: 2014939036

Typesetting: Camera-ready by author, data conversion by Scientific Publishing Services, Chennai, India

Printed on acid-free paper

Springer is part of Springer Science+Business Media (www.springer.com)

Preface

The inaugural Asia Pacific Requirements Engineering Symposium (APRES 2014) was held at the Auckland University of Technology (AUT), in the beautiful city of Auckland, in New Zealand during April 28–29, 2014. Requirements engineering (RE) has become a well-established discipline of research and practice in software and systems development. The importance of eliciting and documenting high-quality requirements and following effective RE practices has long been recognized by researchers and practitioners alike. The main aim of this initiative is to develop and expand the RE research and practice community specifically in the Asia Pacific region and to foster collaborations among researchers and practitioners in Asia, Australia, and New Zealand.

We sought submissions on all aspects of RE. In particular, papers that present novel ideas, methods, tools, and techniques for improving and enhancing RE products and processes. We were also interested in reflections on current industrial RE practices. A total of 30 submissions were received, of which 27 entered the review process (after discarding three papers, two were out of scope and one was an abstract only). Each paper was reviewed by three members of the APRES Program Committee. All the reviews were assessed for quality by the program chairs. Sixteen papers written by authors from ten different countries were selected for publication and were presented in four sessions.

This volume serves as a record of APRES 2014 proceedings but it also represents a snapshot of the state of RE research in the Asia Pacific region. We believe that these proceedings will be of interest to the entire RE community, whether students or experienced researchers.

We would like to express our gratitude to the Auckland University of Technology, especially the Software Engineering Research Lab (SERL), and its director Jim Buchan for hosting the inaugural APRES. We would also like to acknowledge the support provided by the Centre for Human Centred Technology Design Research from the University of Technology, Sydney (UTS).

April 2014

Didar Zowghi
Zhi Jin

Organization

General Chair

Jim Buchan Auckland University of Technology, New Zealand

Program Co-chairs

Didar Zowghi University of Technology, Sydney, Australia
Zhi Jin Peking University, China

Website Manager and Publicity Chair

Muneera Bano University of Technology, Sydney, Australia

Program Committee

Mikio Aoyama Nanzan University, Japan
Muhammad Ali Babar Adelaide University, Australia
Muneera Bano University of Technology, Sydney, Australia
Tony Clear Auckland University of Technology, New Zealand
Mohamed El-Attar King Fahd University of Petroleum and Minerals, Saudi Arabia
Smita Ghaisa Tata Research Design and Development Center, India
Aditya Ghose University of Wollongong, Australia
Asif Gill University of Technology, Sydney, Australia
John Grundy Swinburne University of Technology, Australia
Naveed Ikram Riphah International University, Pakistan
Massila Kamalrudin Universiti teknikal Malaysia Melaka, Malaysia
Seok-Won Lee Ajou University, South Korea
Lin Liu Tsinghua University, China
Stephen MacDonell University of Otago, New Zealand
Stuart Marshall Victoria University of Wellington, New Zealand
Mahmood Niazi King Fahd University of Petroleum and Minerals, Saudi Arabia

Table of Contents

A Process-Oriented Conceptual Framework on Non-Functional Requirements

Lianshan Sun[1] and Jaehong Park[2]

[1] Dept. of Comp. Sci., Shaanxi Univ. of Sci. & Tech., Xi'an, China, 710021
[2] Institute of Cyber Security, Univ. of Texas at San Antonio, TX, USA, 78249

Abstract. Non-Functional Requirements (NFR), as its emergence, is a buzzword that is mostly overused while remaining obscure. There is no consensus on what NFR is, how to identify NFR during software development, and what capabilities a desired NFR modeling approach should deliver. To this end, this paper proposes a process-oriented conceptual framework on NFR. It explicitly distinguishes NFR from application-independent domain knowledge, such as quality attributes, tactics, and various constraints, then defines NFR as the composition in specific contexts of domain knowledge and various system abstractions, which include not only the target system, but software models that conceptually define the target system at early stages of software development. Enlightened by the framework, we produce a checklist for NFR identification in the whole development process. We also analyze the methodological implications of our framework and discuss the fundamental capabilities of a desired NFR modeling approach.

1 Introduction

Software requirements, derived from stakeholders' needs and environment constraints, guide software development and determine whether a target software meets the intended purposes [1,2]. Requirements engineering, also called software analysis, is the process of eliciting, analyzing, specifying, validating, and managing software requirements. The primary focus of requirements engineering has been functional requirements, which specify functions that a system or system component must deliver to users [3]. Increasingly, both researchers and practitioners realized that there exist many other requirements that play important role in shaping the target system, defining the development process, and managing the development project [4]. Non-Functional Requirements (NFR), as an umbrella term, then was coined to name these requirements [5].

Noticed the importance of NFR, researchers have paid much efforts on clarifying NFR from functional requirements and have proposed plenty of NFR definitions over the last three decades [6,7]. For example, Chung et al. define NFR as any *"-ilities"*, *"ities"*, *along with many other things that do not necessarily end with either of them, such as performance, user-friendliness and coherence, as well as concerns on productivity, time, cost and personal happiness* [6]. Unlike Chung's broad NFR definition, Glinz rules out the process requirements

D. Zowghi and Z. Jin (Eds.): APRES 2014, CCIS 432, pp. 1–15, 2014.

and project requirements from system requirements, which include functional requirements and NFR. Glinz defines NFR as *an attribute of or a constraint on a system, where an attribute is a performance requirement or a specific quality requirement and a constraint is requirement that constrains the solution space beyond what is necessary for meeting the given functional, performance, and specific quality requirements* [7]. Unfortunately, none of these definitions has been adopted as consensus in the community partly due to the diversity, subjectiveness, and relativeness of NFR [4,6,7,8].

Although it is not clear what NFR exactly is, it has been widely agreed that NFR should be explicitly handled during software development and maintenance process in order to get software systems with high quality [6]. However, existing NFR definitions, such as the two afore-mentioned ones, provide very little operable guidance on identifying and specifying NFR, and on clarifying relationships between NFR and functional requirements, other NFR, and other artifacts in software development. To this end, requirements engineering community took a *process-oriented* approach to elicit and model NFR in software development process, such as the well-known NFR-Framework [9]. NFR-framework models intermediate artifacts of analyzing and operationalizing NFR as an AND/OR tree [9,10], which could then be used to justify design decisions [6].

Software architecture community also noticed the fact that NFR plays an important role in shaping software architecture while usually remaining implicit or obscure. They also took a process-oriented point and argued that software architects should analyze and refine NFR before or during software architecting [11]. However, an aftermath is that the borderline between NFR and design knowledge-related artifacts, such as design issues, tactics, design rationale, and even design decisions, is likely to be blurred in practice [8]. Furthermore, the two threads of research efforts that share the fundamental idea of process-orientation differ from each other in terms of understanding, modeling, and managing NFR. This partially hinders the adoption of these approaches in practice because stakeholders in one community usually do not understand (hence cannot use) an approach initially invented to solve problems of another community.

We argue that the idea of *process-orientation* requires a revamped NFR definition that helps stakeholders unambiguously understand NFR in whole software development process. This paper proposes a process-oriented conceptual framework that concisely characterizes the essence of NFR identified in different development phases in a unified manner. Specifically, it explicitly distinguishes NFR from application-independent domain knowledge, such as quality attributes, tactics, and other constraints, and then defines NFR as the composition in specific contexts of domain knowledge and various system abstractions, which include not only the target system, but requirements model and software architecture that conceptually define the system at early stages of software development.

The proposed conceptual framework of NFR has two main benefits. First, it uniformly models the relationships between NFR and functional requirements, other NFR, and other intermediate artifacts produced in software development, which provides stakeholders an operable and consistent guideline, a checklist, for

NFR identification and management in software development process. Second, it implicitly regulates the fundamental capabilities that a desired NFR modeling approaches should deliver, which can guide the improvement to the existing approaches or the invention of more practical approaches for better adoption. We analyze the methodological implications of our framework and then discuss the fundamental capabilities of a desired NFR modeling approach.

The rest of this paper is organized as follows. Section 2 analyzes what *process-orientation* means to NFR. Section 3 proposes the process-oriented conceptual framework on NFR. Section 4 defines the checklist for NFR identification. Section 5 analyzes the methodological implications of the proposed framework on understanding, modeling, and managing NFR. Section 6 introduces related work and finally section 7 concludes this paper and foresees our future work.

2   NFR in Software Development Process

Software development is going through a transition from the code-centric paradigm to a so-called model-centric paradigm [12]. The model-centric development is concerned with the construction of software models at various level of abstractions and the transformations from software models at higher level to those at lower level, such as from requirements to software architecture, and up to implementation model, i.e. the target system. Requirements engineering and software architecting are two closely-related early phases in software development process [8], which produces requirements model and software architecture respectively. However, the two phases usually weave together with each other and the line separating them is very fuzzy [8,13]. In particular, as important driving factors of software architecting, NFR is usually identified and refined not only in requirements engineering but also in software architecting [10,11,14,15,16].

From the requirements engineering perspective, NFR should ideally be elicited from stakeholders' needs and expectations. These needs and expectations cannot be well satisfied and some of them may even be totally failed when a target system does not fulfill NFR. For various reasons, most stakeholders tend to use obscure terminologies, such as *security*, *usability* or *performance*, to denote their non-functional expectations. Some stakeholders may even propose unattainable NFR or conflicting NFR, which could not be identified until software architecting stage. It is the responsibility of requirements engineers to define NFR with specificity necessary for downstream development activities according to various domain knowledge, such as various quality models [17], tactics repositories [10,11], and NFR-related artifacts documented in domain models [18].

From the software architecting perspective, most NFR are architecturally significant requirements that shape software architecture and finally the target system. In real settings, software architects usually have to identify and refine NFR before or during software architecting [15] due to the fact that NFR is often not well documented in requirements specification [11]. Traditionally, software architecture is considered to be a high-level structural model that consists of components and connectors. A NFR such as usability or performance usually affects multiple modules (components or connectors) scattered across the whole system. This makes it very difficult to establish and manage the traceability of NFR [19] and to evaluate how NFR are impacted by software architecture changes. Even worse, design knowledge about why software architecture changes happened was usually vaporized after a change is done. The newly identified or refined NFR that drive the evolution of software architecture are usually not documented in either requirements model or software architecture [15].

To address the design erosion problem, software architecture has been increasingly seen as a set of design decisions that led to the software architecture that consists of components and connectors. Design decisions document the designers' knowledge gained in the design process and are modeled as first-class entities in software architecture [20,21]. However, an aftermath is that NFR-related knowledge is usually captured and mixed in a set of architecture-level artifacts, including *design issue, tactic or solution, design decision,* and *design rationale* [20,21]. *Design issue* describes problems that need to be solved in software architecture; *tactic or solution* has pros and cons in solving design issues; *design decision* records which solutions are selected to solve design issues; and *design rationale* models the reason of making design decisions [20,21].

In fact, before design decision oriented solutions are proposed to compile design knowledge produced during software architecting, Mylopoulos and Chung et al. have proposed a comprehensive *NFR-Framework* to model NFR-related design knowledge in a set of requirement-level terminologies [9,10]. In the *NFR-framework*, NFR is modeled as a set of *softgoals*. Each *softgoal* may be inter-related with *goals* that mainly representing functional requirements and other *softgoals*. Each *softgoal* can be refined into multiple child *softgoals* or *operationalization goals* that contribute to their parents, or into *argument goals* that justify their parents. All *softgoals* and their *operationalizations* and *arguments* form a AND/OR tree, called Softgoal Interdependency Graph (SIG). Operationalization is a concept similar to tactic and argument is a concept similar to design rationale. A SIG finally serves as justifications of making decisions on selecting right operationalizations to meet NFR [6].

Although the above two threads of research efforts are both closely related to NFR, there exist subtle differences between them in terms of their understanding on NFR and terminologies used to document NFR-related knowledge. For example, design issue is similar but not identical to NFR. Some functional requirements may introduce challenging design issues, such as a requirement of enabling the *undo/redo* function in an editor. Meanwhile some NFR may not introduce design issue because they can be satisfied by commonly adopted practices, such as a time requirement on retrieving a specific item in a small-size address book. It is very difficult for people from one field to understand and use approaches from another field to handle NFR. This partially hinders the adoption of these approaches in practice [15]. We argue that it is inappropriate to understand and identify NFR only at requirements engineering stage, software architecting stage, or system implementation stage. It is natural and even imperative to identify NFR and clarify the relationships among NFR and other related artifacts in the whole software development process, in particular in the iterative process of requirements engineering and software architecting. We believe that an unified view on NFR across the whole software development process would shed a light on integrating achievements from different communities, and as a result on producing a more adoptable approach in practice.

3   A Process-Oriented Conceptual Framework on NFR

This section first overviews the fundamental components of the process-oriented conceptual framework on NFR and then presents a formal NFR definition to clarify how these components can be composed into NFR at different stages.

3.1   Framework Overview

As shown in Figure 1, the proposed framework has four key components: stakeholders' needs, system abstractions abstractly defining the target system, NFR-related domain knowledge base that will be reified in system abstractions, and the contexts where the target system would be operated in.

First, stakeholders' needs are main sources of both functional requirements and non-functional requirements. Ideally, any NFR should be traced back to one or more stakeholders' needs, no matter at which stage it is identified. For example, NFR related to availability of an e-shop could be derived from the need that the e-shop should be online 24-7 to keep its competence in market. Note that a target system may have many stakeholders with various needs. These needs could not be completely identified before identifying NFR. In practice, some NFR could be identified first and then corresponding stakeholders' needs should be identified by requirements engineers and confirmed by stakeholders.

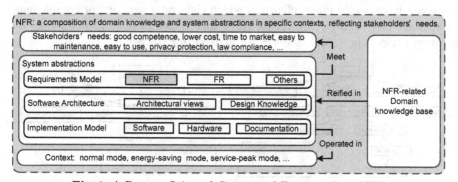

Fig. 1. A Process-Oriented Conceptual Framework on NFR

Second, according to Glinz [7], we confine NFR as a part of system requirements, not including requirements related to the development process or project management. However, the target system does not exist and is only imagined and modeled as various system abstractions when modeling NFR. System abstractions usually include a stack of software models produced at different development stages, such as requirements model and software architecture, and implementation model. We believe that identifying NFR of a target system at a specific development stage is actually identifying NFR of the system abstractions produced at that stage. Note that system abstractions will keep evolving during the whole development process. So it is necessary to explicitly state which part of system abstraction NFR is targeting when we identify and specify NFR. Note that the relationship between NFR and system abstractions is very tricky. On one side, NFR is a part of requirements model, i.e. a part of a system abstraction. On the other side, NFR itself is usually identified on the basis of available system abstractions. In addition, NFR could drive the evolution of some system abstractions, such as software architecture.

Third, NFR with enough specificity usually cannot be easily derived from stakeholders' needs and system abstractions. The degree to which NFR specification is analyzable or useful in software development process is heavily influenced by NFR-related domain knowledge of requirements engineers, which is accumulated during the construction of similar systems before or learned from literature. Domain knowledge is application independent but important for identifying and elaborating NFR in a specific application. Typical NFR-related domain knowledge includes standardized quality models [17,22], tactics (design patterns/architectural styles) repositories [23,24], catalogues of conflictions among quality attributes [25], as well as constraints regulated by various parties. Note that public domain knowledge bases, such as the standardized quality models [17], may be either too verbose in terms of irrelevant knowledge or too general in terms of relevant knowledge to fully meet the requirements of a specific application development. So developers need to create and maintain a tailored knowledge base to capture the consensus on NFR-related knowledge in a specific project, organization, or domain [6]. NFR-related knowledge items with different specificity can be organized into a hierarchy. Each item in a hierarchy could have one or more offsprings which elaborate, support, or complement the parent. For example, we create three hierarchies of domain knowledge on security, performance, and usable(CAPTCHA) in Figure 2.

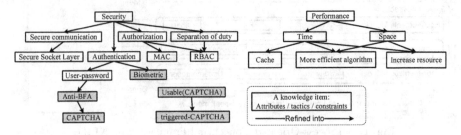

Fig. 2. Two hierarchies of domain knowledge

The security hierarchy in Figure 2 tells that security can be refined into secure communication, authentication, authorization, and separation of duty. Secure communication could then be refined into secure socket layer, which encrypts and decrypts the transmitted messages across networked components. Authentication concerns user identification. Authorization concerns user rights on services and resources and is usually implemented by various access control systems [26], such as mandatory access control (MAC) and role-based access control (RBAC). RBAC supports separation of duty. The most common authentication solution is to check user passwords. Performance hierarchy elaborates performance into several possible solutions/tactics, including employing cache, increasing computation power or storage, and improving algorithm efficiency. Note that these hierarchies keep evolving along with NFR modeling and software architecting. For example, if customers realize that user-password based authentication has to be free from brute force attacks (*Anti-BFA*), two possible solutions might be added into the security hierarchy, including *CAPTCHA* [27] and *Biometric* authentication [28]. Note that these tactics come at a cost of usability and performance. Researchers have compiled the correlations among quality attributes into catalogues [25], which are also important domain knowledge.

Fourth, the context of a NFR is the set of circumstances in which system abstractions are analyzed for NFR identification. NFR identified in one context could be different from ones identified in other contexts. For example, security threats to a system that runs on an isolated network may be different than the threats to a system that runs on the public network. Performance-related NFR of an online ticketing system in peak period might be different from those in off-peak period. A change request that arrives after the code has been frozen for a release may be treated differently than one that arrives before the freeze [11].

The framework in Figure 1 only defines the fundamental components that have to be considered when identifying and refining NFR. Note that none of them can independently be treated as NFR. A specific enough NFR is usually the refinement of the composition of an item in domain knowledge base and a specific part of system abstractions in a set of explicitly defined contexts and can be traced back to one or more stakeholders' needs. For example, we can analyze *performance* issue with regard to a *downloading* function to identify a NFR such as *the download speed should be as fast as possible*. We can also analyze the *RBAC* issue with regard to a function of adding goods onto an online store inventory to identify a NFR that *only users with a manager role can add goods*. Note that the knowledge items in a hierarchy, either the general ones at the top level or the specific ones at the bottom level, can be composed with modules in a system model to define NFR. As a result, some NFR could be implicitly declared by automatically refining the composition of a general knowledge item with subordinate offsprings and a module with inside structure.

3.2 Formal Definition

This section defines a formal process-oriented NFR definition to concisely clarify how the four components in the framework are composed together to form NFR.

Definition 1. *Stakeholders' Needs* $\mathbb{U}$*: Let* $\mathbb{U}$ *be the set of stakeholders' needs. The subset* $U \in 2^{\mathbb{U}}$ *denotes a subset of stakeholder's needs.*

Definition 2. *Domain Knowledge* $\mathbb{K}$*: Let* $\mathbb{K}$ *be the set of domain knowledge, which includes one or more hierarchies. A hierarchy* $H \subseteq \mathbb{K}$ *is a directed acyclic* *graph capturing a subset of domain knowledge. Given a hierarchy H, we can define a refinement function $\Psi_H : H \to 2^H$.*

Beside domain knowledge, system abstractions can also be viewed as several hierarchies corresponding to software models at different level. Each hierarchy has the most general element *the whole system* as its root, which is then iteratively refined into subsystems or modules in smaller granularity.

Definition 3. *System Abstractions $\mathbb{S}$: Let $\mathbb{S}$ be the set of system abstractions, which includes functional requirements model $\mathbb{R}$, software architecture $\mathbb{A}$, and implementation model $\mathbb{I}$. For each hierarchical software model $\mathbb{M} \in \mathbb{S}$ ($\mathbb{R}$, $\mathbb{A}$, or $\mathbb{I}$), we can define a refinement functional $\Phi_\mathbb{M} : \mathbb{M} \to 2^\mathbb{M}$. For each module $m \in \mathbb{M}$, $\Phi_\mathbb{M}(m)$ is the set of offsprings of m in the hierarchy $\mathbb{M}$.*

Definition 4. *Context $\mathbb{C}$: Let $\mathbb{C}$ be the set of contexts. Each $C \in 2^\mathbb{C}$ is a subset of contexts where a NFR is identified.*

With the above notations, we can formally define the set of NFR ($\mathbb{N}$) as the following recursive equations.

Definition 5. *Context specific, Process-Oriented NFR*

$$N := \{n|n = (u,c,k,m), m \in M, k \in K, C \in 2^\mathbb{C}, u \in \mathbb{U}\}, \tag{1}$$

$$N := \{n|n = (u,c,k,r), r \in N, k \in K, C \in 2^\mathbb{C}, u \in \mathbb{U}\}. \tag{2}$$

Definition 5 includes two equations. Equation 1 defines NFR as the composition of a subset of domain knowledge k with a module in system abstractions ($r \in R$, $a \in A$, and, and $i \in I$) in specific contexts C. For example, in web-based systems, a functional requirement *Log-on* must be secure enough to prevent brute force attacks on user identification and password. So we need a NFR *Anti-BFA(Log-on)*, where *Anti-BFA* is an item from domain knowledge shown in Figure 2. Equation 2 recursively defines NFR as the composition of the NFR and a knowledge item k in specific contexts C. For example, *Anti-BFA(Log-on)* also needs to be efficient and usable to allow a legitimate user to log on in an easy and efficient way. In that, *usable(Anti-BFA(Log-on))* and *time(Anti-BFA(Log-on))* could also be modeled as NFR, which imply the potential conflicts between security and performance or usability.

Note that Definition 5 suggests that there exists complex iterations among defining system abstractions, collecting domain knowledge, and analyzing NFR in real setting, and that any intermediate version of $\mathbb{R}$, $\mathbb{A}$, $\mathbb{I}$, $\mathbb{C}$, $\mathbb{U}$ or $\mathbb{K}$ that are produced during software development process could be used as the basis of analyzing NFR. In theory, all possible compositions of domain knowledge and system abstractions should be analyzed for NFR identification during software development process. However, it is not possible to do so due to limited time-to-market and human resources. That means, the recursive equations in Definition 5 would not achieve the fixed point in a desired speed. In practice, the iterative process of NFR identification is interweaved with the whole software development process and should be increasingly dropped out when the target system is increasingly emerged.

4   A Checklist for NFR Identification

This section further clarifies what NFR is and what NFR is not according to Definition 5 and presents a checklist for NFR identification at different software development stages. We explain the checklist with regard to the account management subsystem in an e-commerce system (eStore) that sells goods online.

4.1   An Account Management Subsystem in eStore

There are many eStores deployed on the Internet, such as Amazon and eBay. An eStore usually allows users to register new accounts, log on the eStore, and maintain their accounts. A usable interface is very important for the success of an eStore. Users may want to log on an eStore as easy and fast as possible. In addition, user account profile, which might include billing addresses or credit card number, needs to be securely protected from illegitimate accesses and abuses.

4.2   A Checklist for NFR Identification

Definition 5 suggests that the initial set of system abstractions, stakeholders' needs, the NFR-related domain knowledge base, and system operating contexts, should be available before identifying NFR at a specific stage. Generally, Essential functional requirements, such as creating account and editing account profiles, and some typical NFR, such as those directly related to the well-known quality attributes, such as security, performance, and usability [17], can be easily identified from stakeholders' needs. For example, an account management subsystem in eStore must provide functions of account management and be easy-to-use, fast, and secure. However, it is not obvious to identify and elaborate NFR that is not directly elicited from quality attributes. To that end, we give the following checklist for NFR identification. Note that the following discussion will continuously refer to tactics defined in hierarchies in Figure 2.

First, *a newly identified requirement item is NFR if it is the composition of domain knowledge and functional requirements*. This rule is obvious for high-level knowledge items directly related to quality attributes, such as performance and security. For example, *Security(Log-on)* is definitely a NFR where *Log-on* is a functional requirement of an eStore and security itself is an item in security related knowledge. However, for some low-level operationalizable tactics, such as *CAPTCHA* contributing to security, things get tricky. Some may argue that *CAPTCHA(Log-On)* composed of *CAPTCHA* and *Log-on* is a functional requirement because it does accept user inputs and produce outputs. However, we argue that it is not an essential functional requirement that is proposed by users as a fixed feature in the eStore and users can achieve their purpose of logging onto the eStore without *CAPTCHA(Log-On)*. In fact, it is only a tactic identified to support security of Log-on and is deployed in a context where malicious attackers would appear. So this rule suggests to model *CAPTCHA(Log-on)* as a NFR that can be traced back to the stakeholders' security need rather than a functional requirement. Categorizing *CAPTCHA(Log-on)* as NFR can explicitly drive related downstream developers to pay more attention to make it secure, such as choosing longer string of characters or exerting more distortion on characters. After all, a secure software does not only come from the adoption of the right tactic but also from corresponding good implementation.

Second, *a requirement item is NFR if it is the composition of domain knowledge and existing NFR.* For example, after adopting *CAPTCHA*, it is difficult for users to recognize the intentionally blurred digits and alphabets in a picture. Even the words are recognizable, it is still annoying for an user to pass the *CAPTCHA* every time he/she logs on. From this point of view, *usable(CAPTCHA(Log-on))* is definitely a NFR that can be traced back to the users' needs that *Log-on* should be secure and usable simultaneously. Apparently, *usable(CAPTCHA(Log-on))* also models a possibility of confliction among security and usability. Our framework enables the uniform treatment on individual NFR as well as on conflictions among multiple NFR. Note that before adopting *CAPTCHA*, usability of Log-on is tacitly acceptable and usually neglected. So *usable(CAPTCHA(Log-on))* is optional because it depends on the binding state of *CAPTCHA*, which could be tailored off when developers adopt *biometric* authentication. By modeling conflictions among NFR as separate NFR, our framework enables explicit management of the binding state of conflictions among NFR and suggests explicit treatment on these conflictions later.

Third, *a requirement item is NFR if it is refined from another NFR.* For example, the NFR *usable(CAPTCHA(Log-on))* can be further refined to the composition of appropriate tactics and Log-on, such as *triggered-CAPTCHA* that limits the application of *CAPTCHA* only after three failed log-on attempts. A tactic that contributes a NFR in a specific application often deserves to be reused as domain knowledge in later development. So we add *triggered-CAPTCHA* into domain knowledge hierarchy as a child node of *usable(CAPTCHA)* in Figure 2.

Fourth, *a requirement item is NFR if it is the composition of domain knowledge and architectural elements.* NFR that are not clearly specified in requirement engineering stage could be further refined in software architecting stage. For example, *triggered-CAPTCHA(Log-On)* could be identified on the basis of the Log-on module in software architecture at software architecting stage when some stakeholders noticed the importance of usability of Log-on. Also, software architects may identify new NFR that is overlooked in requirements engineering. Suppose after *Biometric(Log-on)* was modeled as a NFR, a software architect finds out that the *Biometric* technologies to be used, such as those based on fingerprint recognition, are not reliable enough because they may fail to authenticate a legitimate user. So the software architect may explicitly model *reliable(Log-on)* as NFR and try to find out tactics satisfying it. Note that the NFR *reliable(Log-on)* cannot be directly elicited from stakeholders because the most common authentication solution *user-password* is inherently reliable.

Fifth, *a requirement item is NFR if it is the composition of domain knowledge and an implementation model.* After implementation is done, both customers and developers can evaluate the target system in use. The identified NFR could be used to drive the evolution of the system in the future. For example, many security leaks in Windows XP has been identified and fixed.

Sixth, *design knowledge captured in software architecture is not NFR*. Software architecture includes not only architectural views, but also design knowledge [20]. In fact, NFR is a part of requirements model that describe the system to be at requirements level. However, Design knowledge describes issues identified, solutions used, rationale abided by, and decisions made during designing software architecture to satisfy requirements. They are closely related to NFR. NFR may introduce design issues, enlighten design tactics, or serve as design rationale for making design decisions. However, all these design knowledge are not NFR. They should be documented and maintained independently.

Seventh, *domain knowledge is not NFR*. NFR we are discussing is a part of requirements model of a specific application. Apparently, application-independent domain knowledge is not NFR. They are important components that can be composed with system abstractions to form NFR in specific contexts.

Eighth, *process requirements and project requirements are not NFR*. Process requirements and project requirements are non-system requirements but could be as relevant as system requirements in some situations [15]. However, being consistent with Glinz's definition [7] that NFR is part of system requirements, our NFR definition does not cover the non-system requirements, such as constraints on project and process in terms of cost, time, and scope. One benefit of doing so is to achieve a consist framework that defines NFR as the composition of domain knowledge with system abstractions in specific contexts.

In practice, the initial set of essential functional requirements should be identified first. Then most NFR should be identified on the basis of these functional requirements. Later, these functional requirements and NFR are used to drive the software architecting. Again on the basis of the produced software architecture model, developers can refine and identify NFR at software architecting stage. Finally, developers can implement the target system under the guidance of software architecture and can identify and refine NFR on the basis of implementation model during this process. The final set of NFR is the union of NFR identified on the basis of system abstractions produced at different stages.

5   Methodological Implications

Definition 5 impacts the way stakeholders understand, model, and manage NFR in software development process. This section defines the fundamental capabilities of a desired NFR modeling approach on top of Definition 5.

First of all, the desired approach should enable the explicit specification of contexts where the target system would be operated and NFR would be analyzed. For example, it does not make sense to discuss security without knowing what kind of threats would arrive.

Second, the desired NFR modeling approach should document NFR independently from both domain knowledge and functional requirements while explicitly model the relationships among them. In fact, it is a well-known myth to abuse some typical quality attributes, such as security and performance, as NFR. And it is a long recognized challenge to consistently and efficiently distinguish NFR from functional requirements. In addition, automation facilities are required to make the desired approach more efficient and thus more practical due to the complexity of real requirements model.

Third, the desired approach should enable iterative NFR identification across the whole software development process. System abstractions must be explicitly specified before corresponding NFR can be identified and the newly identified NFR would also drive the evolution of system abstractions. It is a huge challenge to systematically create and manage the complex relations among NFR and related system abstractions across the whole software development process due to the varieties of modeling languages and tools used in different stages.

Fourth, it is better for a the desired approach to take a hierarchical view on both domain knowledge and system abstractions and to manage and evolve them in a relatively independent process than modeling NFR. As a result, the desired approach could enable implicit NFR identification by automatically composing the offsprings of either system abstractions or knowledge items composing NFR.

Fifth, the desired approach should carefully design the semantics of refining functional requirements or NFR for easier management of relationships among functional requirements and NFR. On one side, no functional requirements should be refined into NFR. All functional requirements can only be composed with various domain knowledge to form NFR, which suggests that functional requirements have to be implemented while meeting corresponding NFR. On the other side, no functional requirements should be refined from a NFR. NFR should only be refined into NFR. In fact, NFR mainly elaborates stakeholders' expectations on quality of a target system. A refinement of NFR contributes to the original stakeholder's needs no matter how it is represented, whether it is 'soft', 'operationalizable', 'cross-cutting' or not. As a result, the original *'support'* relationship from functional requirements (usually operationalizations of a NFR) to the NFR is modeled as the *'contribute-to'* relationships from child NFR to their parents. Note that the original *'hurt'* relationship from an operationalization of a NFR to another NFR is modeled as a new NFR that substitutes for the operationalization. For example, *usable(CAPTCHA(Log-on))* can be introduced to substitute for the *CAPTCHA (Log-on)* which hurts usability of Log-on.

Finally, the desired approach should model conflictions among multiple NFR as special NFR for easier management on their traceability and optionality. Note that potential conflictions among multiple NFR must be carefully solved in requirements model, software architecture, or ultimately a target system [11]. That is to say, a so-called confliction can only exist in the process of analyzing NFR but not in the final requirements model. Two conflicting NFR are just two interacting NFR that need to be satisfied simultaneously and can be reasonably seen as a new NFR to be satisfied. For example, as *CAPTCHA(Log-on)* contributes to security while hurts usability, the confliction among security and usability can be modeled as another NFR *usable(CAPTCHA(Log-on))*. Modeling conflictions as a new NFR will explicitly drive developers to consider possible correlations among multiple NFR during downstream development activities and enable easier NFR traceability management.

In addition, a desired NFR should enable the explicit management of optionality of a NFR (modeling its binding-state) because some NFR are optional due to the optionality of domain knowledge items (tactics) or system abstractions they are associated with. In fact, conflictions among NFR are also optional due the optionality of NFR. So modeling conflictions as a new NFR would enable the uniform management on the optionality of NFR as well as of conflictions among multiple NFR.

6   Related Work

The concept of NFR has been proposed for almost three decades [5]. Although there is no consensus on NFR, two most popular and influential working NFR definitions suggest that NFR are mainly concerned with constraints or attributes of a system [7], such as various "ilities" and "ities", along with many other things that do not end with either of them [6]. These definitions focus on characterizing NFR from the product perspective and lack of operable guidance for understanding and handling NFR in the process of software development.

From process-oriented perspective, some researchers argued that there are no clear-cut distinction between requirements engineering and software engineering [8,13]. Some researchers even argued that functional requirements, NFR, and software architecture should not be separated [16]. Researchers also proposed to represent and use NFR from the process-oriented perspective [9,10] or to record NFR-related design knowledge along with software architecting [20,21]. However, no researchers have discussed how to concisely and uniformly characterize the essence of NFR observed across different development stages in a formal definition to clarify relationships between NFR and functional requirements, NFR and NFR, NFR and other system abstractions, and NFR and domain knowledge. In contrast, this paper unified some essential characteristics of NFR that are identified in process-oriented perspective across different development stages into a concise NFR definition, which forms a theoretical foundation for inventing more practical NFR modeling approaches.

Note that there are some controversial requirements that could be categorized into either functional requirements or non-functional requirements, such as *CAPTCHA* or *undo/redo*. These requirements on one side can take inputs and produce outputs, which makes them deserve to be treated as functional requirements. They on the other side usually influence NFR positively or negatively and also deserve to be modeled as NFR. Some researchers noticed the particularity of these requirements and name them as neither functional requirements nor NFR, but as operationalizations [10] or responsibilities [11]. By doing so, additional types of relationships had to be introduced to record the inherent connections among operationalizations or responsibilities and NFR. Our strategy is to uniformly model the controversial requirements as operationalizable NFR. As a result, the possible types of relationships among functional requirements and

NFR and those among NFR in requirements model would be simplified. Furthermore, traditional NFR definitions did not reveal that multiple NFR might interfere with each other. As a result, existing NFR modeling approaches model conflictions among NFR as new relationships and then manage and trace them separately [10,25]. This makes the NFR modeling approaches unnecessarily complex in terms of managing various relationships among functional requirements and NFR and those among NFR and makes it difficult to trace conflictions to software architecture [19]. In contrast, our definition models the refinements of NFR or the possible *conflictions* among multiple NFR as special NFR, which drives developers to focus on NFR-related issues during downstream development activities and is also conducive for NFR traceability management.

7   Conclusion

It is long believed that explicitly identifying, modeling, managing Non-Functional Requirements (NFR) is necessary for developers to build software with satisfiable quality. However, existing NFR definitions cannot provide operable guidance for developers to identify and manage NFR. This paper proposes a conceptual framework on NFR to concisely and uniformly characterize the essence of NFR observed from the process-oriented perspective, and presents a checklist to guide NFR identification in software development process. It suggests developers to identify NFR as the composition of domain knowledge and system abstractions, such as functional requirements, NFR, architectural components and connectors, and modules in a target system, in specific contexts. This paper also analyzes the fundamental capabilities that a desired NFR modeling approach should deliver. In the future, we will explore more practical NFR modeling and managing approaches on the basis of the proposed conceptual framework.

Acknowledgment. This work is supported by National Science Foundation of China (No. 61202019).

References

1. Nuseibeh, B., Easterbrook, S.: Requirements engineering: A roadmap. In: ICSE 2000, pp. 35–46. ACM, New York (2000)
2. Cheng, B.H.C., Atlee, J.M.: Research directions in requirements engineering. In: FOSE 2007, pp. 285–303. IEEE Computer Society Press, Washington, DC (2007)
3. Software & Systems Engineering Standards Committee: IEEE Std 1061-1998, IEEE Standard for a software quality metrics methodology. IEEE Computer Society, Tech. Rep. (1998)
4. Sommerville, I., Kotonya, G.: Requirements Engineering: Processes and Techniques. John Wiley & Sons, Inc., New York (1998)
5. Yeh, R.T., Zave, P., Conn, A.P., Cole, G.E.: Software requirements analysis - new directions and perspectives. In: Vick, C.R., Ramamoorthy, C. (eds.) Handbook of Software Engineering, Van Nostrand Reinhold Co. (1984)
6. Chung, L., do Prado Leite, J.C.S.: On Non-Functional Requirements in Software Engineering. In: Borgida, A.T., Chaudhri, V.K., Giorgini, P., Yu, E.S. (eds.) Mylopoulos Festschrift. LNCS, vol. 5600, pp. 363–379. Springer, Heidelberg (2009)

7. Glinz, M.: On non-functional requirements. In: RE 2007, pp. 21–26 (October 2007)
8. de Boer, R.C., van Vliet, H.: On the similarity between requirements and architecture. Journal of Systems and Software 82(3), 544–550 (2009)
9. Mylopoulos, J., Chung, L., Nixon, B.: Representing and using nonfunctional requirements: A process-oriented approach. IEEE Transactions on Software Engineering 18(6), 483–497 (1992)
10. Chung, L., Nixon, B.A., Yu, E., Mylopoulos, J.: Non-Functional Requirements in Software Engineering, 1st edn. The Kluwer International Series in Software Engineering, vol. 5. Springer (October 1999)
11. Bass, L., Clements, P., Kazman, R.: Software architecture in practice. Addison-Wesley Professional (2003)
12. Forward, A., Lethbridge, T.C.: Problems and opportunities for model-centric versus code-centric software development: A survey of software professionals. In: MiSE 2008, pp. 27–32. ACM, New York (2008)
13. Nuseibeh, B.: Weaving together requirements and architectures. Computer 34(3), 115–119 (2001)
14. Taylor, R.N., Medvidovic, N., Dashofy, E.M.: Software Architecture: Foundations, Theory, and Practice. Wiley Publishing (2009)
15. Ameller, D., Ayala, C., Cabot, J., Franch, X.: How do software architects consider non-functional requirements: An exploratory study. In: RE 2012, pp. 41–50 (September 2012)
16. Paech, B., Dutoit, A.H., Kerkow, D., Knethen, A.V.: Functional requirements, non-functional requirements, and architecture should not be separated -a position paper. In: REFSQ 2002, Essen, Germany (2002)
17. ISO/IEC: ISO/IEC 9126. Software engineering – Product quality. ISO/IEC (2001)
18. Pohl, K., Böckle, G., Linden, F.V.D.: Software product line engineering: foundations, principles, and techniques. Springer (2005)
19. Cleland-Huang, J., Marrero, W., Berenbach, B.: Goal-centric traceability: Using virtual plumblines to maintain critical systemic qualities. IEEE Transactions on Software Engineering 34(5), 685 (2008)
20. Jansen, A., Bosch, J.: Software architecture as a set of architectural design decisions. In: WICSA 2005, pp. 109–120. IEEE Computer Society (2005)
21. Kruchten, P.: An Ontology of Architectural Design Decisions in Software Intensive Systems. In: 2nd Groningen Workshop Software Variability, pp. 54–61 (October 2004)
22. Bøegh, J.: A new standard for quality requirements. IEEE Software 25(2), 57–63 (2008)
23. Kienzle, D., Elder, M., Tyree, D., Edwards-Hewitt, J.: Security patterns repository version 1.0. Technical report (2002)
24. Fielding, R.T.: Architectural styles and the design of network-based software architectures. PhD thesis, University of California, Irvine (2000)
25. Mairiza, D., Zowghi, D.: Constructing a catalogue of conflicts among non-functional requirements. In: Maciaszek, L.A., Loucopoulos, P. (eds.) ENASE 2010. CCIS, vol. 230, pp. 31–44. Springer, Heidelberg (2011)
26. Sandhu, R., Samarati, P.: Access control: principle and practice. IEEE Communications Magazine 32(9), 40–48 (1994)
27. von Ahn, L., Blum, M., Hopper, N.J., Langford, J.: CAPTCHA: using hard AI problems for security. In: Biham, E. (ed.) EUROCRYPT 2003. LNCS, vol. 2656, pp. 294–311. Springer, Heidelberg (2003)
28. Wayman, J.L., Jain, A.K., Maltoni, D., Maio, D.: Biometric Systems: Technology, Design and Performance Evaluation, 1st edn. Springer (2010)

Capturing Security Requirements Using Essential Use Cases (EUCs)

Syazwani Yahya[1], Massila Kamalrudin[1,**], Safiah Sidek[1], and John Grundy[2]

[1] Innovative Software System and Services Group,
Universiti Teknikal Malaysia Melaka, Malaysia
[2] Faculty of Science, Engineering and Technology
Swinburne University of Technology
Melbourne, Australia
{massila,safiahsidek}@utem.edu.my, syazwaniyahya13@gmail.com,
jgrundy@swin.edu.au

Abstract. Capturing security requirements is a complex process, but it is crucial to the success of a secure software product. Hence, requirements engineers need to have security knowledge when eliciting and analyzing the security requirements from business requirements. However, the majority of requirements engineers lack such knowledge and skills, and they face difficulties to capture and understand many security terms and issues. This results in capturing inaccurate, inconsistent and incomplete security requirements that in turn may lead to insecure software systems. In this paper, we describe a new approach of capturing security requirements using an extended Essential Use Cases (EUCs) model. This approach enhances the process of capturing and analyzing security requirements to produce accurate and complete requirements. We have evaluated our prototype tool using usability testing and assessment of the quality of our generated EUC security patterns by security engineering experts.

Keywords: Software Engineering, Requirements Capturing, Security Requirements, Secure Software Development, Essential Use Case (EUC).

1 Introduction

There is an increasing need to look at the cost, reliability and safety of software systems. With the increase of threats and vulnerabilities in many software systems, security issues involving software have become widespread, frequent and serious. We believe that enumerating accurate security requirements can help system architects and security engineers to develop realistic and meaningful secure software [1]. Security requirements elicitation is usually conducted during the early phase of the system life cycle. Often these are only generic lists of security mechanisms, such as password protection, firewalls, virus detection tools and SSL layer (for cryptographically protecting communications) [1, 2] [12]. However, these security requirements often do

---

* Corresponding Author.

D. Zowghi and Z. Jin (Eds.): APRES 2014, CCIS 432, pp. 16–30, 2014.
© Springer-Verlag Berlin Heidelberg 2014

not present a complete solution to the security problems of the target application under development. It is crucial for software engineers to accurately capture the essential security mechanisms (such as access control) and implement the correct design solutions for security (such as robust design and good technology choices) that makes software attacks much more difficult. In our experience, we have found that security requirements elicitation and analysis necessary for a better set of security requirements seldom happens. According to Salini [12], even if it is done, the security requirements are often developed independently from the rest of the requirements engineering activities: They are not integrated into the mainstream of the requirements engineering activities. As a consequence, security requirements that are specific to the application of software or system and the protection of essential services and assets are often neglected. A lot of requirements engineering research and practice have tried to address the security capabilities that a software or system should provide. However, they have limited focus since they tend to describe design solution in terms of protection mechanisms only. They lack of making declarative propositions [12] with regards to the required level of protection that can be accurately established by capturing the correct security requirements in the first place.

A lot of attention has been given to the functional requirements of the system from the user's view, whilst less attention is given to security requirements. [6][12]. Many practices do not tackle security requirements at all, but rather focus on the implementation mechanisms intended to satisfy unstated requirements and assumptions. As a result, security requirements that are specific to the system and that provide protection of essential services and assets are often neglected. This can cause substantial security problems at a later stage [2, 3]. In practice, when capturing security requirements from clients, requirements engineers frequently use some forms of natural language, written either by clients or themselves. This forms a human-centric representation of the requirements accessible to both the engineers and clients. However, due to the ambiguities and complexities of the natural language and the process of capture, these requirements often have inconsistencies, redundancies, incompleteness and omissions which can lead to the development of inaccurate secure software. Our research described in this paper introduces a new, more effective approach using semi-formal models called Essential Use Cases (EUCs) that support requirements engineers in capturing security requirements. This study is an extension of our earlier work [34] [36] to provide better supports for the capturing of security requirements that can enhance the correctness and completeness of the captured security requirements.

This study contributes to the enhancement of the quality of software intended to be developed. The essence of the approach is to support capturing security elements from the normal business requirements expressed in natural language. To allow requirements engineers and stakeholders to detect security requirements, we adopted the concept of essential interactions patterns and essential use case patterns. We highlighted the potential of this tool for quality security requirements by annotating a visual, semiformal model of the security requirements and normal business requirements depicted in our support tool. We evaluated the usability of our prototype tool using a survey conducted with a sample of selected end-users. An evaluation of our security requirements patterns by experts was also conducted.

2   Background

The Essential Use Case (EUC) approach was developed by Constantine and Lock-wood [37]. EUCs are designed to resolve problems which occur in conventional Use Case modeling and they have important benefits over that approach [41]. An EUC is defined as a "structured narrative, expressed in a language of the application domain and of users, comprising a simplified, generalized, abstract, technology free and inde-pendent description of one task or interaction that is complete, meaningful, and well-defined from the point of view of users in some role or roles in relation to a system and that embodies the purpose or intentions underlying the interaction" [37]. An EUC is thus a form of dialogue between a user and a system which supports better commu-nication between the developers and the stakeholders. An EUC is shorter and simpler as compared to a conventional use case since it comprises an abstraction of only es-sential steps and the user's intrinsic interest. An EUC aims to identify "what the sys-tem must do" without being concerned on "how it should be done".

EUCs are made up of a set of organized "abstract interactions" and EUCs extracted from natural language specifications can be compared against templates of "interac-tion patterns" to detect requirements quality problems. Requirements engineers need to derive appropriate essential interactions from the requirements at a correct level of abstraction. Biddle et al. [42] and Kamalrudin et al. [5] found that almost all users have problems defining the right level of abstraction and exerted that the abstraction process to be time consuming. These problems are some of the reasons why it is diffi-cult to check security requirements for consistency and completeness. In this case, we anticipate that a Security Essential Interaction Library can mitigate these prob-lems. This library consists of important key phrases (security essential interactions) and mappings to appropriate essential security requirements (security abstract interactions).

A key reason for choosing the EUC model is that it lends itself to a deeper analysis that enables the identification of security requirements by extracting from the normal business requirements. Once a EUC model has been extracted, it can be compared against a pattern in our SecEUC Interaction Pattern Library.

3   Motivation

Many studies have found that most software engineers have poor training in eliciting, analyzing, and specifying the security requirements. This is due to a considerable lack of security knowledge [1] [15] [16] [17] [18]. New security challenges are growing along with today's complexity and interoperability software systems development. Requirements are provided by a variety of project partners; thus, the specifications are voluminous and contain many requirements. Further, the process of manually eliciting requirements is tedious [3]. To correctly capture security requirements, good skills and knowledge in both the requirements and security areas are required. Shielding security loopholes and establishing correct and accurate security requirements are considered to be a difficult task. Yet, this essential element is taken for granted by many. It is important for requirements engineers to understand that security requirements are more than just dealing with security solutions that provide strong passwords, configure SSL, or validate user input. It involves a process of accurately capturing the right security controls for what the applications and business really needs. However, requirements engineers often fail to pay sufficient attention to security concerns, treating them as non-functional requirements [4]. The majority of software projects deal with the security when the system has already been designed and sometimes even when it has been put into operation. In extreme cases, the actual security requirements themselves are never well understood [4]. Requirements engineers without sufficient experience in security face the risk of over-looking security requirements leading to security vulnerabilities that are easily exploited [3]. It is widely known that security requirements need to be considered at the early stage of software development.

Recognizing the importance of security requirements in achieving a secure software development, Microsoft has adopted a systematic security assurance process, the Security Development Lifecycle (SDL). As a company-wide initiative and a mandatory policy since 2004, the SDL has a significant role in embedding security and privacy in the software and culture at Microsoft. During the software development life cycle (SDLC), security requirements are elicited at the most early phase, which is at the requirement phase, as shown in Figure 1 [13]:

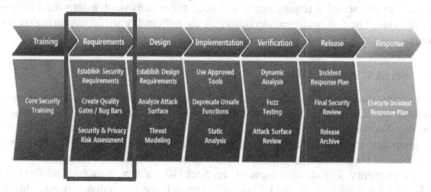

Fig. 1. The Microsoft Security Development Lifecycle – Simplified [13]

In a software organization, it is common to have a project team that consists of requirements engineers and security engineers. The primary responsibilities of requirements engineers or system analysts are to gather, analyze, document and validate the needs of the project stakeholders [14]. They are responsible at the requirement phase which is to capture security requirements from clients. Security engineers, on the other hand are responsible for designing, developing and deploying security related systems and security in systems. Their responsibilities and skills can be very specific such as designing a hardware security appliance [19]. The task of a security engineer is usually centered at the implementation or design phase.

Although both engineers have complementary responsibilities in capturing requirements, they do not communicate effectively with each other; hence, there is a lack of integration on the work done between them. This condition can lead to inconsistency and incorrectness of the developed software and it fails to fulfill the needs of the stakeholders. Additionally, the existing standard, such as the Common Criteria (ISO) has been identified as extensive, complex and difficult to comprehend by requirements engineers [27]. The existing techniques, such as interviews and brainstorming are found to be time consuming and fail to accurately identify security requirements. In this case, captured security requirements using the existing standards and techniques are prone to be inaccurate, inconsistent and incomplete, and this can lead to insecure software systems.

4   Our Approach

We explored the use of semi-formal model Essential Use Cases (EUCs) to develop a new approach for capturing security requirements. We automate the capturing process of security requirements from the business requirements using (EUCs) model. Further, a rapid prototyping approach was adopted to ensure the production of accurate and secure software. Next, pattern libraries called Security Essential Use Cases (SecEUC), Security Essential Interactions (SecEI) and Security Controls Patterns (SecCtrl) library were developed to assist the capturing process for security requirements. This is a lightweight approach that allows requirements engineers to identify and capture the security requirements and keep them consistent within the business requirements. The following section describes the pattern library for capturing security requirements.

4.1   SecEUC Pattern Libraries

Our security pattern library consists of three library patterns, which are the Security Essential Use Cases (SecEUC), Security Essential Interaction (SecEI), and Security Controls (SecCtrl) patterns. The SecEUC library patterns which is based on EUCs was generated from the normal business requirements, while the SecEI library patterns is based on the essential interactions found in the textual requirements related to security elements. The development of the SecEUC patterns was adapted from the works of Kamalrudin et al. 2011 [34] [36]. Through the extraction process, phrases from the textual natural language requirements were analyzed and matched to the essential interaction pattern library to find an appropriate abstract interaction. The abstract interactions associated with security are called SecEUC. Essential Interactions that contain the security elements are called SecEI.

The identification of associated security elements are based on the definitions from the basic security services [38]. It was found that multiple SecEI are associated with one SecEUC. For example, the essential interaction "key in username and password" and "log in" were identified as security related and they were mapped to a SecEUC "identify self". This is because all of them have the attributes of security. Other examples of the pattern library are shown in Table 1.We then designed our SecCtrl library patterns based on basic security services [38], such as the access control (authorization), authentication (integrity), confidentiality (privacy), availability and accountability (non-repudiation). The SecCtrl was developed for the purpose of mapping it to the prototype generation and providing the mandatory security controls. This pattern library helped us to identify the security controls that are relevant to a particular SecEUC. The association between the SecEUC and SecCtrl is that one Se-cEUC can have one or more than one SecCtrl. For example, "Identify Self" of SecEuc was mapped to "Authentication" and "Authorization" SecCtrl. Other examples of the pattern library are shown in Table 1.

Table 1. Examples of our security-oriented EUC pattern libraries

SecEI	SecEUC	SecCtrl
Check password	Identify Self	Authentication
Check username		Authorization
Verify username		
Make payment	Make payment	Authentication
Complete payment form		Transaction

4.2 Using Our Approach

Figure 2 shows the overview of our approach that enhances the process of capturing security requirements. The process of our approach begins after the requirement engineer gathered the requirements from the stakeholders. The collected requirements are in the forms of textual natural language requirements. The followings are the sequence of the process.

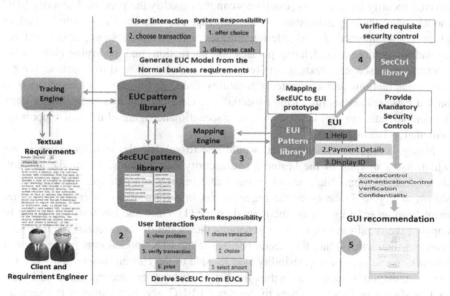

Fig. 2. Overview of our approach

The process starts when the textual requirements are analyzed and traced to the EUCs patterns library for appropriate abstract interaction in a form of EUC model (1). Then, SecEUC are derived from the generated EUC Models based on the categorization of their attribute related to the security element as defined in the SecEUC pattern library (2). Each SecEUC is mapped to EUI pattern library (3) for the generation of abstract prototype in a form of EUI model. Then, each EUI model is verified with a defined mandatory security control in the SecCtrl library patterns (4). Next, a recommendation of graphical user interfaces (GUI) is provided to visualize the security requirements based on the generated SecEUC (5). This helps to ensure the consistency and correctness of the captured security requirements with the original business requirements provided by the end-user.

5   Tool Support and Usage Example

5.1   SecMEReq : Prototype Tool

We have developed a prototype tool to support our EUC-based requirements capture and analysis process, an extension of our earlier MEReq [7] tool. Figure 3 shows our extended version of MEReq, called SecMEReq. The tool allows requirements engineers to automate the elicitation process for capturing security requirements. The selected phrases in the textual requirements show the resulting extracted security essential interactions. Meanwhile, the selected essential interactions show the sources from which the textual natural language phrases were derived. This provides a traceability support mechanism between the textual natural language requirements and the derived security EUC models. Engineers can then modify the generated security EUC model and/or the original textual natural language requirements. This includes adding phrases and interactions, re-ordering phrases and interactions, uploading and re-uploading requirements, deleting phrases and interactions and modifying phrases and interactions descriptive texts. Users (engineers) are also allowed to re-extract the essential interactions and associated traceability links. In this case, engineers need to have a basic understanding of the Essential Use Case concept and methodology only. To demonstrate, our tool key features, user scenario and figure of the tool support are provided as below:

Nancy, a requirements engineer, would like to validate the security requirements which has a mixture of the business and security requirements, which she has collected from a client, Nick, who is a car rental information manager. To do this, as shown in Figure 3, she types the requirements in a form of user scenario or copies them from an existing file on the textual editor (1). Once she has finished typing or copying the requirements, the tool generates the model of the essential requirements (abstract interactions) and the screen will show the EUC models containing the user interaction and system responsibility side by side to the chosen requirements (2). On the same display screen, she verifies the list of abstract interactions provided by the tool as shown in figure 4. From the generated EUC, she then captures the security requirements from the business requirements in a form of SecEUC which is presented in the green color boxes. Further, she checks the consistency and dependencies between the SecEUC components and the SecEI by performing a trace back using the "capture SecEI" (3) event handler. From here, she could verify the consistency between the captured security requirements with the original textual requirements. At this stage, the associated SecEI are highlighted with yellow colors at the textual requirements (3A). In order to further validate her captured security requirements and to ease the discussion process with Nick, she has the tool map the SecEUC model to the low-fidelity prototype - EUI prototype (3B). As shown in Fig 3(3B), the EUI model that has the relation with security is also colored in green. From the EUI prototype, the tool then provides her with a set of mandatory security control for the captured SecEUC (4). In order to visualize the captured security requirements, she then has the tool that translates the EUI prototype to a more concrete UI view (5). From here, she then verify the consistency and the correctness of the captured security requirements with the client-stakeholder.

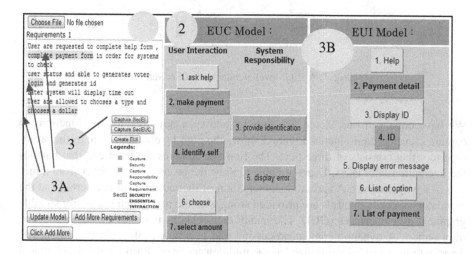

Fig. 3. Requirements Example and a SecMereq Usage Example

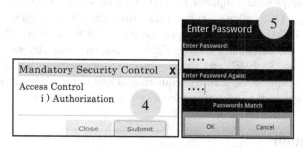

Fig. 4. SecMereq Tool Support in use

5.2   Tool Architecture

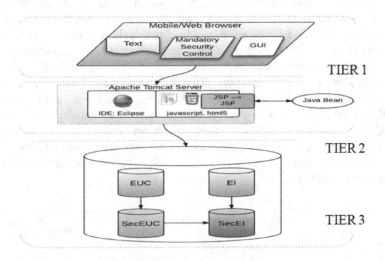

Fig. 5. A High-level architecture of SecMereq

We have enhanced our Mereq [7] tools by adding a new module and functions to capture security requirements. Figure 5 shows the high-level architecture of the prototype tool that consists of three tiers. The first tier contains the front-end that handles the interaction with users. Users are able to view the prototype tool either from a mobile or a web browser. A textual documentation of the requirement is inserted and the mandatory security controls are provided along with the recommendations for suitable graphical user interfaces (GUI). The middle-tier contains the rules for the processing information. A dynamic content processing and generation takes place at this level. Apache tomcat servers are utilized as the middleware or platform for the development at this stage. To build the Java applications, Eclipse Juno was selected for the IDE as it is recognized to provide a superior Java editing with validation and code assistance. Java Server Pages (JSP) allows writing a text using client's languages, which are the JavaScript and HTML5. Tier 3 manages the access to the database that stores the patterns library: the essential use cases (EUCs), essential interactions (EI), security essential use cases (SecEUC) and security essential interactions (SecEI). These patterns are used to capture the security requirements and to recommend the mandatory security controls as well as to generate security requirements prototype.

6   Evaluation

6.1   Tool Usability

We conducted a preliminary evaluation of our developed prototype to evaluate its usability. The participants of this study were 40 students, comprising 16 males and 24 females. The average age of the students was 22 years old. They were final year students from the Bachelor of Computer Science majoring in Software Engineering. They have sufficient understanding of requirements engineering and were familiar with the concept and methodology of essential use cases and security .To explore the functionality of the tool, the students were provided with a set of requirements on "online car rental registration". They were informed that they will be observed and they are free to say aloud their responses of the tool while completing the task. The purpose of the observation was to identify the problems and misconceptions faced by the participants when using the tool. Further, the say aloud evaluation of the tool provided us with the users' spontaneous responses and suggestions for improvement. After the completion of the task, students were requested to answer four questions related to the usability [5] which consists of the usefulness, ease of use, ease of learning and satisfaction of the tool based on a five-level Likert scale. Students' responses for these questions were analysed and the results of the survey are shown in Figure 6.

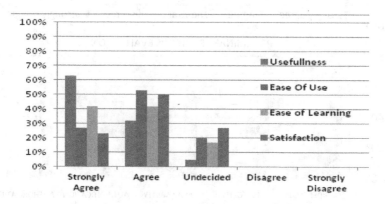

Fig. 6. Preliminary Usability Test Results

More than 90% of the participants agreed that the tool is useful, 70% agreed that the tool is easy to use, 80% agreed that the tool is easy to learn, and 70% were satisfied with the tool. None of the participants expressed disagreement to the four aspects evaluated in this survey. It can be concluded that our prototype tool is useful, easy to use, easy to understand and able to satisfy users. There are some enhancements that we need to consider for the refinement of our tool. Based on the say aloud responses, the suggestions given by the participants were mostly related to the improvement of the interface design of the tool and the provision of a user manual or a tutorial for users. Therefore, we plan to integrate the tool with existing security tools with the security features to ease the design and development phase. This stage is closely related to the work of the security engineers. Key threats to the validity of this findings are the selection bias due to our method of selecting the sample. The selection of participants for the preliminary study was based on one group of students. Hence, the subjects in the group were not homogenous with regards to the preference of the interface design. However, they were similar in one or more of the subject-related variables, such as the agreement towards the easiness of using the tool.

6.2   Preliminary SecEUC Patterns Evaluation

We also conducted an evaluation of our SecEUC patterns using five experts in security requirements from IBM Corporation from India, Austria, France and Malaysia. They were invited to evaluate the correctness of our new SecEUC patterns library by evaluating the classification of security controls with the associated SecEUC and SecEI. They were given five sets of requirements from a small size security application requirements document. This consisted of 10 SecEUC, 50 SecEI and five basic security controls: confidentiality, integrity, availability, authentication and authorization. They were asked to answer a few questions using likert-scale and some open ended questions. The results of this expert evaluation are shown in Figure 7.

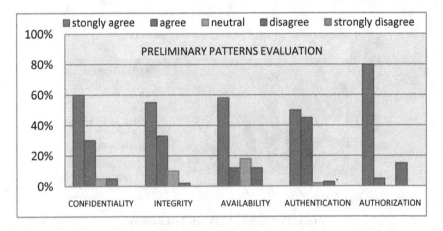

Fig. 7. Preliminary Patterns Evaluation Results

As shown in Figure 7, all of the general security controls rating have some disagreement. Based on this feedback, the disagreement does not mean that we have provided incorrect selection, but they would prefer some other security control classifications for each of the SecEUC. They requested more options for security controls for more complex requirements. For example, the security requirements "login" are currently mapped to the security controls "Authorization". Some experts think it should be mapped to another security control such as Authentication. They also offered some recommendations for correct and relevant security controls associated to a particular SecEUC. Here, we will update the security patterns from time to time in accordance with this feedback. Based on this study, the dependency on basic security services is not purely relevant for capturing more complex security requirements. Therefore, a further study on the patterns relates to more establish security standards is required.

7   Related Work

Many methods, approaches, techniques and tools have been used to capture security requirements. Viega [22], showed how to build security requirements in a structured manner that is conducive to iterative refinement. If this structured procedure is followed correctly according to the metrics for evaluation, it would serve as a framework that provides a significant improvement for the traditional methods that do not consider security at all. They also provided an example using a simple three-tiered architecture. The basic idea behind the way that CLASP handles security requirements is the performance of a structured walkthrough of resources, determining how they address each core security service throughout the lifetime of that resource. While it is obviously far more effective than any ad-hoc treatment of security requirements, this methodology is still new and immature.

Hussein and Zulkernine [23], proposed a framework for developing components with intrusion detection capabilities. The first stage of this framework is requirements elicitation, in which developers identify services and intrusions. In this framework, they capture users requirements regarding the services and functionalities provided by the components, and identify the unwanted or illegal usage of components by intruders. Intrusion scenarios are elicited through the use of misuse-cases of a UML profile called UMLintr. Yet, their proposed framework still needs an extension scope on UMLintr to other security requirements. UMLintr can be extended by exploring how to specify and handle other security requirements like authentication, authorization, integrity, etc. Their framework is also considered as complex intrusion scenarios. While Agile Security Requirements Engineering proposes the extension of agile practices to deal with security in an informal, communicative and assurance-driven spirit, it has its own limitation. It is only partially support consistency and does not support correctness and validation checking between security and business requirements.

i* frame is a modeling and analysis framework for organizational environments and their software systems, and is based on the intentionality relations between agents. Tropos [26] adopts the i* modeling framework and is an agent- oriented software system development methodology. However, it focuses on describing both organizational environment of a system and a system itself. A secure Tropos framework to model and analyze the security requirements is then built using the Secure Tropos methodology [27]. It especially addresses the problem of modeling security requirements through ownership, permission and delegation among the actors or agents involved in the software system. In our previous research [26] we reviewed a few related tools, such as STS-Tool [27], SecTro [28], SecReq [31], SREPPLine [30] and ST-Tool [31]. Many researchers have done great works on their research of security requirements engineering, particularly involving a tool that supports the security requirement engineering. We found that most work used a modeling approach, such as use cases, misuse cases, and UMLsec, to handle security requirements. UML models are the most commonly used [34], especially use case diagrams that are widely used by developers and requirements engineers to elicit and capture requirements. Kamalrudin et al. [7], [34] have shown that EUCs are useful to capture and validate the quality of requirements. EUCs also benefit the development process as they fit a problem-oriented rather than solution–oriented approach, thus they have the potential to allow designers and implementers of the user interface to explore more possibilities. This approach allows for a more rapid development, whereby when using EUCs, it is no longer necessary to design an actual user interface. Although EUCs simplify captured requirements as compared to the conventional UML use cases, and it is beneficial to integrate the requirements and design [35][39], they have not explored the process of capturing security requirements.

8 Conclusion and Future Work

We have described a new approach to supporting security requirements capture and analysis using Essential Use Case models. Our prototype tool, SecMereq, provides support for extracting EUCs and security requirements from natural language text, prototype generation including security interfaces, and validation of extracted security requirements using a library of security related patterns. We have evaluated our tool in terms of both its usability for target end users, and for quality of the encoded EUC-based security patterns.

In future, we plan to enhance our security pattern library using a-well-established standard: Common Criteria. Then we intend to compare the efficacy of our tool with manual approaches of extracting security requirements. Additionally, we will work on the possibility of automating currently complicated usage of the standard to produce a simpler practice by using our tool support. This would then create the possibility of allowing a complete and consistent capture of security requirements from normal business requirements.

Acknowledgments. The authors also would like to acknowledge Universiti Teknikal Malaysia Melaka and the Ministry of Education Malaysia of the scholarship Mybrain15. We also would like to thank the funding of this ERGS research grant: ERGS/2013/FTMK/ICT01/UTEM/E00026 for funding this research.

References

1. Alam, M.: Software Security Requirements Checklist. International Journal of Software Engineering, IJSE 3(1), 53–62 (2010)
2. McGraw, G.: Building Security. In: Software Security. IEEE Security and Privacy, pp. 80–83 (2004)
3. Schneider, K., Knauss, E., Houmb, S., Islam, S., Jürjens, J.: Enhancing security requirements engineering by organizational learning. Requirements Engineering 17(1), 35–56 (2011)
4. Paja, E., Dalpiaz, F., Poggianella, M., Roberti, P., Giorgini, P.: STS-tool: Socio-technical Security Requirements through social commitments. In: Conference on IEEE International Requirements Engineering, pp. 331–332 (2012)
5. Kamalrudin, M., Hosking, J., Grundy, J.: Improving requirements quality using essential use case interaction patterns. In: Proceeding of the 33rd International Conference on Software Engineering - ICSE 2011, p. 531 (2011)

6. Elahi, G., Yu, E.: A Semi-automated Decision Support Tool for Requirements Trade-Off Analysis. In: IEEE 35th Annual Computer Software and Applications Conference, pp. 466–475 (2011)
7. Kamalrudin, M., Grundy, J., Hosking, J.: Tool Support for Essential Use Cases to Better Capture Software Requirements, pp. 327–336 (2010)
8. Mellado., D., et al.: A systematic review of security requirements engineering. Computer Standards and Interfaces (2010)
9. Ding, W., Marchionini, G.: A Study on Video Browsing Strategies. Technical Report, University of Maryland (1997)
10. Fröhlich, B., Plate, J.: The cubic mouse: A new device for three-dimensional input. In: Proceedings of the SIGCHI (2000)
11. Firesmith, D.: Specifying reusable security requirements. Journal of Object Technology (2004)
12. Salini, P.: Survey and analysis on Security Requirements Engineering. Journal Computers and Electrical Electrical Engineering, http://linkinghub.elsevier.com/retrieve/pii/ S0045790612001644 (accessed October 1, 2012)
13. Corporation, M.: Simplified Implementation of the SDL. pp. 1–17 (2010)
14. Wiegers, K.E.: Software Requirements. O'Reilly (2009)
15. Souag, A., Salinesi, C., Comyn-Wattiau, I.: Ontologies for Security Requirements: A Literature Survey and Classification. In: Bajec, M., Eder, J. (eds.) CAiSE Workshops 2012. LNBIP, vol. 112, pp. 61–69. Springer, Heidelberg (2012)
16. Rodríguez, A., Fernández-Medina, E., Piattini, M.: Towards a UML 2.0 extension for the modeling of security requirements in business processes. In: Fischer-Hübner, S., Furnell, S., Lambrinoudakis, C. (eds.) TrustBus 2006. LNCS, vol. 4083, pp. 51–61. Springer, Heidelberg (2006)
17. Backes, M., Pfitzmann, B., Waidner, M.: Security in Business Process Engineering. In: van der Aalst, W.M.P., Weske, M. (eds.) BPM 2003. LNCS, vol. 2678, pp. 168–183. Springer, Heidelberg (2003)
18. Herrmann, G., et al.: Viewing Business Process Security from Different Perspectives. In: 11th International Bled Electronic Commerce Conference, Slovenia, pp. 89–103 (1998)
19. The SANS Institute, Determining the Role of the IA / Security Engineer, InfoSec Reading Room (2010)
20. Kamalrudin, M.: Automated Support for Consistency Management and Validation of Requirements". PhD thesis. The University of Auckland (2011)
21. Myagmar.: Threat Modeling as a Basis for Security Requirements. In: Proceedings of the ACM Workshop on Storage Security and Survivability, pp. 94–102 (2005)
22. Viega, J.: Building Security Requirements with CLASP. In: Proceedings of the Workshop on Software Engineering for Secure Systems Building Trustworthy Applications, SESS 2005, pp. 1–7 (2010)
23. Hussein, M., Zulkernine, M.: Intrusion detection aware component-based systems: A specification-based framework. Journal of Systems and Software 80(5), 700–710 (2007)
24. Du, J., et al.: An Analysis for Understanding Software Security Requirement Methodologies. In: Third IEEE International Conference on Secure Software Integration and Reliability Improvement, pp. 141–149 (2009)
25. Giorgini, P., et al.: Modeling security requirements through ownership, permission and delegation. In: 13th IEEE International Conference on Requirements Engineering (RE 2005), pp. 167–176 (2005)

26. Yahya, S., Kamalrudin, M., Sidek, S.: A Review on Tool Supports for Security Requirements Engineering. In: IEEE Conference on Open Systems, Sarawak, Malaysia (2013)
27. Paja, E., et al.: STS-tool: Socio-technical Security Requirements through social commitments. In: 2012 20th IEEE International Requirements Engineering Conference (RE), pp. 331–332. IEEE (2012)
28. Pavlidis, M., Islam, S.: SecTro: A CASE Tool for Modelling Security in Requirements Engineering using Secure Tropos. In: Proceedings of the CAiSE forum, CAiSE 2011, pp. 89–96 (2011)
29. Houmb, S.H., Islam, S., Knauss, E., Jürjens, J., Schneider, K.: Eliciting security requirements and tracing them to design: An integration of Common Criteria, heuristics, and UMLsec. Requirements Engineering 15(1), 63–93 (2010)
30. Mellado, D., Fernández-medina, E., Piattini, M.: Security Requirements Engineering Process for Software Product Lines: A Case Study and Technologies SREPPLine. pp. 1–6 (2008)
31. Giorgini, P., Massacci, F., Mylopoulos, J., Zannone, N.: ST-Tool: A CASE tool for security requirements engineering. In: Proceedings of 13th IEEE International Conference on Requirements Engineering, pp. 451–452 (2005)
32. Kamalrudin, M., Hosking, J.G., Grundy, J.C.: Improving Requirements Quality using Essential Use Case Interaction Patterns. In: ICSE 2011, Honolulu, Hawaii, USA (2011)
33. Kaindl, H., Constantine, L., Pastor, O., Sutcliffe, A., Zowghi, D.: How to Combine Requirements Engineering and Interaction Design? In: 16th IEEE International Requirements Engineering, RE 2008, Barcelona, Catalunya, Spain, pp. 299–301 (2008)
34. Kamalrudin, M., Grundy, J., Hosking, J.: Managing Consistency between Textual Requirements. Abstract Interactions and Essential Use Cases, 327–336 (2010)
35. Yahya, S., Kamalrudin, M., Sidek, S.: The Use of Essential Use Cases (EUCs) to enhance the Process of Capturing Security Requirements for Accurate Secure Software. In: Proceeding of Software Engineering Postgraduates Workshop, SEPoW (2013)
36. Kamalrudin, M.: Automated Software Tool Support for Checking the Inconsistency of Requirements. In: 24th IEEE/ACM International Conference on Automated Software Engineering, ASE 2009. IEEE (2009)
37. Constantine, L.L., Lockwood, A.D.L.: Software for Use: A Practical Guide to the Models and Methods of Usage-Centered Design. ACM Press/Addison Wesley Longman, Inc. (1999)
38. Develop functional security requirements in Document security-relevant requirements retrieve, https://www.owasp.org/index.php/ Document_security-relevant_requirements (accessed July 15, 2013)
39. Blackwell, A.F., et al.: Cognitive Dimensions of Notations: Design Tools for Cognitive Technology. In: Beynon, M., Nehaniv, C.L., Dautenhahn, K. (eds.) CT 2001. LNCS (LNAI), vol. 2117, pp. 325–341. Springer, Heidelberg (2001)
40. What is the Common Criteria (CC) in Common Criteria and Mutual Recognition retrieve from, http://www.cybersecurity.my/myc (accessed August 5, 2013)
41. Biddle, R., Noble, J., Tempero, E.: Essential use cases and responsibility in object-oriented development. In: Proceeding of the Twenty-Fifth Australasian Conference on Computer Science, Melbourne, Victoria, Australia, pp. 7–16. ACM (2002)
42. Biddle, R., Noble, J., Tempero, E.: Patterns for Essential Use Case Bodies. In: Proceedings of the 2002 Conference on Pattern languages of programs, CRPIT 2002, vol. 13, pp. 85–98. Computer Society, Australian (2002)

Utilizing TOPSIS: A Multi Criteria Decision Analysis Technique for Non-Functional Requirements Conflicts

Dewi Mairiza[1], Didar Zowghi[1], and Vincenzo Gervasi[1,2]

[1] Faculty of Engineering and Information Technology,
University of Technology, Sydney (UTS), Australia
[2] Dipartimento di Informatica
Università di Pisa, I-56125 Pisa, Italy
`mairiza@it.uts.edu.au, Didar.Zowghi@uts.edu.au,`
`gervasi@di.unipi.it`

Abstract. Experience shows that many software systems suffer from inherent conflict among Non-Functional Requirements (NFRs). It also confirms that resolution strategies for handling NFRs conflicts often result in changing overall design guidelines, not by simply changing one module. Therefore, in software system development, software developers need to analyse the NFRs and conflicts among them in order to make decisions about alternative design solutions. This paper presents the use of Multi Criteria Decision Analysis (MCDA) approach for NFRs conflict decision analysis. TOPSIS (Technique for Order of Preference by Similarity to Ideal Solution), as one of the essential MCDA techniques has been adopted to resolve such conflict. We show how the systematic application of TOPSIS can assist software developers select the most preferable design solutions with respect to the conflicting NFRs. The quantitative result generated with this technique will be used as the basis for decision support. An example that shows the application of TOPSIS is also presented.

Keywords: Non-Functional Requirements, design solution, conflict resolution, MCDA, TOPSIS, decision analysis.

1 Introduction

Non-Functional Requirements play a critical role in the success of software projects. They address the essential issue of software quality [1-3] and they are also considered as the qualifications of operations [4, 5]. Prior study reveals that there are 252 types of NFRs listed in the literature [6]. Among them, 114 types correspond to the NFRs perspective in relation to the "quality". This huge number reflects how NFRs can be more critical than individual Functional Requirements (FRs) in the determination of a system's perceived success or failure. Neglecting NFRs may lead to software failure, as discussed in a series of systemic failures in the literature [6-9].

NFRs are interacting, which means that they tend to interfere, conflict, and contradict with one another [1]. Achieving a particular type of NFR can hurt the

D. Zowghi and Z. Jin (Eds.): APRES 2014, CCIS 432, pp. 31–44, 2014.

achievement of the other type(s) of NFRs. Unlike FRs, this inevitable conflict arises as a result of inherent contradiction among various types of NFRs [1, 2]. Certain combinations of NFRs in the software systems may affect the inescapable trade offs [2, 8, 10]. Dealing with and managing NFRs conflict is essential [11], not only because conflict among software requirements are inevitable [1, 12, 13], but also because conflicting requirements are one of the three main problems in the software development in term of the additional effort or mistakes attributed to them [13]. A study of two-year multiple-project analysis conducted by Egyed & Boehm [14, 15] reports that between 40% and 60% of requirements involved are in conflict, and among them, NFRs involved the greatest conflict, which was nearly half of the total requirements conflict [16]. Therefore, since conflict among NFRs have also been widely acknowledged as one of NFRs characteristics, managing this conflict as well as making this conflict explicit is important [17].

This paper presents the outcome of our longitudinal study of investigating conflicts among NFRs. Utilizing TOPSIS, an MCDA technique to resolve the NFRs conflicts is presented as the novel contribution of the paper. Integrating TOPSIS with our foregoing sureCM Framework can assist software developers performing NFRs conflict decision analysis quantitatively.

This article is organized in five sections. The first section is the introduction to NFRs and conflicts among them. The second section describes the research background and some earlier works. The use of TOPSIS for NFRs conflict decision analysis is presented in section three, continued by illustrating an example of how TOPSIS can be applied in NFRs conflict management in section four. Then, section five concludes this paper by highlighting some open issues that have emerged from the investigation.

2   Study Background

A number of techniques to manage NFRs conflict have been discussed in the literature [11]. Majority of them provide documentation, catalogue, or list of potential conflicts. These catalogues represent the interrelationships among various types of NFRs. Some examples are: the QARCC win-win approach [8, 18, 19], trace analyzer of the requirements traceability technique [20], and a technique that adopts a hierarchical constraint logic programming approach [21]. Apart from strength and weaknesses of each technique, NFRs can be viewed, interpreted, and evaluated differently by different people and different context within which the system is being developed. Consequently, the positive or negative relationships among NFRs are not always obvious. These relationships might change depending on the meaning of NFRs in the context of the system being developed. Due to this relative characteristic, cataloguing the NFRs relationships in order to represent the conflict among them would inevitably produce disagreement. Identifying the NFRs conflict without understanding the meaning of NFRs in the system may produce erroneous conflict identification and analysis.

This study is conducted as part of a long-term project of investigating the relative conflicts among NFRs. The project's ultimate goal is to develop a novel framework to effectively identify, characterize and resolve the NFRs conflict. Earlier versions of the framework have been published in [22-24]. The sureCM Framework utilizes an experimental approach as the basis to attain the evidence for managing the NFRs conflict. As shown in Figure 1, sureCM Framework has five-layer sequential process: P1 (Define Case); P2 (Identify Metrics and Measure); P3 (Setup and Run Experiments); P4 (Characterize Conflict); and P5 (Conflict Decision Analysis). Each process has different roles and outputs. Here, NFRs are characterized as the associated system functionality and systems operationalizations, and NFRs metrics and measures are used as parameters to gather the quantitative evidence in the experiments. Then, this empirical evidence will be used to perform conflict decision analysis. Conflict Decision Analysis (P5) process is currently limited to translating the experimental result into the conflict categorization. The decision about which alternative design solutions to be implemented within the system is not defined yet. Given the above context, we are motivated to perform further research into extending the framework for NFRs conflict decision analysis. The objective is to select the best design solution with respect to those conflicting NFRs. The main research question that we address is as follow:

"How can we use the Multi Criteria Decision Analysis (MCDA) approach to perform NFRs conflict decision analysis?"

The utilization of MCDA approach for conflict decision analysis is presented as the novel contribution of this paper. This approach will be applied to analyze the alternative design solutions, with the ultimate goal to select the one that best satisfices[1] the conflicting NFRs.

3   NFRs Conflict Decision Using TOPSIS

Every decision requires the balancing of multiple factors, i.e. criteria. Therefore a formal analysis is needed to promote a good decision-making. Multi Criteria Decision Analysis (MCDA) assists decision makers to structure and solving decision problems involving multiple criteria. It provides guideline that help decision makers to organize and synthesize such information so that they will feel comfortable and confident about making the decision [26, 27]. It also helps to structure the problem. Based on these characteristics, we propose to apply MCDA to perform the NFRs conflict decision analysis in sureCM Framework. It can be used to evaluate and analyze the alternative design solutions. It can also be used to decide the best design solution that best satisfices the conflicting NFRs.

---

[1] Satisfice is the term first coined by Hebert Simon [25]   H. A. Simon, "The science of the artificial," 1996.

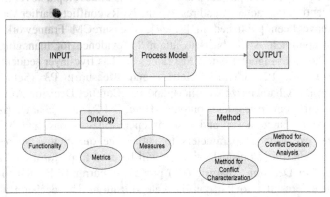

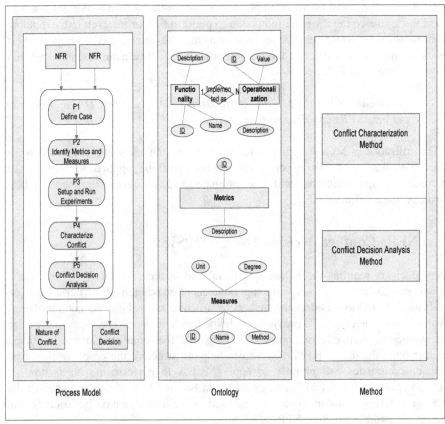

sureCM Framework

Fig. 1. sureCM Framework [23]

TOPSIS (Technique for Order of Preference by Similarity to Ideal Solution) is a goal-based technique in MCDA for finding the alternative that is closest to the ideal solution. The fundamental idea of TOPSIS is that the best solution is the one, which has the shortest distance to the ideal solution and the farthest distance from the negative-ideal solution. Therefore, the best solution is the one that can maximize all criteria.

TOPSIS consists of 6 steps as shown in Figure 2: (1) construct the normalized decision matrix; (2) construct the weighted normalized decision matrix; (3) determine the positive ideal solution and negative ideal solution; (4) determine separation from ideal solution; (5) calculate the relative closeness to the ideal solution; and (6) rank the preference order and select the closest option to ideal solution.

Some basic principles of TOPSIS are:
→ The chosen alternative should be as close as possible to the ideal solution and as far as possible from the negative-ideal solution.
→ The positive-ideal solution is formed as a composite of the best performance values exhibited (in the decision matrix) by any alternative for each attribute.
→ The negative-ideal solution is the composite of the worst performance values; this means the one that has the worst attribute values.
→ Proximity to each of these performance poles is measured in the Euclidean sense (e.g., square root of the sum of the squared distances along each axis in the "attribute space"), with optional weighting of each attribute.

Figure 2 shows the six steps of TOPSIS. It starts with creating an evaluation matrix $X_{ij}(mxn)$ consisting of m alternative, n attributes/criteria and the score of each alternative with respect to each attribute. The matrix $X_{ij}(mxn)$ is then normalized using such formula in step 1 to form the matrix r_{ij}. A normalized decision matrix will be formed. Next step is calculating the weighted normalized decision matrix V_{ij} by multiplying the normalized scores r_{ij} by their corresponding weights w_j. Weight is defined as a certain points that estimate the relative importance of each criteria. And weight is optional. Continue to step 3 to determine the positive ideal solution and negative ideal solution, that is, the worst alternative and the best alternative. A^+ is the maximum value of each attribute, and A^- is the minimum value of each attribute.

Step 4 is then calculating the distance for each alternative to the ideal solution. This step is taken to calculate the similarity to the worst condition, by calculating the separation measures for each alternative from the positive (S^+) and negative (S^-) ideal solution. This is then continued by calculating the relative closeness to the ideal solution (C_i^*) and rank the preference order of alternative based on its relative closeness to the ideal solution, i.e. a set of alternatives would be preference-ranked according to descending order of C_i^*.

Step 1: Construct the normalized decision matrix.

$$r_{ij} = \frac{x_{ij}}{\sqrt{\sum_{i=1}^{m} x_{ij}^2}}$$

Step 2: Construct the weighted normalized decision matrix.

$$V = \begin{bmatrix} v_{11} & v_{12} & \cdots & v_{1j} & \cdots & v_{1n} \\ \cdot & & & & & \cdot \\ v_{i1} & v_{i2} & & v_{ij} & & v_{in} \\ \cdot & & & & & \cdot \\ \cdot & & & & & \cdot \\ v_{m1} & v_{m2} & \cdots & v_{mj} & \cdots & v_{mn} \end{bmatrix} = \begin{bmatrix} w_1 r_{11} & w_2 r_{12} & \cdots & w_j r_{ij} & \cdots & w_n r_{1n} \\ \cdot & & & & & \cdot \\ w_1 r_{i1} & w_2 r_{i2} & & w_j r_{ij} & & w_n r_{in} \\ \cdot & & & & & \cdot \\ \cdot & & & & & \cdot \\ w_1 r_{m1} & w_2 r_{m2} & \cdots & w_j r_{mj} & \cdots & w_n r_{mn} \end{bmatrix}$$

Step 3: Determine the positive ideal (S+) and negative ideal (S---) solutions.

$$A^* = \{ (\max_i v_{ij} | j \in J), (\min_i v_{ij} | j \in J') | i = 1,2,...m \}$$

$$= \{ v_1^*, v_2^*, ..., v_j^*, ..., v_n^* \}$$

$$A^- = \{ (\min_i v_{ij} | j \in J), (\max_i v_{ij} | j \in J') | i = 1,2,...m \}$$

$$= \{ v_1^-, v_2^-, ..., v_j^-, ..., v_n^- \}$$

$$\text{where} \quad J = \left\{ j = 1,2,....,n \middle| j \quad \text{associated} \quad \text{with} \quad \text{benefit} \quad \text{criteria} \right\}$$

$$J' = \left\{ j = 1,2,....,n \middle| j \quad \text{associated} \quad \text{with} \quad \text{cost} \quad \text{criteria} \right\}$$

Fig. 2a. – NFRs Conflict Decision Analysis with TOPSIS (Step 1 – 3)

Step 4: Calculate the separation measures for each alternative.

— **Ideal Separation**

$$S_i^+ = \sqrt{\sum_{j=1}^{n}(v_{ij} - v_j^+)^2} \qquad i = 1,2,...,m$$

— **Negative-Ideal Separation**

$$S_i^- = \sqrt{\sum_{j=1}^{n}(v_{ij} - v_j^-)^2} \qquad i = 1,2,...,m$$

Step 5: Calculate the relative closeness to the ideal solution C_{i*}.

$$c_i^* = \frac{S_i^-}{(S_i^+ + S_i^-)}, \qquad 0 < c_i^* < 1, \qquad i = 1,2,...,m$$

$$c_i^* = 1 \quad if \quad A_i = A^+$$

$$c_i^* = 0 \quad if \quad A_i = A^-$$

Step 6: Rank the preference order.

Select the option with C_{i*} closest to 1 (the highest one).

Fig. 2b. NFRs Conflict Decision Analysis with TOPSIS (Step 4 – 6)

Figure 3 shows how TOPSIS can be implemented in sureCM Framework. In the framework, input for TOPSIS is the conflict relationship diagram, which is obtained from the previous sureCM process (P3 and P4). Conflict relationship diagram (as shown in Figure 4) is a two-dimensional conflict relationship graph that uses quantitative data obtained in process P3, i.e. running the experiments, as the evidence of existence of conflict [23]. Each operationalization taken in the experiments will be plotted based on its NFRs metrics calculation result. By plotting all of the defined operationalizations, a conflict relationship characterization will be created. In the context of this framework, the criteria refer to the conflicting NFRs, and the alternatives refer to the alternative design solutions/operationalizations. Output of this conflict decision process is a decision, which is the ranking of each alternative design solution based on its closeness to the ideal solution, i.e. maximum satisficing for each conflicting NFRs.

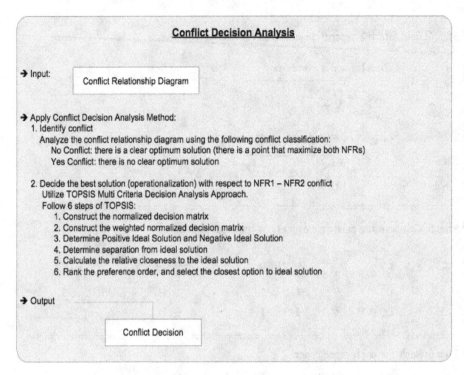

Fig. 3. sureCM Framework Conflict Decision Analysis

4   Applying TOPSIS: An Example

To show how TOPSIS can be applied for NFRs conflict decision analysis, in this paper we use two statement of NFR from the Chemical Tracking System [23]. We consider the two NFRs given in the specification document. NFR1 is considered a security requirement, while NFR2 is a usability requirement.

NFR 1: The Chemical Tracking System shall have identified/authenticated the user and protect user's personal information.

NFR 2: A chemist who has never used the system before shall be able to learn using the system easily and independently.

The sureCM Framework supports the characteriz and identification of conflict, as well as performing conflict decision analysis. The details of NFRs conflict characterization and identification (process P1; P2; P3; P4) have been presented previously in [23], so here we only focus on conflict decision analysis (process P5). As described in [23], the first four processes of sureCM Framework produce a set of experimental data and the conflict relationship diagram. By using 7 types of alternative design solutions for implementing security and usability, i.e. (1) Fixed Key; (2) Smart Card; (3) Scrambled Key; (4) Geometrical Pin Code; (5) Finger Print; (6) Palm Scanner; (7) Retina Scanner, the nature of conflict is illustrated as follow:

Exp. ID	Ops.	Security	Usability	Note
GA.T.1	Fixed Key	4	0.0641	---
GA.T.2	Smart Card	1	0.1053	---
GA.T.3	Scrambled Key	7	0.0503	---
GA.T.4	Geometrical Pin Code	9	0.0500	---
GA.T.5	Finger Print	1	0.1563	---
GA.T.6	Palm Scanner	1	0.1370	---
GA.T.7	Retina Scanner	1	0.1266	---

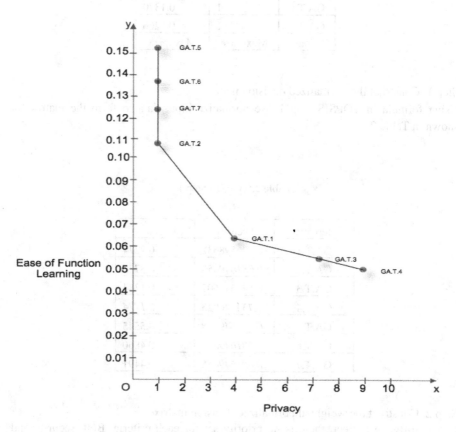

Fig. 4. Conflict Relationship Diagram of Security – Usability Conflict [23]

This will be used as the input for NFRs conflict decision analysis with TOPSIS, presented in Table 1. Then each TOPSIS step is described.

Table 1. TOPSIS Input

Weight	1	1
	Security	Usability
GA.T.1	4	0.0641
GA.T.2	1	0.1053
GA.T.3	7	0.0503
GA.T.4	9	0.0500
GA.T.5	1	0.1563
GA.T.6	1	0.1370
GA.T.7	1	0.1266
Goal	Maximize	Maximize

Step 1: Construct the normalized decision matrix.

Using formula in TOPSIS step 1, we normalize input data to form the matrix r_{ij}, shown in Table 2.

Table 2. TOPSIS Step 1

Alternative	Security	Usability
GA.T.1	0.326598632	0.2274
GA.T.2	*0.081649658*	0.3736
GA.T.3	0.571547607	0.1784
GA.T.4	**0.734846923**	*0.1774*
GA.T.5	*0.081649658*	**0.5545**
GA.T.6	*0.081649658*	0.4860
GA.T.7	*0.081649658*	0.4491

Step 2: Construct the weighted normalized decision matrix.

In this software project, there is no priority set for each criteria. Both security and usability have the same priority level. Therefore, the weighted normalized decision matrix gives the same result as generated in step 1.

Step 3: Determine the positive ideal (S+) and negative ideal (S-) solutions by determining A^+ and A^- for each criteria. This is done by selecting the highest element (for A^+) and the lowest element (for A^-) in each criteria of the matrix in Table 2. The result is presented in Table 3.

Table 3. Positive Ideal and Negative Ideal Solutions

A+

Security	Usability
0.734846923	0.55450207

A-

Security	Usability
0.081649658	0.1773839

Step 4: Calculate the separation measures for each alternative
Euclidean distance is used to measure the separation of each alternative design solution from the ideal alternative (positive ideal) and negative ideal alternative.

Table 4. Separation Measures

Alternative	(S+)	(S-)
GA.T.1	0.523123696	0.250004453
GA.T.2	0.677792669	0.196186593
GA.T.3	0.409979485	0.489899105
GA.T.4	0.377118171	0.653197265
GA.T.5	0.653197265	0.377118171
GA.T.6	0.656776090	0.308647985
GA.T.7	0.661640891	0.271752134

Step 5: Calculate the relative closeness to the ideal solution C_i^*
The higher C_i^* is the better, which means the closer the alternative to the ideal solution. Using TOPSIS step 5 formula, C_i^* is calculated and presented in Table 5.

Table 5. Relative Closeness

Alternatives	C*
GA.T.1	0.323367417
GA.T.2	0.224475112
GA.T.3	0.544405779
GA.T.4	0.633977947
GA.T.5	0.366022053
GA.T.6	0.319701977
GA.T.7	0.291144381

Step 6: Rank the preference order

A set of alternatives can now be preference ranked according to the descending order of $Ci*$. The best solution is the alternative with C_i^* closest to 1, which is the highest one. The result of step 6 is presented in Table 6.

Table 6. Final Result

Alternatives	C*	Ranked	Ranked	Design Solutions
GA.T.1	0.323367417	4	1	Geometrical Pin Code
GA.T.2	0.224475112	7	2	Scrambled Key
GA.T.3	0.544405779	2	3	Finger Print
GA.T.4	0.633977947	1	4	Fixed Key
GA.T.5	0.366022053	3	5	Palm Scanner
GA.T.6	0.319701977	5	6	Retina Scanner
GA.T.7	0.291144381	6	7	Smart Card

As shown in Table 6, the highest C_i^* is the alternative 4 ($C_i^* = 0.633977947$), that means GA.T.4 is the design solution that has maximum security and maximum usability, among other alternatives. Therefore, according to TOPSIS, software developer should consider taking alternative 4 (Geometrical Pin Code) as the design solution that can maximize the satisfaction of those conflicting NFRs, security and usability.

5   Conclusion

This paper describes a novel idea of utilizing TOPSIS, an MCDA technique, to resolve the conflict among NFRs, particularly to perform conflict decision analysis that can assist software developer deciding the best alternative design solution that can maximize the satisficing of NFRs in conflict. Conflict decision analysis using TOPSIS will be integrated as part of our foregoing sureCM Framework [22-24], i.e. an integrated experimental-based framework for NFRs conflict management and analysis. Requirements statement from a Chemical Tracking System has been used as an example to show how TOPSIS can be applied.

As part of a long-term project of investigating conflict among NFRs, a number of important task remain to complete:

1) Conducting empirical evaluation

The effectiveness of the framework will be empirically evaluated through controlled experiments. The reason for conducting controlled experiments is because: (a) "controlled experiments make it possible for the careful observation and precise manipulation of independent variables (e.g. proposed framework); (b) allowing for greater certainty; and (c) encourage the researcher to try out novel frameworks in a safe and exploratory environment before implementing them in the real world settings" [28]. Effectiveness and efficiency will be used as the evaluation criteria. Effectiveness means that this framework can be used to manage the NFRs conflict by considering NFRs relative characteristic, while efficiency represents how fast people can identify the conflict using the framework.

2) Developing a semi-automatic tool

To support the framework utilization, we also plan to develop a semi-automatic tool that can assist software developers, particularly requirements engineers to perform conflict management among NFRs.

Acknowledgments. We would like to thank The International Schlumberger Foundation Paris for funding this research through Faculty for the Future Award Program. We would also like to thank The Centre for Human Centered Technology Design (HCTD) at UTS for partially funding Dr Gervasi's trip for research collaboration.

References

[1] Chung, L., Nixon, B.A., Yu, E., Mylopoulos, J.: Non-functional requirements in software engineering. Kluwer Academic Publishers, Massachusetts (2000)
[2] Ebert, C.: Putting requirement management into praxis: Dealing with nonfunctional requirements. Information and Software Technology 40, 175–185 (1998)
[3] Firesmith, D.: Using quality models to engineer quality requirements. Journal of Object Technology 2, 67–75 (2003)
[4] Kotonya, G., Sommerville, I.: Non-functional requirements (1998)
[5] Mittermeir, R.T., Roussopoulos, N., Yeh, R.T., Ng, P.A.: Modern software engineering, foundations and current perspectives. Van Nostrand Reinhold Co., New York (1989)
[6] Mairiza, D., Zowghi, D., Nurmuliani, N.: An investigation into the notion of non-functional requirements. In: 25th ACM Symposium on Applied Computing, Switzerland (2010)
[7] Breitman, K.K., Prado Leite, J.C.S., Finkelstein, A.: The world's a stage: A survey on requirements engineering using a real-life case study. Journal of the Brazilian Computer Society 6, 1–57 (1999)

[8] Boehm, B., In, H.: Identifying quality-requirements conflict. IEEE Software 13, 25–35 (1996)

[9] Leveson, N.G., Turner, C.S.: An investigation of the Therac-25 accidents. IEEE Computer 26, 18–41 (1993)

[10] Wiegers, K.E.: Software requirements, 2nd edn. Microsoft Press, Washington (2003)

[11] Mairiza, D., Zowghi, D., Nurmuliani, N.: Managing conflicts among non-functional requirements. In: 12th Australian Workshop on Requirements Engineering (AWRE 2009), Sydney, Australia (2009)

[12] Chung, L., Nixon, B.A., Yu, E.: Dealing with change: an approach using non-functional requirements. Requirements Engineering 1, 238–260 (1996)

[13] Curtis, B., Krasner, H., Iscoe, N.: A field study of the software design process for large systems. Communication of the ACM 31, 1268–1287 (1988)

[14] Boehm, B., Egyed, A.: WinWin requirements negotiation processes: A multi-project analysis. In: 5th International Conference on Software Processes (1998)

[15] Egyed, A., Boehm, B.: A comparison study in software requirements negotiation. In: 8th Annual International Symposium on Systems Engineering, INCOSE 1998 (1998)

[16] Robinson, W.N., Pawlowski, S.D., Volkov, V.: Requirements interaction management. ACM Computing Surveys 35, 132–190 (2003)

[17] Paech, B., Kerkow, D.: Non-functional requirements engineering - quality is essential. In: 10th International Workshop on Requirements Engineering: Foundation for Software Quality, pp. 27–40 (2004)

[18] Boehm, B., In, H.: Aids for identifying conflicts among quality requirements. IEEE Software (March 1996)

[19] In, H., Boehm, B., Rodgers, T., Deutsch, M.: Aplying WinWin to quality requirements: A case study. In: 23rd International Conference on Software Engineering, Toronto, Ontario, Canada, pp. 555–564 (2001)

[20] Egyed, A., Grünbacher, P.: Identifying requirements conflicts and cooperation: how quality attributes and automated traceability can help. IEEE Software 21, 50–58 (2004)

[21] Guan, Y., Ghose, A.K.: Use constraint hierarchy for non-functional requirements analysis. In: Lowe, D., Gaedke, M. (eds.) ICWE 2005. LNCS, vol. 3579, pp. 104–109. Springer, Heidelberg (2005)

[22] Mairiza, D., Zowghi, D.: An ontological framework to manage the relative conflicts between security and usability requirements. In: The Third International Workshop on Managing Requirements Knowledge (MaRK 2010), in conjunction with the 18th IEEE International Requirements Engineering Conference (RE 2010), Sydney, Australia (2010)

[23] Mairiza, D., Zowghi, D., Gervasi, V.: Conflict characterization and analysis of non functional requirements: An experimental approach. In: 12th International Conference on New Trends in Software Methodologies, Tools and Techniques (SOMET 2013), Budapest, Hungary, pp. 83–91 (2013)

[24] Mairiza, D.: Non-functional requirements in software development projects: A systematic review. Presented at the ACS – BRASIG 29, Sydney, Australia (September 2011)

[25] Simon, H.A.: The science of the artificial (1996)

[26] Belton, V., S.T.J.: Multiple criteria decision analysis: An integrated approach. Kluwer Academic Publishers (2002)

[27] Zopounidis, C., Pardalos, P.M.: Handbook of multicriteria analysis. Springer, Heidelberg (2010)

[28] Damian, D.: Empirical studies of computer support for distributed requirements negotiation. University of Calgary (2001)

Analysis of Economic Impact of Online Reviews: An Approach for Market-Driven Requirements Evolution

Wei Jiang[1], Haibin Ruan[2], and Li Zhang[1]

[1] School of Computer Science and Engineering, Beihang University, Beijing, China
jiangwei@cse.buaa.edu.cn, lily@buaa.edu.cn
[2] Investment Department, Central University of Finance and Economics, Beijing, China
nivadacufe@gmail.com

Abstract. As a novel market data, online reviews can manifest user demands in real contexts of use. Thereby, this paper proposes a demand-centered approach for requirements evolution by mining and analyzing online reviews. In our approach, it is challenging to improve the accuracy of opinion mining techniques for huge volume of noisy review data. Furthermore, how to quantitatively evaluate the economic impact of user opinions for determining candidate requirements changes is also a challenging problem. In this paper, an opinion mining method augmented with noise pruning techniques is presented to automatically extract user opinions. After automatic synthesizing the information extracted, a utility-oriented econometric model is employed to find causal influences between the system aspects frequently mentioned in user opinions and common user demands for revising current requirements. A case study shows that the presented method of opinion mining achieves good precision and recall even if there is a large amount of noisy review data. The case study also validates the effectiveness of our approach that it discovers the candidate requirements changes related to the software revenue, especially the ones that are ignored by software developers.

Keywords: Electronic market, requirements evolution, online reviews, opinion mining, econometric analysis.

1 Introduction

Evolution is an inherent attribute of software requirements due to changing user needs and application environment [1]. In today's competitive market, it is crucial for the software system to respond to the social environment where users form opinions based on their experience with it [2]. With user generated content becoming mainstream in Web platforms, consumers are willing to publish online reviews to express their opinions about software systems. As market data, these reviews manifest user demands in real contexts of use, which have become a very important resource for eliciting requirements for designing future systems. Therefore, our goal is to explore a demand-centered approach for requirements evolution through mining and analyzing online reviews. We first automatically extract software features and relevant user

D. Zowghi and Z. Jin (Eds.): APRES 2014, CCIS 432, pp. 45–59, 2014.
© Springer-Verlag Berlin Heidelberg 2014

opinions from online reviews. Second, we determine candidate requirements changes by econometric analysis of user opinions.

Currently, some automated techniques, such as text mining, information retrieval, and machine learning are utilized in identifying the aspects of the software system and associated opinions mentioned in user comments [3, 4]. However, due to different content quality of reviews, it is challenging to ensure the accuracy of automated techniques for huge volume of review data. In this paper, we augment the existing opinion mining method with noise pruning techniques. Experiment results show that our method achieves good performance even if large amounts of noisy review data.

Furthermore, the system aspects frequently commented on in user opinions are useful evidence to design requirements for future systems. Several approaches have provided a set of techniques and processes about how to analyze and determine requirements in accordance with user feedback [5, 6]. However, content analysis in these approaches relies more on the manual effort. Moreover, the evaluation models of user opinions cannot consider market elements. How to quantitatively evaluate the economic impact of user opinions for determining candidate requirements changes is also a challenging problem. In our approach, we first adopt the text clustering technique and heuristic method to group and rate user opinions. Then, we employ a utility-oriented econometric model to find causal influences between the system aspects frequently commented on in user opinions and common user demands for revising current requirements. A case study validates the effectiveness of our approach that it discovers the candidate requirements changes related to user demands, especially the ones that tend to be ignored by software developers.

The contributions of our research are as follows: (1) our opinion mining method can accurately deal with large amounts of noisy reviews; and (2) our approach can support analysts to make wise decision on requirements evolution in the open market by suggesting the requirements changes that are more economically valuable.

The rest of this paper is organized as follows. Section 2 describes the method for opinion mining. Section 3 elaborates econometric analysis for requirements evolution according to the exracted user opinions. To evaluate our approach, Section 4 presents a case study in which the candidate requirements changes for the future system are derived from the review data of Kaspersky Internet Security 2011. Finally, Section 5 and Section 6 discuss related work, conclusions and future work.

2   User Opinion Mining

The user opinion in a review of the software system is defined as a pair of *feature* and *opinion*. The feature refers to a software feature that is a prominent or distinctive user-visible aspect, quality, or characteristic of the system [10]. The opinion is a subjective user evaluation expressed on the feature. Opinions and features are often related syntactically and their relations can be modeled using the dependency grammar [4]. Therefore, we adopt the syntactic relation-based propagation approach (SRPA) [7] for fine-gained opinion mining. However, once there is a large amount of noisy review data, SRPA may introduce much noise and result in the decrease in the accuracy. We augment SRPA with pruning noisy opinion words and features. Finally, we recover complete expressions of user opinions according to the extracted individual words.

2.1 Extracting User Opinions Using SRPA

SRPA is a bootstrapping approach, which uses the syntactic relations that link opinion words and features to expand the initial opinion lexicon and extract features. A rule-based strategy is used to iteratively perform the extraction task through propagation. The extration rules modeling noun features and adjective opinion words are defined according to the syntactic dependency relations in which people often express their opinions. Through the identification of extration rules, the propagation algorithm is first bootstrapped by the seed opinion lexicon to extract opinion words and features, then applies newly extracted words to further extraction, and finally stops until no more new words are extracted. In this way, SRPA has good results of precision and recall even if the initial opinion lexicon is small.

For opinion extraction, we first redefine the exraction rules based on Stanford syntactic parser[1]. Second, we take raw review data of the software system and a seed lexicon as the input of SRPA and then obtain the set of extracted features and the expanded opinion lexicon. Third, we identify the reveiw sentences matching the extraction rules and extract <feature, opinion> pairs whose features and opinion words are respectively involved in the extracted feature set and expanded opinion lexicon. Finally, we adopt the noise pruning method in SRPA to remove the user opinions for other competitive systems.

2.2 Pruning Noisy Opinion Words

Although some adjectives modify features, they do not have any positive, negative or neutral sentiment polarity. For example, in the sentence "The latest version is good", good is a positive opinion word whereas latest is an ordinary adjective. However, latest is extracted incorrectly. This means that SRPA may introduce noisy opinion words, as the extraction rules are unconstrained.

We determine whether the extracted adjectives are noise using the following heuristic rules, which are defined from observing contexts of the reviews.   **Rule 1**: When two adjectives modify the same feature in a clause, the adjective before it as the adjectival modifier is an ordinary adjective if the adjective after it as the predicative adjectives is an opinion word.   **Rule 2**: Two adjectives in a clause that are connected by a coordinating conjunction or have a coordinating relation are either opinion words or ordinary adjectives. **Rule 3**: When two adjectives modify the same feature in different sentences, the adjective after it as the predicative adjectives is also an opinion word if the adjective before it as the adjectival modifier is an opinion word.

---

[1] http://nlp.stanford.edu/software/lex-parser.shtml

The extracted adjectives are initially recognized as opinion words if they are involved in an opinion word lexicon, such as MPQA[2] and Liu's opinion words[3]. The reasoning is performed according to the above three rules. Most adjectives may be identified as either ordinary adjectives or opinion words. However, some adjectives are still not determined on the context evidence. Such adjectives are regarded as opinion words for avoiding that excessive pruning decrease the recall of opinion mining.

2.3   Pruning Noisy Features

In expressions of user opinions, features refer to domain-specific nouns that appear more frequently in a certain domain and less in other domains. However, most opinion words are domain-independent adjectives that can modify any object. As a result, SRPA increases the risk of introducing ordinary nouns when using opinion words to extract features. For example, there are two sentences "*Kaspersky occupies many resources*" and "*I have used Kaspersky for many years*". The ordinary noun *years* is incorrectly extracted through the opinion word *many* modifying the feature *resources*.

Observing the way in which people express their opinions, we can see that features are frequently modified by opinion words. Based on such observation, we count the numbers of opinon words and ordinary adjectives modifying each extracted noun and employ the standard Support Vector Machine (SVM) algorithm [8] to identify correct features. The SVM inputs a set of pre-classified nouns with high frequency opinion words or ordinary adjectives, and then trains a binary linear classifier to predict the category of a new noun.

In the training phase, suppose $F=\{f_1, f_2, ..., f_n\}$ is the training feature set. For $\forall f_i \in F$, it is assigned a $(\mathbf{x}_i, y_i)$ where $\mathbf{x}_i$ is a 2-dimensional integer vector $\mathbf{x}_i=\{x_{i1}, x_{i2}\}$ corresponding to the nubmers of opinon words and ordinary adjectives of f_i and $y_i \in (1, -1)$ determines whether f_i is a feature. The SVM model trains a classifier as

$$L(\mathbf{x}_i)=\mathbf{w}\mathbf{x}_i +b \tag{1}$$

where $\mathbf{w}=\{w_1, w_2\}$ is the weight vector, b is a real offset. In accordance with maximal margin that wants to find decision boundary that is as far away from the data of both classes as possible, we can get the optimal vector. Furthermore, when a new noun comes, we can determine whether it is a feature through the trained SVM classifier.

2.4   Recovering Expressions of User Opinions

Base on the propagation algorithm, the extracted features and opinion are individual words. However, the feature can be a noun phrase and the opinion may be an adjective phrase including an opinion word and its adverb modifiers. For example, in the sentence "*The user interface is not very intuitive*", the feature *user interface* is a noun phrase and the opinion *not very intuitive* is a negative adjective phrase. We thereby

---

[2] http://mpqa.cs.pitt.edu/lexicons/subj_lexicon/
[3] http://www.cs.uic.edu/~liub/FBS/sentiment-analysis.html

use shallow parsing techniques to recover complete expressions of user opinions. The Stanford parser can output the phrase structure tree of a sentence. In the tree, the noun/ adjective phrase that contains the extracted feature/opinion word is recognized as the feature/opinion phrase. Moreover, a negative word in the clause modifying the opinion word is also identified as a part of the opinion phrase even if it is not directly contained in the adjective phrase.

3   Econometric Opinion Analysis

High ratings of user satisfaction are widely believed to be the best indicator of the company's future profits [9]. In requirements analysis, we thereby emphasize the economic benefits that result from the system improvement with changing user demands. A utility-oriented econometric model is employed to find the candidate requirements changes for system improvement. The detailed steps are as follows: (1) organizing the similar extracted features into a system aspect relevant to an overall, functional or quality requirement, (2) rating the associated opinions with the extracted features, (3) analyzing the causal relationships between the utilities of system aspects and software sales and then determine the important aspects for revising current requirements, and finally (4) generating a meaningful report on the candidate requirements changes.

3.1   Categorizing Features

As what features may be mentioned in the reviews is unknown, the k-means clustering [20] is adopted to categorize the extracted features into system aspects that depict their semantic commonalities. The k-means clustering aims to divide n data points into k clusters so as to minimize the mean squared distance from each point to the center within a cluster. There are two potential problems using the k-means algorithm for categorizing features: how to compute the distance between features and how to choose k seeds for avoiding poor clusters.

For the first issue, the distance between features is defined as the difference between 1 and their semantic similarity. We rely on an explicit semantic analysis algorithm (ESA) to compute semantic similarity. The idea of ESA is to use machine learning techniques to represent the meaning of any text as a weighted vector of Wikipedia-based concepts and then assess the relatedness of texts in this space amounts to comparing the corresponding vectors using conventional metrics [10]. ESA can enhance the feature representations described by nouns/noun phrases and further improve the accuracy of clustering. For the second issue, we now choose a larger value (50-100) for k to cover as more feature categories as possible and then use k-means++ algorithm [21] for optimizing k seeds to cluster the extracted features.

Each feature category can represent an overall description or a user-perceived functional/quality aspect of the software system. As the value of k is larger, there may be duplicated feature categories. To solve the problem, we regard the feature that is nearest to the center within a cluster as the name of each feature category and manually merge those categories whose names are similar.

3.2 Rating User Opinions

We propose a two-stage strategy for rating the associated opinion with an extracted feature on a five-point scale. In the first stage, a heuristic method based on the context evidence [7, 11] is adopted for assigning polarities to opinion words. The heuristic rules are defined according to the observations about the consistent manner in which people often express their opinions. The same polarity is propagated between features and opinion words based on the extraction rules unless there are explicit *contrary words* or *negative words* in the clauses. There are new opinion words extracted by some features without polarities. Their polarities are inferred using the overall review polarity. In the second stage, the opinion word is rated based on its polarity and the ratings that users place on the reviews. The steps are indicated in Fig. 1.

Input: Opinion word o and its polarity p,
     Review data set R, Ratings of review data Rat
Output: Rating of o $Rat(o)$
1.   **if** p is neutral
2.   **then** $Rat(o)=3$
3.   **else if** p is positive
4.   **then**
5.   compute the sum S_4 of o mentioned in R with its $Rat=4$
6.   compute the sum S_5 of o mentioned in R with its $Rat=5$
7. $Rat(o)=S_5>S_4?5:4$
8.   **else**
9.   compute the sum S_1 of o mentioned in R with its $Rat=1$
10.   compute the sum S_2 of o mentioned in R with its $Rat=2$
11. $Rat(o)=S_2>S_1?2:1$
12.   **endif**
13. **endif**

Fig. 1. Rating opinion words

3.3 Econometric Model-Based Requirements Analysis

The importance of a system aspect represents its priority for requirements evolution. It is stated that its importance to revising the requirements for future releases lies on the proportional to the number of reviews relevant to the system aspect [4, 12]. From the market's perspective, however, the importance of a system aspect depends more on its economic benefits. If changes in the system aspect can improve the ability of the software system satisfying changing user demands, its improvement will result in the company's future profits. Thus, we present a utility-oriented econometric model to analyze which system aspects are required in the requirements for future releases.

In economics, utility is the ability that a good or service satisfies consumer wants. The rating of a user opinion represents the degree to which the system satisfies a certain user about the feature. Thus, the utility of a system aspect is measured by average ratings of user opinions related to the aspect. It is computed as follows:

$$U(a) = \frac{1}{n_a} \sum_{i=1}^{n_a} Rat(f_i, \ o_i) \qquad (2)$$

where n_a is the number of features belonging to aspect a and $Rat(f_i, o_i)$ is the rating of associated opinion o_i with feature f_i.

In marketing communication, online reviews are a novel word-of-mouth that has positive impact on the product sales [13]. Furthermore, the change in software sales is triggered by the change in user satisfaction of some system aspects frequently mentioned on in the reviews. In order to estimate the importance of a system aspect from the market's perspective, we need to find the causal influence between the utilities of system aspects in real contexts of use and software sales. We adopt the Granger causality model (GCM) to analyze whether the utility of a system aspect is useful in forecasting the software sales. GCM is a linear regression method often used in econometrics to quantify the causal influence from time series variables. It has better results than Bayesian network and information theory [14]. Its improvement of prediction may reduce the influence of coincidental causality.

Suppose there are two time series X and Y. X is said to Granger-cause Y if Y can be better predicted using the histories of both X and Y than the history of Y alone [15]. We test whether X causes Y or not by estimating the following regressions:

$$Y(t) = \alpha_0 + \sum_{i=1}^{n} \alpha_i Y(t-i) + \varepsilon_1 \tag{3}$$

$$Y(t) = \alpha_0 + \sum_{i=1}^{n} \alpha_i Y(t-i) + \sum_{i=1}^{n} \beta_i X(t-i) + \varepsilon_2 \tag{4}$$

where n is the maximal time yield, ε_i is a random distribution. If (4) is a significantly better than (3) through hypothesis testing, time series X causes time series Y.

Estimating the importance of a system aspect based on GCM follows a series of steps. First, the review set R of a software system S is divided into a set of sequential groups $G=\{g_1, g_2, ..., g_z\}$ according to the chosen time yield. The relevant sales $S(S)_{t=i}$ and utility of a system aspect $U(a)_{t=i}$ to group g_i are measured and then the time series $X=\{U(a)_t\}_{t \in Z}$ and $Y=\{S(S)_t\}_{t \in Z}$ ($Z=\{1, 2, ..., z\}$) are constructed based on their measurements from the group set G. Second, Equation (3) and (4) are used for examining the Granger causal relationships between time series X and Y without considering the correlations among system aspects. Finally, in light of the Granger causality test, the system aspects whose utilities have significant positive correlations with the software sales are discovered as the useful evidence to revise the requirements for future releases. The correlations of system aspects indicate their importance for market-driven requirements evolution.

3.4 Generating Report

The goal of generating the report is to provide a meaningful information for developers to improve the software system. The report contains system aspects and associated statements that describe candidate requirements changes for system improvement. The statements are used to interpret the meanings of candidate requirements changes. They can be mapped to the user opinions mentioned in the reviews through the corresponding system aspects. Although system aspects for designing furture systems are discovered in previous analysis, whether they are related to candidate requirements changes cannot be determined through the Granger causality test. We distinguish these system aspects in accordance with the statistical characteristics of their utilities. We first compute the mean $EU(a)$ and standard deviation $SU(a)$ of the utility of each system aspect and the overall user satisfaction $OS(R)$ over review set R. $OS(R)$ is measured by the average of ratings that users place on the reviews. Second, we determine the system aspects relevant to candidate requirements changes using the following steps depicted in Fig. 2.

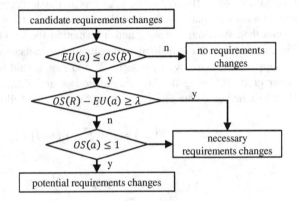

Input: aspect a, mean $EU(a)$ and standard deviation $SU(a)$ of its utility overall user satisfaction $OS(R)$ over review set R
Output: the category of candidate requirements changes relevant to aspect a $Req(a)$
Note: λ is the threshold

Fig. 2. A strategy of determining candidate requirements changes

We therefore check the software requirements specification (SRS) to revise the corresponding statements to the system aspects relevant to candidate requirements changes. We conclude the new statement based on several negative review sentences revelant to such system aspect with the highest probability to alter the old one in SRS.

4   Case Study

A case study was carried out to elicit the requirements for system improvement using the reviews of Kaspersky Internet Security 2011 (KIS 2011). In the study, we first evaluate the validity of the opinion mining technique on dealing with large amounts of noisy review data and then evaluate the effectiveness of the generated report for system improvement.

4.1   Experiments for Mining User Opinions of KIS 2011

Experimental Design.
Correct user opinions derived from large amounts of noisy review data are the evidence to requirements elicitation for system improvement. Based on the review data of KIS 2011, we compare our method P-SRPA with SRPA and discuss the advantages and disadvantages according to all metrics including recall, precision and F-score.

The raw review data of KIS 2011 used in this paper was scraped from Amazon.com. The data set contains 380 reviews and 3200 sentences from September 2, 2010, to February 25, 2012. Each review has a user rating on a five-point scale. All sentences of the review data are descended by the helpfulness of a review that is computed through our previous work [16]. Then these ordered sentences are divided into five subsets $D=\{d_1, .., d_5\}$. For each subset, the potential features and opinions in the sentences are manually labeled as the testing data for the comparison experiment.

We perform P-SRPA and SRPA using the seed opinion lexicon provided by Hu and Liu [11], which involves 654 positive and 1098 negative opinion words. Recall is computed as the number of true positives divided by the sum of the number of true positives and the number of false negatives. Precision is computed as the number of true positives divided by the sum of the number of true positives and the number of false positives. F-score is computed as follows:

$$F\text{-score} = 2\times\frac{\text{precision}\times\text{recall}}{\text{precision}+\text{recall}} \tag{5}$$

Comparison Results and Discussion.
The Fig. 3 shows the results of recall, precision and F-score of P-SRPA and SRPA using different subsets. From Fig. 3 (a), the average recall of P-SRPA is 0.86 and that of SRPA is 0.77. This shows that the propagation is reasonable in achieving high recall. Clearly, the recall may be affected by natural language processing (NLP) techniques. The sentences in high noisy data subsets often have many errors of spelling and grammatical structure so that automatic tagging and parsing don't work correctly. Fortunately, the recall values of P-SRPA do not decrease significantly with the increase of noisy data, only from 0.92 to 0.82.

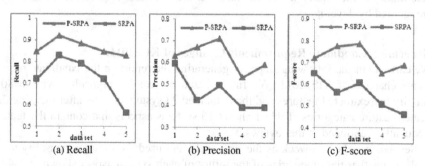

(a) Recall   (b) Precision   (c) F-score

Fig. 3. Results of mining user opinions from KIS 2011 review data

Observing Fig. 3 (b), we can see P-SRPA outperforms SRPA in precision. In the low noisy data subsets, the precision values of P-SRPA and SRPA are more than 0.70. This indicates that dependency relation-based extraction rules are effective for identifying correct features and opinions. However, the precision values of SRPA decrease obviously with the increase of noisy data, from 0.60 to 0.40, while our precision values decrease from 0.71 to 0.53. In addition to NLP problems, the causes are as

follows. First, there are many ordinary nouns and adjectives irrelevant to user opinions in the high noisy data subsets. Due to unconstrained dependency relations, the
words match the extraction rules so as to be extracted incorrectly. Second, the expressions of user opinions are flexible and diverse in the reviews. The descriptions of
the same feature do not usually have a unified term. Thus, noisy feature pruning
in SRPA does not produce obvious effect, as it relies on the frequency of terms.
Moreover, SRPA does not still provide a method for noisy opinion word pruning. To
address these problems, P-SRPA employs a heuristic method to distinguish opinion
words from ordinary adjectives and then filters incorrect features through the SVM
classifier.

Fig. 3 (c) shows P-SRPA archives better average F-score than that of SRPA. We
can draw the conclusion that P-SRPA is useful to provide user feedback for requirements evolution analysis even if dealing with large amounts of noisy review data.

4.2   Requirements Analysis   for KIS 2011 Improvement

Evaluation of Generated Report.
We organize a human subject study to determine the usefulness of the generated report for system improvement. In the study, five participants are the developers that
work in the computer security companys. All of them have more than three years of
experience in software development. The participants are required to use KIS 2011
and read its SRS for developing a set of candidate requirements changes. As the SRS
of KIS 2011 is not open to users, we create it according to understanding of the application and other information, such as product introduction, user manual and AV-Test
results. The SRS contains 21 functional statements and 14 quality statements that are
appreciable to users. We compare the generated report and participants' results to
determine whether our approach can discover the candidate requirements changes that
are ignored by developers.

Generating Candidate Requirements Changes of KIS 2011.
We carried out the following steps for generating the report on the candidate requirements changes of KIS 2011. We first utilized k-means++ algorithm with $k=80$ to
classify the extracted features and then obtained 23 system aspects after merging duplicated feature categories. Table 1 shows 15 systems aspects that contain the features
frequently mentioned in the reviews.

Second, we chose a week as the time yield and used the Granger causality test to
analyze whether the time series of the utility of each system aspect shown in Table 1
were useful in forecasting the time series of the sales rank of KIS 2011. As the exact
sales of KIS 2011 are not available, we modify the utility-oriented GCM in Section
3.3 by replacing the software sales with the software sales rank that is publicly available information in most Web platforms. As the prior research in marketing experi-
mentally observed that the distribution of sales in terms of associated sales rank has a
Power distribution [17], we select the principal system aspects whose utilities have
the negative correlations with the sales rank as shown in Table 2. These system

aspects are related to the requirements of KIS future releases. Note that the system aspects of *scan*, *safe run*, and *parental control* have not the causal influences on the sales rank, although they receive many user opinions in the reviews. Such system aspects do not have to be changed from the economic perspective, since the software revenue is not significantly enhanced by improving their utilities.

Table 1. Results of categorizing features

Perspective	Aspect	Feature
Overall		Software, product, application, package, program, suit, version, Internet security, Kaspersky, Kaspersky internet security, KIS
Function	Protection	Computer protection, Virus protection, Malware protection, Protection
	Antivirus	Antivirus, Anti-virus, Anti virus
	Firewall	Two-way firewall, Personal firewall, Firewall
	Scan	Scan, Computer scan, System scan, Virus scan, Malware scan, Scanning
	Safe run	Safe run, Safe desktop, Safe mode
	Parental control	Parental control
	Installation	Installation, Installation process, Installing
	Update	Update, Upgrade
Quality	Performance	Performance, Speed, Time, Slowdown
	Resource	Resource utilization, System resource, Resource, Memory, CPU, Footprint
	Reliability	Reliability, Bug, Crash, Reboot
	Usability	Usability, Easy to use, Use friendly
	User interface	User interface, Window, Setting, Look
	Flexibility	Flexibility, Configuration, Customization

Table 2. Causal relationships of KIS 2011

Function				
Protection	Antivirus	Firewall	Installation	Update
-0.738*	-0.625*	-0.226**	-0.558*	-0.387**

Quality					
Performance	Resource	Reliability	Usability	User interface	Flexibility
-0.815*	-0.764*	-0.317*	-0.832*	-0.629*	-0.315**

$*p=0.05; **p=0.1$

Table 3. Statistics of Utilities of System Aspects of KIS 2011

	Function		Quality				
	Installation	Update	Performance	Resource	Reliability	Usability	User interface
$EU(a)/SU(a)$	3.79/0.96	3.75/1.29	3.44/1.24	3.50/1.02	2.83/0.58	3.71/0.95	3.85/0.97

Finally, we generated the report on the candidate requirements changes through observing the overall user satisfaction $OS(R)$ of KIS 2011 (4.08) and the statistics ($EU(a)$ and $SU(a)$) of the utility of each system aspect. We used the strategy in section 4.4 ($\lambda=1.36$) to find the system aspects relevant to the candidate requirements changes of KIS 2011 that are shown in Table 3. The categories of potential/necessary requirements changes are distinguished through yellow/red colors. Through the above analysis, we checked the SRS of KIS 2011 and revised the associated statements with the system aspects in Table 3 to generate the report shown in Table 4.

Table 4. Candidate requirements changes of KIS 2011

ID	Statement	Aspect	Type
1	Automatic configuration during installation	Installation	#necessary
2	Update databases and application modules more smoothly	Update	#potential
3	Make less impact on the computer in daily use.	Performance	#necessary
4	Reduce the resource footprint when performing the user's task	resource	#necessary
5	Fix bugs and issues that are causing crashing and rebooting	Reliability	#necessary
6	Improve usability	Usability	#potential
7	Make user interface more intuitive and reduce needless pop-up messages	User interface	#potential

Analysis and Discussion of Requirements Changes.
Fig. 4 indicates the requirements changes designed by the participants, which contains 4 functional and 3 quality aspects of KIS 2011. Only quality aspects are consistent with those in our report whereas functional aspects are completely different.

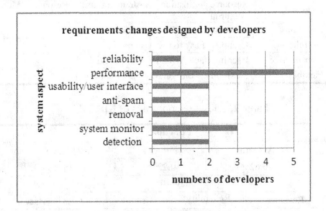

Fig. 4. Requirements changes designed by developers

We investigated the decision-making processes of participants. They stated that the changed functional requirements were designed based on the evaluation criteria for Internet security technology and personal experience. For functional requirements, developers paid more attention to key and special features while users were more concerned with the features closely related to user habits. As KIS 2011 is one of best sellers in the Internet security domain, its main functional aspects implicitly meet mass user desires in the open market. The improvement of such aspects cannot have significant impact on software revenue only when they have serious issues and bugs. In terms of KIS 2011, however, automatic remote *installation* and regular online *update* often fail in different contexts of use in the real world. The improvement of those aspects can promote the purchase of most users. Developers often ignore the requirements changes in these aspects as they may not be regarded as important modules of the software from the perspective of technology.

We showed the participants the report generated by our approach and told them that changes in the functional aspects of *installation* and *update* could bring about significant growth in the software revenue. Three participants admitted to lose sight of these aspects, and the other two participants tried to revise them. Thereby, our approach can discover the requirements changes that developers sometimes overlook.

From Fig. 4, we find that the participants have obvious disagreements in the quality aspects of *reliability* and *usability*. Few participants determined the changes in them. The other participants stated that it was hard to well implement *reliability* and *usability* because their user preferences were diverse. Considering huge development costs, the participants gave up their improvement. However, the report generated by our approach shows that changes in such quality aspects are necessary from the economic perspective. Therefore, it is a trade-off between economic factors and technical levels for requirement evolution. Our approach suggests the requirements changes that are more economically valuable. Further, the analysts are required to make decision on how to meet user interests through a certain technical level as far as possible.

5   Related Work

Several researchers have developed techniques for eliciting requirements from online user feedback. Gebauer et al found the factors significantly related to overall user evaluation through the content analysis of online user reviews and then resulted in user requirements of mobile devices [5]. Lee et al. gathered customer's opinions from social network service to facilitate requirements elicitation [6]. These approaches capture changing requirements without limited range of users and insufficient expressions. However, they rely more on the manual content analysis of user opinions.

Cleland-Huang et al utilized a classification algorithm to detect non-functional requirements from stakeholder comments [19]. Hao et al. adopted machine learning techniques to extract the aspects of service quality from Web reviews for conducting automatic service quality evaluation [3]. Carreño et al. adapted topic modeling techniques to deal with available user feedback of mobile applications for extracting new/changed requirements for next versions [4]. Our previous research compared the changes in user satisfaction before and after software evolution to provide instructive information for designing future systems [18]. Although the existing approaches validate that automated techniques can efficiently explore user feedback for requirements evolution, they lack the deep analysis about how valuable user feedback of different system aspects are for determining changes in requirements.

In our research, opinion mining techniques make it possible to automatically elicit requirements from huge volume of user feedback data. Common approaches generally fall into two categories. One category is to identify user opinions through grammatical structures [7, 20-22]. Such approaches have good performance for mining fine-gained features and related opinion words. However, the completeness of extraction rules/templates and domain knowledge have obvious impact on the accuracy of algorithms.

The other category is to use topic modeling techniques for simultaneously extracting and grouping user opinions [23-25]. These approaches are governed by how often feature terms and opinion words co-occur in different context. As expressions of user opinions are diverse, topic models are appropriate for mining coarse-gained features. A protential problem is that the extracted features may be not meaningful.

6   Conclusions

This paper has presented a novel approach for requirements evolution from the economic perspective. We explore a broad spectrum of online reviews and combine the techniques of opinion mining, machine learning, and text clustering with a utility-oriented econometric model to find system aspects significantly related to software sales for revising the requirements. A case study in the Internet security domain was carried out to show that our opinion mining method achieved good recall and precision in large amounts of noisy review data. Moreover, our approach supported analysts by suggesting the requirements changes that were more economically valuable. Therefore, it is useful to improve existing approaches for requirements evolution in understanding user demands in an open market.

Future work will refine our opinion mining method for improving the accuracy and efficiency of automated user feedback acquisition in the big data era. Furthermore, we will evaluate our approach using a broader data set from different domains.

Acknowledgments. The work in this paper was partially fund by National Natural Science Foundation of China under Grant No. 61170087 and State Key Laboratory of Software Development Environment of China under Grant No. SKLSDE-2012ZX-13.

References

1. Zowghi, D., Offen, R.: A Logical Framework for Modeling and Reasoning about the Evolution of Requirements. In: 3rd IEEE International Symposium on Requirements Engineering, pp. 247–257. IEEE Computer Society (1997)
2. Godfrey, M.W., German, D.M.: The Past, Present, and Future of Software Evolution. In: 2008 Frontiers of Software Maintenance, FoSM 2008, pp. 129–138 (2008)
3. Hao, J., Li, S., Chen, Z.: Extracting Service Aspects from Web Reviews. In: Wang, F.L., Gong, Z., Luo, X., Lei, J. (eds.) WISM 2010. LNCS, vol. 6318, pp. 320–327. Springer, Heidelberg (2010)
4. Galvis, L.V., Winbladh, K.: Analysis of User Comments: An Approach for Software Requirements Evolution. In: 35th International Conference on Software Engineering, pp. 582–591. IEEE Press, New York (2013)
5. Gebauer, J., Tang, Y., Baimai, C.: User Requirements of Mobile Technology: Results from A Content Analysis of User Reviews. Inf. Syst. E-Bus. Manage 6, 361–384 (2008)
6. Lee, Y., Kim, N., Kim, D., Lee, D., In, H.P.: Customer Requirements Elicitation based on Social Network Service. KSII Trans. on Internet and Information Systems 5(10), 1733–1750 (2011)

7. Qiu, G., Liu, B., Bu, J., Chen, C.: Opinion Word Expansion and Target Extraction through Double Propagation. Comput. Linguist. 37(1), 9–27 (2011)
8. Cortes, C., Vapnik, V.: Support-Vector Networks. Mach. Learn. 20(3), 273–297 (1995)
9. Kotler, P.: Marketing Management: Analysis, Planning, Implementation, and Control. Prentice Hall College Div. (1999)
10. Gabrilovich, E., Markovitch, S.: Computing Semantic Relatedness Using Wikipedia-based Explicit Semantic Analysis. In: 20th Int'l Joint Conf. on Artificial Intelligence, pp. 1606–1611. Morgan Kaufmann Publishers Inc. (2007)
11. Qiu, G., Liu, B., Bu, J., Chen, C.: Expanding Domain Sentiment Lexicon through Double Propagation. In: 21st Int'l Joint Conf. on Artificial Intelligence, pp. 1199–1204. Morgan Kaufmann Publishers Inc. (2009)
12. Pagano, D., Brügge, B.: User Involvement in Software Evolution Practice: A Case Study. In: 2013 Int'l Conf. on Software Engineering, pp. 953–962. IEEE Press, New York (2013)
13. Chevalier, J.A., Mayzlin, D.: The Effect of Word of Mouth on Sales: Online Book Reviews. Journal of Marketing Research 43(3), 345–354 (2006)
14. Cantone, I., Marucci, L., Iorio, F., Ricci, M.A., Belcastro, V., Bansal, M., Santini, S., di Bernardo, M., di Bernardo, D., Cosma, M.P.: A Yeast Synthetic Network for In Vivo Assessment of Reverse-Engineering and Modeling Approaches. Cell 137(1), 172–181 (2009)
15. Granger, C.W.J.: Testing for Causality: A Personal Viewpoint. Journal of Economic Dy-namics and Control 2, 329–352 (1980)
16. Jiang, W., Zhang, L., Dai, Y., Jiang, J., Wang, G.: Analyzing Helpfulness of Online Reviews for User Requirements Elicitation. Chinese Journal of Computers 36(1), 119–131 (2013)
17. Goolsbee, A., Chevalier, J.: Measuring Prices and Price Competition Online: Amazon.com and Barnesand Noble.com. Quantitative Marketing and Economics 1, 203–222 (2003)
18. Lew, P., Olsina, L., Becker, P., Zhang, L.: An Integrated Strategy to Systematically Understand and Manage Quality in Use for Web Applications. Requirements Engineering 17(4), 299–330 (2012)
19. Cleland-Huang, J., Settimi, R., Xuchang, Z., Solc, P.: The Detection and Classification of Non-functional Requirements with Application to Early Aspects. In: 14th IEEE Int'l Requirements Engineering Conf., pp. 39–48. IEEE CS (2006)
20. Hu, M., Liu, B.: Mining and Summarizing Customer Reviews. In: Tenth ACM SIGKDD Int'l Conf. on Knowledge Discovery and Data Mining, pp. 168–177. ACM, New York (2004)
21. Popescu, A., Etzioni, O.: Extracting Product Features and Opinions from Reviews. In: Conf. on Human Language Tech. and Empirical Methods in Natural Language Processing, pp. 339–346. ACL (2005)
22. Wu, Y., Zhang, Q., Huang, X., Wu, L.: Phrase Dependency Parsing for Opinion Mining. In: Conf. on Empirical Methods in Natural Language Processing, pp. 1533–1541. ACL (2009)
23. Mei, Q., Ling, X., Wondra, M., Su, H., Zhai, C.: Topic Sentiment Mixture: Modeling Facets and Opinions in Weblogs. In: 16th Int'l Conf. on World Wide Web, pp. 171–180. ACM, New York (2007)
24. Zhao, W., Jiang, J., Yan, H., Li, X.: Jointly Modeling Aspects and Opinions with A Max-Ent-LDA Hybrid. In: Conf. on Empirical Methods in Natural Language Processing, pp. 56–65. ACL (2010)
25. Jo, Y., Oh, A.H.: Aspect and Sentiment Unification Model for Online Review Analysis. In: 4th ACM Int'l Conf. on Web Search and Data Mining, pp. 815–824. ACM (2011)

An IT-Driven Business Requirements Engineering Methodology

Masahiro Ide[1,2], Tomoko Kishida[1], Mikio Aoyama[2], and Yasuhiro Kikushima[2]

[1] Qunie Corporation, Tokyo, Japan
[2] Nanzan University, Seto, Japan
{idem,kishidat}@qunie.com, mikio.aoyamapnifty.com,
y-kiku@ark.ocn.ne.jp

Abstract. We propose a business requirements engineering methodology in order to rapidly generate a business requirements and its supporting business architecture centered around the IT (Information Technology). As a high-level representation of business requirements along with the business value chain, we propose XBMC, an extension of BMC (Business Model Canvas) of the Business Model Generation. To align the business requirements onto an enterprise information system, we propose a new framework of the SMC (System Model Canvas) and a bidirectional mapping between XBMC and SMC governed by a business meta-model. Based on the mapping, we propose a technique of incrementally aligning business requirements represented in XBMC to and from ITA (IT Architecture) in SMC, which is intended to effectively utilize IT capabilities and resources. We demonstrate the effectiveness of the proposed methodology by applying it to the development of a mobile music delivery business.

Keywords: Business Requirements Engineering, Business Analysis, Business Design, Business Model, Business Model Canvas, System Model Canvas, Business Value Chain.

1 Introduction

The IT is the critical resources for corporate management, and a comprehensive design of the business that utilizes the IT is indispensable to the competitive advantage of the business. Therefore, various business analysis methods have been proposed and draw attentions [2]. In the business analysis transcending the simple business model design, it is required to clarify capability and limitation of the information system to realize a business strategy and to develop a business and information system to realize it. However, conventional methods rather focus on business model design first, utilization of IT capability is postponed after the design.

In this article, we first clarify the problems of the conventional business design from the viewpoints of IT utilization. Then, we propose a set of representations to model the BA (Business Architecture) and ITA (IT Architecture), a technique to align BA and ITA, and a business design technology that combines the above-mentioned representations and techniques. We apply the proposed methodology to mobile music delivery business and evaluate its effectiveness.

D. Zowghi and Z. Jin (Eds.): APRES 2014, CCIS 432, pp. 60–76, 2014.
© Springer-Verlag Berlin Heidelberg 2014

2   Background of Problems

Fierce global competitions and kaleidoscopic environmental changes have raised the importance of agility of the business. Instead of spending time on simply "a design" of business, a new approach is necessary to evolve into the most suitable business by quickly repeating the feedback cycle of "design, execution, evaluation, and re-design". Therefore, the business design methodology to capture the overall business situation and resources is required. In such a situation, as one of the crucial business resources, the importance of IT increases, and the business design that utilizes the IT becomes indispensable to lead business toward success. While authors are engaged in the business development for many companies in different industry sectors, we realized that CIO and IT department strongly need the methodology to design a business that fully utilizes IT. However, the conventional business model development methods focus on the business view of a business model, have some difficulties in the design of a business that utilizes IT capabilities.

3   Problems

3.1   Business Design Framework

In order to realize the business strategy of the company, it is necessary to capture problems from a viewpoint of both business and IT. Therefore, the authors propose the framework of a business design comprised of the business strategy, the BA, and the ITA, as shown in the Fig. 1.

Fig. 1. A Framework of Business Design

The business model design is mainly based on the model that is a static structure of the business. However, to lead the business to a success by improving its value, "a strategic scenario," that utilizes and develops business model to achieve the business goal, should be designed too. In this study, we define "BA (Business Architecture)" in Fig.1 as a set of "a strategic scenario" and "business model." For the information system, we call the model that captures its entire structure as "system model". Also, we call a system behavior to utilize and develop system models as "system scenario." The combination of "system model" and "system scenario" is defined as "ITA (IT Architecture)".

3.2   Conventional Methods of Business Requirements Engineering

The information system is an important resource to control competitive advantage of the business. In business requirements, the BA should be designed considering information system and the capability and constrain of information system environment. However, we may encounter difficulties to execute the BA or problems in the realization of ITA in the current business requirements, because ITA is designed based on a one-way demand from BA after the BA design is completed. As a result, it ends with a re-design of the BA. Also, it implies the BA designed could not fully utilize the capability of the information system and information system environment (Fig. 2).

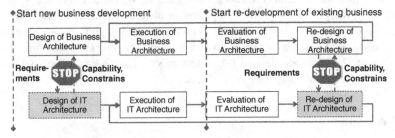

Fig. 2. Conventional methods of Business Requirements Engineering

The BA is designed for not only a new business plan, but also a re-development of the existing business. In the latter case, effective asset utilization is necessary for the restraint of the investment and the improvement of the further competition, superiority by utilizing the existing internal asset as a resource of the company's competitive advantage, are demanded. Therefore, the re-design of the BA in consideration of possibility and constraints of the existing information system and environment is required. The unpractical BA which is not aligned with the existing information system leads to the business failure and the waste of the investment and time.

3.3   Desirable Method of Business Requirements Engineering

In order to develop and operate agile and competitive business that utilize information system and information system environment, ITA needs to be designed by capturing the overall information system and its environment while synchronizing with a design of the BA and aligning with BA as shown in Fig. 3.

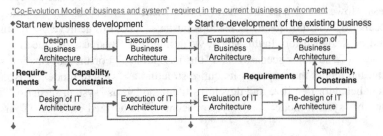

Fig. 3. Desirable method of Business Requirements Engineering

In the case of development of the existing business, not only for the new business development, ITA needs to be aligned with BA in the continuously re-design. Thus, business value is raised through the co-evolution of business and system, and it enables the continuous growth of the business.

3.4   Problem Structure in the Current Business Requirements

The authors, through their consulting experiences in business design for many companies, collected problems of existing business requirements to utilize IT. As a result of the root cause analysis, we identified four problems as shown in the lower part of Fig. 4.

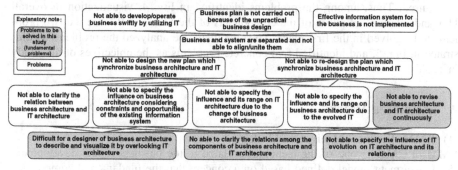

Fig. 4. Root Cause Analysis of Conventional Methods

(1)   Problem 1: Modeling ITA visually
In BA design, ITA, which captures the components by overlooking information system, is not visualized.

(2)   Problem 2: Relations between components of BA and ITA
The relations among components of both ITA and BA, which aligns and synchronize both architectures, are not clarified.

(3)   Problem 3: Relations between IT evolution and ITA components
Relations between IT evolution and ITA components, which utilize evolving IT technology to business and enable business growth, are not clarified.

(4)   Problem 4: Continuous evolution of BA and ITA
For the continuous development of business, continuous evaluation and re-design of both BA and ITA are required. Co-evolution of business and system is not planned through evaluation, re-design, and execution by aligning both models.

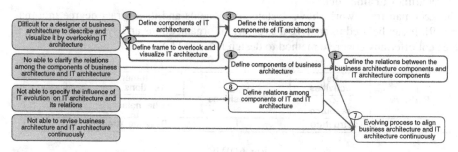

Fig. 5. Problems to be solved in this study

Table 1. Five problems focused in this study

No	Problem
1	Define components of ITA
2	Define frame to overlook and visualize ITA
3	Define the relations among components of ITA
4	Define components of BA
5	Define the relations between the BA components and ITA components

3.5   Problems to be Solved by IT Driven Business Requirements

To realize the framework in Fig.3, visualization of ITA and relation definition of BA is required. Thus, among the problems identified in Fig. 4, visualization of overall ITA and relation definition of the components of the ITA and BA are the two problems to be solved in the first place. To solve them, we analyzed the problems as illustrated in Fig. 5, and identified five concrete problems as the objectives of this study in Table 1.

4   Related Works

(1) BMM (Business Motivation Model)

BMM of OMG is one of the techniques related to the business model development [5]. It is a meta-model defined based on a concept that the fundamental components of a business plan compose a purpose and means. The analysis technique to utilize BMM in information system planning is proposed.

(2) BMG (Business Model Generation)

BMG is one of methodologies to develop business model [1][4]. It is a method to design value generation and its delivery to a customer in a business model. BMC (Business Model Canvas) shown in Fig. 6 is one of the BMG techniques. BMC is a visualized framework to gather important components for business model design, to arrange typical issues for checking, and to examine business model. BMC is comprised of nine blocks covering four areas including customer, value proposition, infrastructure, and fund. BMC enables to share the problems of the business model among stakeholders who related to business development. BMC is a concept of design from the business view, and does not provide any method to examine ITA required to realize business model, to develop ITA, and to design BA that utilize the possibility of information system.

(3) Zachman Framework

The Zachman framework shows system components and its abstract degree in a matrix [9]. It can be used to analyze a structure of organizations and system; However, it does not offer any concrete method to design BA and ITA.

Key Partners	Key activities	Value Propositions	Customer relations	Customer segments
	Key resource		Channels	
Cost structure			Revenue stream	

Fig. 6. BMC

(4) EA(Enterprise Architecture) and TOGAF

EA is the business model development framework is derived from Zachman Framework [6]. TOGAF [8] is one of the representative frameworks of EA. EA is defined as four layers including BA, data architecture, application architecture, and technical architecture; However, it does not offer any method to develop business models and the business model that utilize IT.

(5) ArchiMate

ArchiMate is proposed as EA modeling language [4]. It provides a development method for EA from the business model defined by applying BMC; however, there is no feedback of the possibility and constraints of ITA toward a business model.

(6) BABOK (Business Analysis Body of Knowledge)

BABOK is a body of knowledge for the business analysis [2]. It assumes the business model a given condition, and its object is an analysis of the condition; however, it does not offer any method to design business model.

(7) REBOK (Requirements Engineering Body Of Knowledge)

REBOK is a body of knowledge on the requirement engineering to connect the business requirements to software requirements [3]. However, it does not offer any concrete method for business model development.

(8) Value Chain Analysis

It provides a framework to analyze the value chain of business that utilizes information system [7]. However, it does not offer any method to develop business models.

5   Approach

This study adopts two approaches to solve the five problems in Table 1.

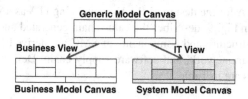

Fig. 7. Extended BMC

(1) Approach 1: Expanded BMC

This approach distinguishes business view, which corresponds to BA, from IT view, which corresponds to ITA, and specialize them to develop a business model that considers constrains by bringing out the capability of information system resources such as information system, organizations related to the information system and a human resource. It extends the BMC, the written framework of BMG, as a method to visualize the overall BA and ITA.

(2) Approach 2: Definition of architecture conversion layer

This approach is to define conversion layer, which converts and to align the visualized BA to ITA. The definition of conversion layer clarifies the requirements of business and system to realize the business model and enables the IT driven business design.

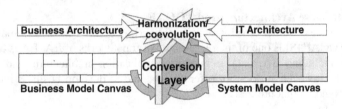

Fig. 8. Architecture conversion layer

6   Business Requirements Engineering Methodology

This study proposes four technologies of IT driven Business Requirements Engineering Methodology.

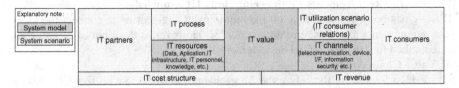

Fig. 9. SMCs

6.1   SMC (System Model Canvas)

In order to solve problem 1, 2, and 3 shown in Table 1, we propose SMC (System Model Canvas), an extension of BMC, as a framework to feed back the capability and constraints of the ITA for the design of BA by visualizing ITA as a whole.

SMC, as shown in Fig. 9, describes the value chain generated and delivered by ITA in one figure. The structure and components of SMC are derived from the extension of BMC, Zachman framework, and software supply chain. Definitions and category of SMC components are in Table 2.

Table 2. Categories and Definitions of SMC Components

No	Components	Category	Definition
1	IT consumer	Scenario	Users who enjoy the value of the system, Place where they use the service
2	IT utilization scenario	Scenario	Relations between users and system such as scenario and ways utilizing system that users enjoy the value
3	IT channel	Model	IT channel that users require to receive the value and utilize the system, such as communication, device, and interface
4	IT value	Model	The value of IT delivered to IT consumer to realize the business value
5	IT revenue	Scenario	Revenue and effects gained by building and operating system
6	IT process	Scenario	A process required to build and operate the system
7	IT resource	Scenario	Assets required to build and operate the system, such as human resource, intellectual property, knowledge
8	IT partner	Scenario	Partners and its role and place required to build and operate the system
9	IT cost structure	Scenario	Cost structure required to build and operate the system (Fixed IT cost factors, variable IT cost factors)

Fig.10 shows SMC meta-model, which defines the relations among SMC components. The relations enable to analyze the formation of value chain throughout the ITA by defining the resources to build ITA on the left side of SMC and the value provided from ITA on the right side. SMC shows the hierarchic structure by placing intangible components such as software and service in the upper part and tangible components such as IT platform in the lower part.

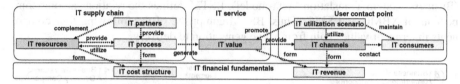

Fig. 10. Meta Model of System Model Canvas

6.2   XBMC

To solve Problem 4 shown in Table 1, we propose XBMC (eXtended Business Model Canvas) as a technology to visualize overall BA for approach 1. This re-defines the components of BA from the business view. XBMC describes the value chain of business that generated and offered by BA in one figure as in Fig. 11. Table 3 presents the definition of the components of XBMC, and Fig.12 shows the relations among XBMC components.

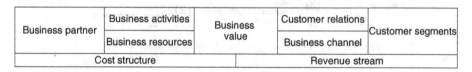

Fig. 11. XMBC

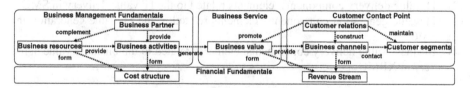

Fig. 12. Meta Model of XBMC

Table 3. Categories and Definitions of XBMC Components

No	Components	Category	Definition
1	Customer segments	Scenario	Segment of target customers to whom the business value is delivered
2	Customer relations	Scenario	A method to build and maintain relations with customer segments
3	Business channel	Model	Business channel to deliver value to customer segment
4	Business Value	Model	Business value to be delivered to customer segments
5	Revenue streams	Scenario	Revenue stream and structure gained by business value delivery
6	Business processes	Scenario	Business process required to deliver business value
7	Business resources	Scenario	Business resources required to deliver business value
8	Business Partners	Scenario	Business partners required to deliver business value
9	Cost structure	Scenario	Cost structure required to deliver business value

6.3   Architecture Conversion between BA and ITA

As shown in Fig.8, BA and ITA are required to be converted each other and aligned to realize business model. We propose the technology of architecture conversion layer that offers architecture conversion function. Architecture conversion layer, as shown in Fig.13, aligns XBMC to SMC. We define the conversion layer as meta-model that describes the relations among components of XBMC and SMC. We call this BSTM (Business-System Translation Meta-model). BSTM defines the relations among components of XBMC and SMC. Thus, BSTM comprised of the following four components in terms of value chain from value generation to delivery.

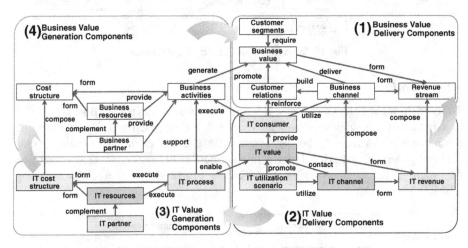

Fig. 13. BSTM (Business-System Translation Meta-model)

(1)   Business value generation components: elements related to the business value generation in XBMC
(2)   IT value delivery components: elements related to the IT value delivery in SMC
(3)   IT value generation components: elements related to the IT value generation in SMC
(4)   Business value delivery components: elements related to the business value delivery in XBMC

6.4   Design Process of BA and ITA

Fig.14 shows the proposed design process of business model. A merit of BSTM is to map BA and ITA on the value chain. Thus, the conversion between XBMC and SMC enables to analyze how BA and ITA contribute to the value chain, while the design of the BA and ITA is in progress. It enables the business design that maximizes the value by bringing out the IT capability and balancing with IT constrains.

(1) Step 1: Value chain analysis of BA
Compose BA from business value delivery component in BMC based on the business goal and strategy. First, we identify customer segments, to which a company delivers its business value. Next, we identify business value to deliver to the customer

segments and business channel or the value chain, in which it is delivered. Furthermore, in order to continuously deliver business value to the customer segments, we evaluate the method to build and maintain the customers in each business channel and revenue from the customer segments.

(2) Step 2: Description of value chain of BA
Describe the analysis results from Step 1 using XBMC, and analyze the alignment among components form XBMC meta-model. If we have some inconsistencies, go back to analyze in Step 1.

(3) Step 3: Analysis of IT Value delivery components through BSTM
Identify IT value delivery component in SMC required to deliver the value in XBMC by referring to the relations among components of XBMC and SMC, which are defined in the business meta-model in conversion layer.

To do so, first, we identify IT consumers from Customer relations, Channels and business activities in BMC. Analyze IT value delivered to identified IT consumers, then we evaluate IT channel, which is IT value chain in which IT value is delivered, the relations with IT consumers (IT utilization scenario), and IT revenue gained in return of IT value delivery.

(4) Step 4: Description of IT value delivery component in ITA
Describe analysis results of IT value delivery components in SMC based on the XBMC through the conversion layer. We clarify the conditions, in which components align, from BSTM and if there is any inconsistency, go back to Step 3 and analyze IT value delivery components again.

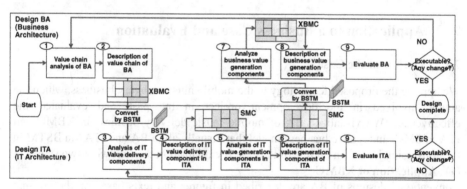

Fig. 14. Design process of BA and ITA

(5) Step 5: Analysis of IT value generation components in ITA
Identify IT value generation components, which are to provide IT value to IT value delivery components visualized in SMC, based on the relations defined in BSTM. We identify IT process which generates IT value and resources, and IT partners that are required to perform IT process and evaluate IT cost structure required for IT value generation.

(6) Step 6: Description of IT value generation component of ITA in SMC
Describe analysis results of IT value generation components in SMC. Analyze the alignment of components from BSTM, and if there is any inconsistency, go back to Step 5 and analyze again.

(7) Step 7: Analyze business value generation components in BMC through BSTM

Based on the relations of XBMC and SMC components defined in the business meta-model in the conversion layer, we identify business value generation components in XBMC, which correspond to the structure of IT value delivery and IT value generation in SMC. Through BSTM, identify required business activities from business value in XBMC, and IT consumer, IT value, and IT process in SMC. Based on the results, we analyze the business cost structure composed of business resources, the cost of the business activities, and IT cost structure defined in BSTM.

(8) Step 8: Description of BA in XBMC

Describe the analysis results of business value delivery components in XBMC. Analyze the alignment among components based on the meta-model in XBMC, and if there is any inconsistency, go back to Step 7 and analyze again.

(9) Step 9: Evaluation of BA and ITA and redesign using XBMC and SMC

Evaluate feasibility and possibility of BA visualized in XBMC and ITA visualized in SMC.

If there is any problem, go back to the related process from Step 1 to Step 8, and repeat processes until the problem is solved and decision of execution is made.

The processes enables to design XBMC and SMC that align BA and ITA.

Designed XBMC, the origin of business requirement, and designed SMC, the origin of information system requirement, leads to requirements definition, design and development of business process, design of organizations, and resource procurement.

7   Application to a Business Case and Evaluation

7.1   Outline of the Case

We applied the proposed technology to the mobile music delivery business, which the author involved in the development project in the past, and evaluated the effectiveness. We visualized BA of mobile music delivery business in XBMC and ITA in SMC, and realize business model that visually align BA and ITA via BSTM in the conversion layer. An outline of the case is explained in the following two stages.

(1) Application of XBMC

Conventional designs of BA are described in figures and texts based on the original idea or experiences on the business designer. So, different designers have different descriptions. In this case, we apply XBMC to design BA.

(2) Application of SMC

In this case, we design ITA by applying SMC in the earlier phase of BA design. Also, we feed back the capability and constraints of ITA in the phase of BA design by applying the conversion layer.

7.2   Design of BA and ITA

Even in the business model development that largely depends on IT, only BA is designed with usual business goals and strategies. Therefore, analysis and design of ITA are postponed, and IT capability is not utilized enough.

The proposed technology enables to analyze BA synchronized with ITA, to visualize as a whole and to align both architectures in order to realize mobile music delivery business as planned. The following chapters provide an example of business model design process, BA, and ITA in this case.

(1) Step 1: Value Chain analysis of BA for mobile music delivery business
The business strategy for mobile music delivery is "deliver music contents utilizing the cutting–edge IT for the cellular phone users who demand latest services other than incoming melody." Through value chain analysis, we analyze and design business value delivery component required to realize the strategy.

We identify the customer segment of mobile music delivery; "users who want to listen to music via cellular phone". We analyze the business value of the mobile music delivery, mobile network as a channel, direct marketing and music delivery as methods to maintain the customer relations, and then we examine the music contents fee as the revenue stream (Fig.15).

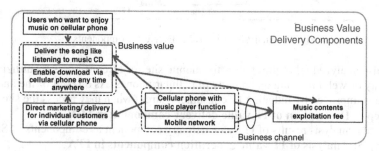

Fig. 15. Analysis of Business Value Delivery Components

(2) Step 2: Description of Value Chain in BA
Describe the analysis results in XBMC and analyze the alignment among components using the XBMC meta-model. We confirmed there is no inconsistency.

(3) Step 3: IT value delivery components analysis in ITA via BSTM
Based on the designed value delivery components in XBMC, we analyzed IT value delivery components in SMC using BSTM in conversion layer.

In this case we analyzed IT consumer in B2C business, based on the customer relations via business channel designed XBMC. Internal users are also extracted as IT consumer involved in business activities. We analyze IT value to be delivered, IT channel required to deliver it, relations with IT or IT utilization scenario, and IT revenue for "cell phone users" who are IT consumers in B2C.

In this case, IT channel, 3G mobile network, has technical limitation of communication capacity. The limitation prevents to meet the requirement of network performance in business channel and causes constrain in the quality of the music contents and download time. The revise of business value was in need. As a result, changes are made to deliver only a main part of music, not a full piece, to slash the length of contents, to lower the quality level of the sound, and to adjust the revenue along with the service changes (Fig.16). BSTM in conversion layer enabled to identify the range of influence and to revise.

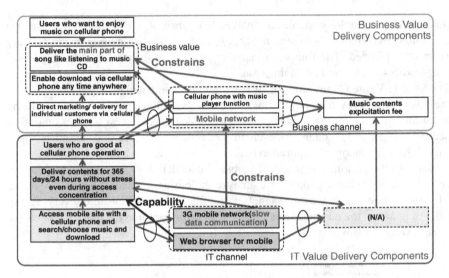

Fig. 16. Analysis of IT Value Delivery Components

We also analyzed UI requirements for mobile site for IT consumers by utilizing the possibility of web browsing technology of cellular phones. As a result of the analysis, IT value is improved by reducing IT consumers' stress when they access the site.

(4)   Step 4: Description of IT value delivery component in ITA

We describe analysis results of IT value delivery component as components of SMC.

(5)   Step 5: Analysis of IT value generation components in ITA

Based on the designed IT value delivery components and BTSM, we analyze IT value generation components. We analyze the IT value generation component sequentially to generate IT value for the mobile music delivery business, "able to deliver music contents for 365 days/24 hours without stress even during access concentration."

IT process, IT resources required to perform IT process, Required IT partner and range of outsourcing to IT partners, based on the preparation status of IT resources and IT process, Required IT cost structure(Fig.17).

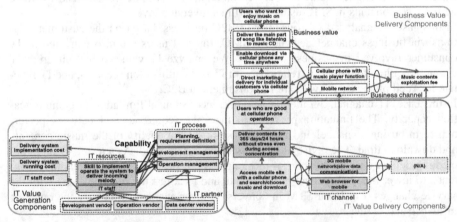

Fig. 17. Analysis of IT Value Generation Components

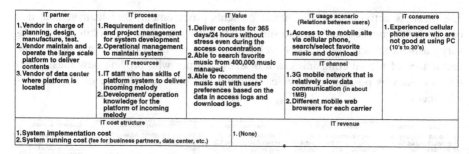

IT partner	IT process	IT Value	IT usage scenario (Relations between users)	IT consumers
1. Vendor in charge of planning, design, manufacture, test. 2. Vendor maintain and operate the large scale platform to deliver contents 3. Vendor of data center where platform is located	1. Requirement definition and project management for system development 2. Operational management to maintain system	1. Deliver contents for 365 days/24 hours without stress even during the access concentration 2. Able to search favorite music from 400,000 music managed. 3. Able to recommend the music suit with users' preferences based on the data in access logs and download logs.	1. Access to the mobile site via cellular phone, search/select favorite music and download	1. Experienced cellular phone users who are not good at using PC (10's to 30's)
	IT resources		**IT channel**	
	1. IT staff who has skills of platform system to deliver incoming melody 2. Development/ operation knowledge for the platform of incoming melody		1. 3G mobile network that is relatively slow data communication (in about 1MB) 2. Different mobile web browsers for each carrier	
IT cost structure			**IT revenue**	
1. System implementation cost 2. System running cost (fee for business partners, data center, etc.)		1. (None)		

Fig. 18. The case study of SMC

According to the analysis, members of the case company who have system planning or management skills and experiences in the mobile music delivery or a similar business, incoming melody business, perform system planning and requirement definition by themselves, and development and operation are outsourced to vendors who are IT partners.

(6) Step 6: Description of IT value generation components of ITA in SMC

Based on the analysis of IT value generation component, we describe ITA of mobile music delivery as shown in Fig. 18 by using SMC, and visualize ITA.

(7) Step 7: Analysis of business value generation components using XBMC via BSTM

We analyzed the designed business value generation component referring to the designed SMC, XBMC, and BSTM (Fig.19).

1) Identify and analyze the request on business activities required to generate business value, business resources, and business partners.

2) Analysis of cost structure to generate business value and IT value

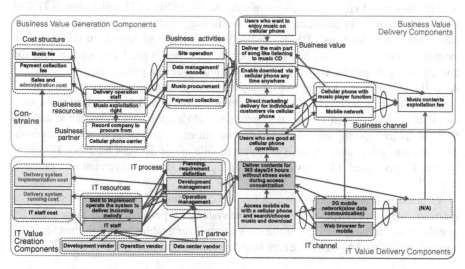

Fig. 19. Analysis of Business Value Generation Components and BSTM in the case study

The business activities such as music contents procurement, data management and encode for the music contents, and site operation are important for mobile music delivery business to generate business value. And as a business partner, we analyze the importance of record companies as a business partner who provide new music contents as many as possible at the release timing and also maintenance of the relations with them.

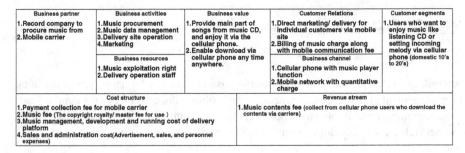

Business partner	Business activities	Business value	Customer Relations	Customer segments
1.Record company to procure music from 2.Mobile carrier	1.Music procurement 2.Music data management 3.Delivery site operation 4.Marketing	1.Provide main part of songs from music CD, and enjoy it via the cellular phone. 2.Enable download via cellular phone any time anywhere.	1.Direct marketing/ delivery for individual customers via mobile site 2.Billing of music charge along with mobile communication fee	1.Users who want to enjoy music like listening CD or setting incoming melody via cellular phone (domestic 10's to 20's)
	Business resources		Business channel	
	1.Music exploitation right 2.Delivery operation staff		1.Cellular phone with music player function 2.Mobile network with quantitative charge	
Cost structure			Revenue stream	
1.Payment collection fee for mobile carrier 2.Music fee (The copyright royalty/ master fee for use) 3.Music management, development and running cost of delivery platform 4.Sales and administration cost(Advertisement, sales, and personnel expenses)			1.Music contents fee (collect from cellular phone users who download the contents via carriers)	

Fig. 20. The case study of XBMC

(8)   Step 8: Description of BA in XBMC
We visualized the analysis results of business value generation components in XBMC. We evaluate the alignment among the components and the feasibility and effectiveness of BA in XBMC. If the evaluation results indicate the re-analysis, perform re-design. When we complete the design, describe in XBMC to create XBMC for mobile music delivery as shown in Fig. 20.

(9)   Step 9: Evaluation and re-design of BA and ITA
We evaluate feasibility and possibility of BA of mobile music delivery based on XBMC shown in Fig. 20. Also, we evaluate the feasibility of IT utilization of ITA of mobile music delivery based on SMC shown in Fig. 18. If the evaluation results indicate needs for re-analysis of SMC and XBMC, perform re-design. In this case, we evaluated that the feasibility and possibility are relatively high. Thus, we conclude the completion of design in XBMC and SMC without re-design processes.

After the completion of design and decision making for execution, designed XBMC and SMC become the origin of requirements of the BA and ITA. They lead to refining the requirements, design the business process, and development. Also, the visualized SMC leads to refining requirements and conditions of information system environment, such as information system to realize mobile music delivery business, IT organization, IT personnel, IT knowledge and IT partners, then procurement and preparation follow.

Visualizing ITA clarifies the capability and constraints of information system environment, such as a purpose of information system, IT personnel, and IT process for mobile music delivery. BSTM of the conversion layer enables feedback the capability and constraints to BA, thus IT driven business model development is realized.

8   Evaluation

As an evaluation of the proposed methodology, we conducted an interview with two consultants who in charge of business model development. We gathered three evaluation comments, which indicate the effectiveness of the proposed methodology.

(1)   The proposed methodology provides frameworks of business and information system to be analyzed in business model development, and they give hints or clues to analyze and design.

(2)   By visualizing an overall picture of the ITA that includes information system resources and environment, it provides hints to utilize IT in the phase of business model design.

It enables to identify information system resources and environments, which are necessary to realize and execute the business, and analyze these requirements in the phase of business model design. Starting preparations for the system implementation and procurement in an earlier phase accelerates the speed toward the business realization.

9   Discussions

Two main roles, a business designer who designs the business model, and the management who make the decision to execute the designed business model, are involved in business model development. We study the proposed technology from those viewpoints.

(1) Improve the quality of BA requirements
The proposed XBMC and SMC visualize BA and ITA as a whole. This helps a business designer design and requirements analysis for BA considering the ITA as prerequisites or constraints. It reduces the rework of the design and improves the feasibility of business.

(2) Improve the quality of ITA requirements
A business designer can design ITA that aligns with BA in the early phase, and that leads to the design and requirements analysis of ITA, which is feasible and effective for the business. It shortens the lead time to business realization by starting design and preparation earlier for the information system that contribute to the business.

(3) Accelerate decision making and facilitate for the agreement
Visualization of business and system in XBMC and SMC in a structured and simple way helps a business designer evaluate it. Also, stakeholders of business model development can easily understand the BA and system architecture to realize the business, and it helps to reach the agreement faster.

(4) Better understanding of information system and its environment
Visualization of ITA in SCM enables managements to capture the required components to realize the business, such as information system, personnel to implement and maintain information system, process and partners. As a result, management is able to evaluate the investment in the information system and make a decision quickly.

10   Future Work

The proposed methodology needs to be applied to the business model development project and to be evaluated quantitatively in comparison with conventional methods.

Also, we think of a future study of the problems, problem 6 and 7 in Fig. 5, in the continuous evolution of parameters of components in XBMC and SMC, a description guideline, and the designed business model.

The relations between BSTM in conversion layer and IT technology enable to design a business model that utilizes more evolving IT. We think it is effective to expand BTSM to correspond to each component of IT technology.

11   Conclusion

In order to develop competitive business model that utilizes IT, since the contribution of information systems to the business success is required, this study technically contributed by proposing four technologies as a practical methodology for business model development: 1) Expansion of BMC to visualize BA, 2) proposing SMC to visualize ITA, 3) BSTM as business meta-model to define the conversion layer to align BA and ITA, and 4) design process of BA and ITA.

We apply the proposed methodology to design mobile music delivery business, where its competitive superiority largely depends on IT utilization, and evaluate the effectiveness.

For future work, we develop the guideline of the proposed methodology and evaluate the effectiveness of the proposed methodology by applying it to actual business model development.

References

1. Osterwalder, A., Pigneur, Y.: Business Model Generation. Wiley (2010)
2. IIBA, A Guide to the Business Analysis Body of Knowledge, Version 2.0 (2009)
3. JISA REBOK WG, Requirements Engineering Body of Knowledge (REBOK), Version 1.0, Kindaikagaku (2011) (in Japanese)
4. Meertens, L.O., Lacob, M.E.: Mapping the Business Model Canvas to Archimate. In: SAC 2012, pp. 1694–1701 (2012)
5. OMG, Business Motivation Model (BMM), Version 1.1,
   http://, http://www.omg.org/spec/BMM/ (May 2010)
6. Sowa, J.F., Zachman, J.A.: Extending and Formalizing the Framework for Information Systems Architecture. IBM Systems J. 31, 590–616 (1992)
7. Barnes, S.J.: The Mobile Commerce Value Chain: Analysis and Future Developments. Int'l J. of Information Management 22, 91–108 (2002)
8. The Open Group, A Guide to TOGAF Version 8.1 Enterprise Edition (2005)
9. Zachman, J.A.: A Framework for Information Systems Architecture. IBM Systems J. 26, 276–292 (1987)

Efficient Identification of Rationales by Stakeholder Relationship Analysis to Refine and Maintain GQM+Strategies Models

Takanobu Kobori, Hironori Washizaki, Yoshiaki Fukazawa, Daisuke Hirabayashi,
Katsutoshi Shintani, Yasuko Okazaki, and Yasuhiro Kikushima

Goal-oriented Quantitative Management Research Group
Waseda University, 3-4-1, Okubo, Shinjuku, Tokyo, 169-8555 Japan
uranus-tk@ruri.waseda.jp

Abstract. GQM+Strategies[1] is an approach that aligns business goals at each level of an organization to strategies to realize overall business goals and assesses the achievement of such goals. Strategies are extracted from business goals based on rationales (contexts and assumptions). Using the proposed approach, which refines the GQM+Strategies model by extracting rationales based on the analysis of the relationships between stakeholders, it is possible to extract rationales exhaustively and to reconsider the GQM+Strategies model even if the business environment changes.

Keywords: Software development, GQM+Strategies, Stakeholder, business goal, organizational change, rationales (contexts and assumptions), Requirements engineering.

1 Introduction

Currently, software is responsible for a lot of business in corporate activities [1]. It is unclear if the IT/software related strategies and an organization's business goals are aligned. One approach to resolve this issue is GQM+Strategies, which aligns the business goals of each level to the overall strategies and goals of the organization as well as assesses the achievement of business goals. It is possible for the entire organization to communicate easily and to work toward common goals.

Nowadays both business and technical environments are changing rapidly. Thus, a model must continuously evolve [2][3]. To understand these changes, an analysis and validation mechanism that adapts the relationships among stakeholders, business goals, and strategies to GQM+Strategies is necessary. Previously, the rationales and business goals have been evaluated using GQM+Strategies for Business Value Analysis [4], but it remains unclear how to extract rationales efficiently and exhaustively. This work proposes the Context-Assumption-Matrix (CAM) to refine business goals and strategies iteratively by analyzing the relationships of stakeholders as a complement to

---

[1] GQM+Strategies® is registered trademark No. 302008021763 at the German Patent and Trade Mark Office; international registration number IR992843.

D. Zowghi and Z. Jin (Eds.): APRES 2014, CCIS 432, pp. 77–82, 2014.
© Springer-Verlag Berlin Heidelberg 2014

GQM+Strategies and the Context Assumption (C/A) extraction sheet to unify the expressive style of contexts and assumptions.

This paper examines the following three research questions.

RQ1: Can CAM and the C/A extraction sheet efficiently extract new rationales?

RQ2: Can CAM exhaustively extract rationales?

RQ3: When the management policy or business environment changes, can the rationales and the GQM+Strategies Grid be easily analyzed via CAM?

The contributions of this paper are two-fold. First, the proposed method may provide a way to efficiently and exhaustively extract contexts and assumptions. Second, when the management or business environment changes, GQM+Strategies, contexts, and assumptions can be easily analyzed.

2   Background

2.1   GQM+Strategies

The GQM+Strategies approach extends the goal/question/metric paradigm to measure the success or failure of goals and strategies, while adding enterprise-wide support to determine actions on the basis of the measurement results [5].

GQM provides support for measurements by developing software-related goals and generating questions to refine goals and to specify measures that need to be considered in order to answer generated questions [6]. Although the GQM approach can measure whether a business goal is achieved in an organization, it does not provide a mechanism to link higher-level business goals to lower-level goals nor does it support and integrate goals at different levels of the organization. On the other hand, GQM+ Strategies creates maps between goal-related data at different levels, so that the insights gained relative to a goal at one level can help satisfy goals at higher levels [4].

The major feature of GQM+Strategies is to determine business goal strategies based on rationales as "contexts" and "assumptions". Contexts are environmental characteristics, and assumptions are aspects of uncertain environments, including estimated ones. Although many strategies are considered for a goal, the best strategy is then selected based on the rationales. Because all of the selected strategies are detailed to lower level goals, it is possible to determine strategies that reflect the actual business environment. Figure 1 overviews the concept of GQM+Strategies. The GQM+Strategies Grid visually confirms the link between a goal and strategy, allowing the entire organization to communicate easily and work toward a common goal. Furthermore, through the GQM paradigm, it is possible to evaluate whether the goals at each level are achieved.

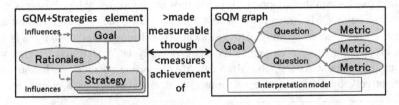

Fig. 1. GQM+Strategies components (based on Basili et al. [5])

2.2 Motivating Example

As an example, we applied GQM+Strategies to a stationary company, which sells stationary to corporations. The company receives orders from corporate customers and then ships based on the order form. Figure 2 overviews the corporate structure of the stationary company. Although the scope of the application is the sales department, the purpose of using GQM+Strategies is to improve accepting orders in the sales department and the shipping business. Figure 3 shows a level 3 business goal, the strategy, and rationales.

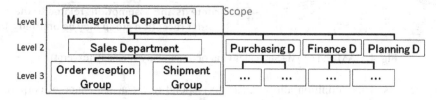

Fig. 2. Corporate structure of a stationary company

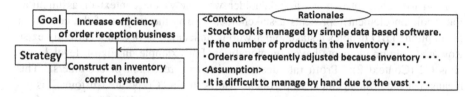

Fig. 3. Business goal, strategy, and rationales (excerpt)

Although the GQM+Strategies process derives business goals, strategies, and rationales, it is unclear whether the contexts and assumptions cover all existing goals and strategies. For example, there may be a context where ensuring the budget of system construction is difficult. The lack of contexts and assumptions tends to be misleading, and incorrect strategies are derived. Therefore, the mechanism must be able to extract contexts and assumptions efficiently and exhaustively.

Business environments are constantly changing. For example, consider a management policy change when a company that began with individuals is sold to a corporation. The GQM+Strategies Grid must be adjusted, and some contexts and assumptions may change. However, it is difficult to grasp exactly what has changed. Thus, the mechanism must also be able to grasp exact changes and adapt GQM+Strategies.

3   Our Approach

3.1   Context-Assumption-Matrix

CAM organizes contexts and assumptions, which are common between stakeholders, into a two-dimensional table. Our approach defines stakeholders as people, systems,

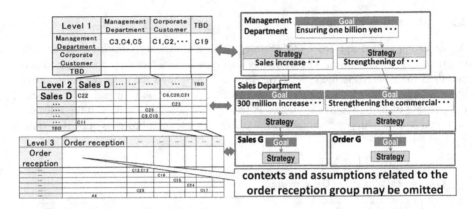

Fig. 4. CAM and GQM+Strategies Grid of a stationary company (excerpt)

or processes. This definition allows CAM to respond to the actual shape of corporations. Figure 4 provides an example of applying CAM to a stationary company and GQM+Strategies Grid.

Each row element denotes a stakeholder who views the context or assumption. Each column element represents a stakeholder who is the subject of the context or assumption. TBD denotes a stakeholder who is undecided or does not currently exist. Row and column elements have commonalities. For example, in Fig. 4, level 1 contains C2 (Context 2): "Profit rate decreases due to a recession of customers." This means that the "Management Department" views that a "Corporate Customer" is experiencing a recession. In CAM, "Context 1" is written as "C1". The details of the contexts and assumptions are described in the CA Extraction Sheet, which is explained in the next section.

CAM has a hierarchy, which corresponds to the corporate structure similar to GQM+Strategies. In this case, CAM has three levels because the example stationary company has three levels. The stakeholders of CAM have the same levels as the corporate structure.

The example in Fig. 4 shows how to use CAM when the order reception group in level 3 lacks contexts or assumptions. It is possible to omit the contexts and assumptions related to the order reception group. In fact, there is a context, "When the order reception group receives an order, it must confirm that the order is placed by a registered customer on the basis of the customer ledger." In addition to the strategy in Fig. 3, it is possible to plan a new strategy, "Construction of a customer information control system" based on this context. By organizing the contexts, assumptions, and stakeholders two-dimensionally in CAM, the contexts and assumptions can be visually reviewed.

3.2   C/A Extraction Sheet

Contexts and assumptions are often described ambiguously. For example, consider the context, "We take an order via telephone, FAX, or email from a corporate company." This context does not clarify who "we" refers to, which may lead to a misunderstanding of the context or assumption even if it is extracted via CAM. There-fore, it is important to unify he expressive style of contexts and assumptions.

To unify the expressive style, we developed the C/A Extraction Sheet. Table 1 shows the definitions and an example of a C/A Extraction Sheet. This expressive style allows contexts and assumptions to be described exactly. Furthermore, the "view-point" in this sheet corresponds to the row elements, while "who" corresponds to the column elements in CAM. Conversely, extracting the contexts and assumptions in this sheet can create CAM.

Table 1. Definitions and an example of the C/A Extraction Sheet

Item	Explanation	Example
Level	Level of corporate structure	Level 3
when	Period of Context and Assumption	until now
viewpoint	Stakeholder who views context or assumption (row element in CAM)	Order Group
who	Stakeholder who are subject of Context or Assumption (column element in CAM)	Order Group
what	Contents of Context and Assumption	We take an order via telephone.
+/-	Context and Assumption are + or - for viewpoint + is positive, - is negative, +- is positive and negative	+-
Source	Source of Context and Assumption	business outline

3.3   Steps of Our Approach

This section explains how we use the GQM+Strategies Grid, CAM, and the C/A Extraction Sheet. Our approach uses the following steps:

1. Collect contexts and assumptions using the C/A Extraction Sheet.
2. Extract stakeholders of CAM from the corporate structure.
3. Apply the collected contexts and assumptions to CAM.
4. Use CAM to extract missing contexts and assumptions.
5. Create a GQM+Strategies Grid based on contexts and assumptions.
6. Update CAM and the C/A Extraction Sheet by referring to the related stake-holders when the management policy or business environment changes.
7. Update the GQM+Strategies Grid based on contexts and assumptions.
8. Repeat steps 6 and 7.

4   Discussion

We applied CAM and the C/A extraction sheet to a stationary company. Thus, the research questions are discussed using this example. In the future, we plan to adapt our method to other examples.

RQ1: Can CAM and the C/A extraction sheet efficiently extract new rationales?

People unfamiliar with GQM+Strategies have difficulties deriving rationales without hints. As shown in Fig. 4, CAM can ascertain information of stakeholders.

Additionally, fitting the items in the C/A extraction sheet can extract rationales (Table 1). Thus, CAM and the C/A extraction sheet can extract new rationales efficiently.

RQ2: Can CAM exhaustively extract rationales?

As shown in Fig. 4, CAM uses stakeholders in the organization as elements. Based on the relationships of stakeholders, rationales are extracted exhaustively.

RQ3: When the management policy or business environment changes, can the rationales and the GQM+Strategies Grid be easily analyzed via CAM?

As shown in Fig. 4, CAM has a mechanism to extract rationales by analyzing the relationships of stakeholders. Accordingly, if changes related to stakeholders occur, elements related to change can be extracted using CAM.

5   Conclusion and Future Work

Often, insufficient requirements management is on top of the list of factors contributing to project failures [7]. GQM+Strategies is an effective approach to align business goals with the systemization of strategies. However, rationales may be ambiguous or omitted. In our approach, ideal rationales are extracted by analyzing the relationships of stakeholders in an organization. Moreover, we propose a mechanism that can respond to changes in the management policy or business environment.

To demonstrate the effectiveness of CAM, an experiment involving 50 students at Shimane University in Japan began in February 2014.

Acknowledgement. In addition to co-authors, I would like to thank other members of Goal-oriented Quantitative Management Research Group (GQM-RG) who provided carefully considered feedback and valuable comments.

References

[1] Adam, T., et al.: Aligning software projects with business objectives. In: 6th IWSM-MENSURA 2011. IEEE (2011)

[2] Munch, J., et al.: "Experiences and Insights from Applying GQM+Strategies in a Systems Product Development Organization. In: 39th SEAA 2013, p. 21 (2013)

[3] Ebert, C., et al.: Requirements Engineering–Industry Needs. In: 6th RE 2008 (2008)

[4] Mandić, V., Basili, et al.: Utilizing GQM+ Strategies for business value analysis: An approach for evaluating business goals. In: 4th ESEM 2010. ACM (2010)

[5] Basili, V.R., et al.: Linking software development and business strategy through measurement. Computer 43(4), 57–65 (2010)

[6] Tatsuya, K., et al.: Application of GQM+ Strategies in the Japanese Space Industry. In: 6th IWSM-MENSURA 2011. IEEE (2011)

[7] Christof, E.: Requirements before the requirements: understanding the upstream impacts. In: 13th RE 2005. IEEE (2005)

Addressing the Challenges of Alignment of Requirements and Services: A Vision for User-Centered Method

Muneera Bano [1] and Naveed Ikram [2]

[1] Faculty of Engineering and IT
University of Technology Sydney, Australia
Muneera.Bano@student.uts.edu.au
[2] Faculty of Computing
Riphah Internaitonal University, Islamabad, Pakistan
naveed.ikram@riphah.edu.pk

Abstract. One of the major challenges in Service Oriented Requirements Engineering is for business analysts to find services that accurately match the customer requirements. Several attempts have been made to propose different methods and techniques for finding the best suitable service to align with customer requirements. However, these solutions are mainly focusing only on the technical side of the problem and the social side of the challenge of alignment has been largely neglected. In this vision paper, we propose a novel user-centered method of alignment, which involves end-users in the process of analysis and decision process for the selection of the service. The analysis and decision for service selection is based on end-user feedback and customer preferences. The aim is to assist the business analysts in making informed decisions for selecting the optimally best-aligned service among available options.

Keywords: Requirements, Services, Alignment, User involvement.

1   Introduction

Service Oriented Software Engineering (SOSE) aims to reuse existing software components in the form of services to reduce the time, cost and effort of the development [1]. In the Service Oriented Requirements Engineering (SORE) there is an additional task of alignment of services and requirements [2]. By aligning a service to the requirements we refer to finding the best matched service for the requirements while making a tradeoff among cost, functional and non functional requirements. Alignment of requirements to services is considered to be the most challenging and problematic task in SORE [3, 12] due to the following major reasons:

Lack of User Involvement: In our previous study of SOSE [3], the practitioners' most frequently mentioned reason for challenges in alignment is the lack of end-user involvement during the analysis and decision process for service selection. The current solutions for the alignment (e.g. [4-9]), are focused primarily on the technological aspect of the problem. Lack the end-user involvement in the process will leads to their dissatisfaction with the resulting system [10, 11]. It has already been acknowledged that a solution may never be complete unless it takes into account multiple perspectives of the problem e.g. organizational, technical and individual [13].

D. Zowghi and Z. Jin (Eds.): APRES 2014, CCIS 432, pp. 83–89, 2014.
© Springer-Verlag Berlin Heidelberg 2014

Mismatch in Granularity Level: Service granularity is the range of functionality offered by a service [4] Services can either be fine-grained (focused, limited functionality) or coarse-grained (broader functionality). Fine granularity offers more flexibility and reusability in customizing the system but also results in increasing the effort and cost of integration [5]. A coarse-grained service is typically expected to carry out more functions but would also exchange more messages and data, and may present a complex interface [6]. This reduces the reusability as the functionality might be too overloaded for the actual need of most consumers [2]. The details provided in the service specifications about their functionality mostly do no provide the same level of details that is needed for matching them against requirements [7].

Context: Services are developed to cover needs of a wide range of customers and thus are developed free of context so to be utilized in various projects from different domains. Aligning context free services to specific project requirements is therefore a challenging task [3].

These identified challenges for the alignment of requirements and services, have motivated to propose a user-centered alignment method in this paper. The construction of our proposed method is grounded in the findings and systematic analysis of the literature [1, 10], a quantitative study (online survey) [22], and qualitative study (interviews with practitioners) [3, 12].

2   Background

Users can have various degrees and levels of involvement in any software project [10], and one form of involvement is where their feedback is utilized in decision making processes [14-18]. Active end-user involvement is required in order to provide personalized systems that can be customized for individual user needs [15]. User feedback analysis from online resources has recently gained a lot of focus in Requirements Engineering research e.g. Requirements Elicitation [15], Software Evolution [16, 17], Software Quality [19]. The end-user comments and feedback has been a major source of evolution in product line release in some cases, e.g. Android Market and Apple's store [16, 19]. The main focus of our proposed method is to make the alignment process user-centered. There are two types of users whose involvement is required in the analysis process of our proposed method and we will be referring to them throughout the paper based on the following definition: *The customers: for whom the service based software system is being developed and who are the project sponsors and will actually use this system in future, **The end-users:** who have experience of using a particular service in the past and have either provided their feedback on online forums or can provide (post deployment) feedback when requested.* The user involvement in our proposed method is of two types based on the two types of users.

Customer Involvement: the involvement of customers in the project is in the form of their actual participation in various activities like for requirements elicitation and modification, providing preferences for service selection as well as reviewing the results before making decisions. For making decision based on customer preferences we will be following the Multi Criteria Decision Analysis (MCDA) [20] approach. MCDA is used for decision making in situations where a trade-off is required among multiple criteria. It helps the analysts in making more informed decisions. This approach has been extensively used in Management Sciences for the selection of suppliers. Our proposed method adopts similar concepts for selection of a service form service providers.

End-User Involvement: the previous users of the service are involved in the process with their feedback based on their past experience of using that service. The feedback is either collected form online resources (if available) or elicited directly from the users (if approachable). There has been a substantial body of research in recent years on utilizing users' feedback from different perspectives and various tools and methods (e.g. data mining, information retrieval, crowd sourcing, parsing, natural language processing), are proposed for extracting useful information form the extensive user comments and feedback available on online resources [14-18].

3   User-Centered Method of Alignment

Besides the three actors that are involved in the alignment process (analyst, service provider, customer), our proposed method (Figure 1) has an additional actor (end-user). These actors are required to perform different activities during alignment process i.e. ***Customers:*** *participate in requirements elicitation, providing preferences and ranking them and reviewing the results before service selection decision making,* ***Analysts:*** *perform requirements elicitation, searching for available services, carry out the alignment process for analyzing and selecting services by involving both customers and end-users,* ***Service providers:*** *publish the specification of services they provide,* ***End-users:*** *provide feedback on services based on their past experience of using them.*

Based on the requirements the services are being searched and the resultant service specifications are analysed along with the end-user feedback. There are five interconnected and iterative steps required for alignment analysis: Granularity Analysis, Perspective based Analysis, Missing information Analysis, End-user Feedback Analysis, and Multi Criteria Decision Analysis.

Granularity Analysis: The first step requires the development of a table where all service specifications are evaluated for granularity level against requirements. The aim is to select the services that provide maximum functional range against requirements, i.e. a service that provides more coverage of requirement set. The table will provide a visual representation of services and requirements in rows and columns showing their level of granularity in quantifiable scores. The scores can be calculated by evaluating a service in one of the three following scenarios: fully aligned, totally misaligned, or partially aligned. Partial alignment has further three cases; *(1) Service functionality fulfils only part of the business requirement (service is too fine grained causing performance related issues e.g. integration problem, delays in interaction among multiple services), (2) Service functionality offers more than business requirement specifies (service is too coarse grained increasing cost), (3) Service functionality and business requirements overlap (causing increase in cost and integration issues).* Considering the format for service specification various methods are available (e.g. [5-9]) for determining the level of granularity of service against requirements

Perspective Based Analysis: A solution cannot be complete unless it takes into account multiple perspectives of the problem [13]. The proposed method will follow multiple perspective evaluation of the services for alignment against requirements, i.e. Organizational, Technical (Functional, non Functional), Economical, and Project related etc. During this step the requirements are analyzed in order to develop a checklist for service evaluation. The checks are assigned weights based on customer preferences for the project. If a particular requirement has more than one criteria then it has to broken down to single or atomic level so that in checklist yes/no/partial type answers for scoring and evaluating the services is possible.

Missing Information Analysis: During this step service specifications are evaluated against checklist developed in previous step, missing information in service specifications are identified. This information will be extracted from the user feedback.

End-user Feedback Analysis: End-user feedback is either collected directly from online resources (if available) or elicited directly from the users (if approachable). Multiple methods and associated tools/techniques are proposed for feedback collection based on the situations and format in which the feedback is available (e.g. feature extraction, information retrieval, crowd sourcing, survey and questionnaire etc.). This feedback is serving two purposes: *(1) providing the information about the users' satisfaction based on their past experience of using the service. This will also reflect users' trust of service provider (if the service is from third party). While analysing user satisfaction it is important to consider the context in which the previous users have used the service. User feedback without context may not be useful at all [21], (2) end-user feedback is also used for filling the gaps in service specification where the information is missing against the checklist that is developed in previous steps. Service specification may not be at the same level of abstraction as customer requirements in giving details about functional and non functional capabilities of service. User feedback can help in identification of missing information in service specification [17].*

Multi Criteria Decision Analysis: Once all the previous steps are executed, the service specifications will have specific scores based on user preferred weights for their criteria. This will help the business analyst to analyze the optimally best available match for the requirements against multiple criteria and to make a better informed decision for service selection. Once all the information is available the total score for all the services is calculated by selected MCDA method. Additive weighting method is the most widely used approach to deal with MCDA problems [20]. In its simplest form weights are multipliers to their respective checks or criteria and then all scores for one option are added. The service with highest score is considered to be possibly best aligned among available options based on customer preferences.

4   Alignment Method Instantiation

In this section we sketch a generic instantiation of the alignment method. The requirements elicitation between analyst and customer results in an initial set of requirements represented by R such that $R = \{R_1, R_2, R_3 \dots R_X\}$ where X is the total number of requirements. Using the requirement set the analyst would search for available related services from service repositories. Available services can be represented by $S = \{S_1, S_2, S_3 \dots S_Y\}$ where Y is number of services found against requirement set R. The analyst converts the requirements into perspective based checklist and assigns the weights to the checks based on customer preferences. The set of checks is represented by $C= \{C_1, C_2, C_3 \dots C_K\}$ and the weights against these checks is represented by $W= \{W_1, W_2, W_3 \dots W_K\}$ where K is the number of checks in the perspective based checklist. The analyst evaluates service specification to provide answers to the checks in the checklist which can be **yes=1** or **no=0** or **partial=0.5**. If there is some missing information then the end-user feedback is either retrieved or elicited to get the required information using suitable methods (e.g. feature extraction, information retrieval, survey questionnaire etc). Once the information is complete the perspective based checklist scores are calculated for all **Y** candidate services. For a service S_i from the set of services **S** the perspective based score is represented by P_i which is calculated by adding all the answers to the **K** number of checks in set **C** for that service according to the following formula:

$$P_i = \sum_{i=1}^{K}((c_i) * (w_i))$$

The next step is to calculate the granularity of the service S_i using a function g_i against all requirements in set **R**. The granularity method is represented by **G-Method** which is selected according to the project situation (e.g. format of service specification) to calculate the functional range of service specifications against requirement set **R**. the scoring can be fully-aligned=1, totally-misaligned=0, and partially-aligned=0.5

$$g_i = G\text{-}Method\,(\,S_i\,,R\,)$$

The next step is to calculate user satisfaction u_i against that service by using suitable method with function **US-Method** by analysing the available end-user feedback. The user comments and ratings are utilized for creating the score for user satisfaction with help of suitable methods. The scores can be selected by the analyst in both positive and negative values.

$$u_i = US\text{-}Method\,(\,S_i\,)$$

The customer provides the preferences for the weights for Perspective based checklist w_p and the level of granularity w_g and user satisfaction w_u to be considered for final decision. The final score for a service S_i in the set **S** can be calculated as following.

$$Score\,(\,S_i\,) = (\,P_i * w_p\,) + (\,g_i * w_g\,) + (\,u_i * w_u\,)$$

When the scores are calculated for all Y number of services, the highest service score among the set S will be the optimally the best aligned service according to the customer preferences and end-user feedback.

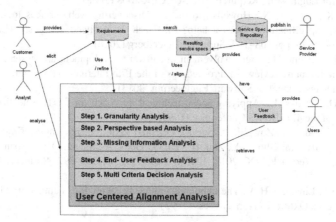

Fig. 1. User-Centered Method for Alignment of Requirements and Services

5   Future Work

In this paper we have proposed a vision for a user –centered method for alignment of requirements and services. By utilizing the design of our alignment method described in this paper, we plan to develop an automated tool to support the business analyst in analyzing and simulating the alignment of the services and requirements. Our aim is to use the method and the supporting tool in an industrial project to empirically evaluate the effectiveness of our proposed method.

References

1. Bano, M., Ikram, N.: Issues and Challenges of Requirement Engineering in Service Oriented Software Development. In: Fifth International Conference on Software Engineering Advances (ICSEA), pp. 64–69 (2010)
2. Heinrich, B., et al.: Granularity of services–an economic analysis. Business & Information Systems Engineering 3(6), 345–358 (2011)
3. Bano, M., Zowghi, D., Ikram, N., Niazi, M.: What makes Service Oriented Requirements Engineering challenging? A qualitative study. IET Software, doi:10.1049/iet-sen.2013.0131
4. Papazoglou, M.P., Van Den Heuvel, W.-J.: Service-oriented design and development methodology. International Journal of Web Engineering and Technology 2(4), 412–442 (2006)
5. Adam, S., Riegel, N., Doerr, J.: Deriving software services from business processes of representative customer organizations. In: IEEE International Workshop on Service-Oriented Computing: Consequences for Engineering Requirements, SOCCER (2008)
6. Steghuis, C.: Service granularity in SOA projects: A trade-off Analysis., Master's thesis,University of Twente (2006)
7. Galster, M., Bucherer, E.: A business-goal-service-capability graph for the alignment of requirements and services. In: IEEE Congress on Services-Part I (2008)
8. Gehlert, A., Bramsiepe, N., Pohl, K.: Goal-driven alignment of services and business requirements. In: IEEE International Workshop on Service-Oriented Computing: Consequences for Engineering Requirements, SOCCER 2008 (2008)
9. Zachos, K., Maiden, N., Howells-Morris, R.: Discovering web services to improve requirements specifications: Does it help? In: Paech, B., Rolland, C. (eds.) REFSQ 2008. LNCS, vol. 5025, pp. 168–182. Springer, Heidelberg (2008)
10. Bano, M., Zowghi, D.: User involvement in software development and system success: A systematic literature review. In: Proceedings of the 17th International Conference on Evaluation and Assessment in Software Engineering (2013)
11. Kunda, D., Brooks, L.: Applying social-technical approach for COTS selection. In: Proceedings of the 4th UKAIS Conference (1999)
12. Bano Sahibzada, M., Zowghi, D.: Service Oriented Requirements Engineering: Practitioner's Perspective. In: Ghose, A., Zhu, H., Yu, Q., Delis, A., Sheng, Q.Z., Perrin, O., Wang, J., Wang, Y. (eds.) ICSOC 2012. LNCS, vol. 7759, pp. 380–392. Springer, Heidelberg (2013)
13. Mitroff, I.I., Linstone, H.A.: The unbounded mind: Breaking the chains of traditional business thinking. Oxford University Press (1993)

14. Hao, J., Li, S., Chen, Z.: Extracting service aspects from web reviews. In: Wang, F.L., Gong, Z., Luo, X., Lei, J. (eds.)WISM 2010. LNCS, vol. 6318, pp. 320–327. Springer, Heidelberg (2010)

15. Seyff, N., Graf, F., Maiden, N.: Using mobile REre tools to give end-users their own voice. In: 18th IEEE International Requirements Engineering Conference, RE (2010)

16. Galvis Carreño, L.V., Winbladh, K.: Analysis of user comments: An approach for software requirements evolution. In: Proceedings of the 2013 International Conference on Software Engineering. IEEE Press (2013)

17. Pagano, D., Maalej, W.: User feedback in the appstore: An empirical study. In: 21st IEEE International Requirements Engineering Conference, RE (2013)

18. Harman, M., Jia, Y., Zhang, Y.: App store mining and analysis: MSR for app stores. In: 9th IEEE Working Conference on Mining Software Repositories, MSR (2012)

19. Chen, M., Liu, X.: Predicting popularity of online distributed applications: iTunes app store case analysis. In: Proceedings of the 2011 Conference. ACM (2011)

20. Vetschera, R.: Preference-based decision support in software engineering. In: Value-Based Software Engineering, pp. 67–89. Springer (2006)

21. Schneider, K., Meyer, S., Peters, M., Schliephacke, F., Mörschbach, J., Aguirre, L.: Feedback in context: Supporting the evolution of IT-ecosystems. In: Ali Babar, M., Vierimaa, M., Oivo, M. (eds.) PROFES 2010. LNCS, vol. 6156, pp. 191–205. Springer, Heidelberg (2010)

22. Bano, M., Ikram, N.: KM-SORE: knowledge management for service oriented requirements engineering. In: The Sixth International Conference on Software Engineering Advances ICSEA (2011)

Evaluating the BPCRAR Method: A Collaborative Method for Business Process Oriented Requirements Acquisition and Refining

Han Lai[1,2,3], Rong Peng[1,*], and Yuze Ni[1]

[1] State Key Lab. of Software Engineering, Computer School, Wuhan University, Wuhan, China
[2] Chongqing Key Lab. of Electronic Commerce & Supply Chain System
[3] School of Computer Science and Information Engineering
Chongqing Technology and Business University, Chongqing, China
{laihan,rongpeng,niyuze}@whu.edu.cn

Abstract. The goal of requirements elicitation is to understand the stakeholders' needs and constraints, and form the system requirements. But gathering requirements correctly, completely and understandably in a natural way is a great challenge to traditional methods, for requirements analysts always play key roles in the elicitation process dominantly while stakeholders participate in passively. Therefore, strategies that help the identification of requirements based on reducing the requirements analysts' dominance and promoting stakeholders' self-expression and self-improvement are welcomed. This paper reports a controlled experiment to evaluate the Business Process oriented Collaborative Requirements Acquisition and Refining (BPCRAR) method. Compared to JAD, the statistical results show that the requirements elicited by BPCRAR are more complete and understandable. Besides that, the perceived usefulness, ease to learn, and ease of use of BPCRAR are all confirmed by the statistical data got from the questionnaire to the participants.

Keywords: Controlled experiment; Requirements elicitation; BPCRAR; JAD; Evaluation.

1   Introduction

Requirements Elicitation (RE) is a critical process in system/software engineering. Its goal is to understand the stakeholders' needs and constraints, which will be analyzed and specified with requirements [1]. RE should consider the analysis of the organization structure with its business domain and processes. The identification and modeling of organization business processes can (i) help the requirements to represent the real business needs, (ii) reduce the number of redundant requirements, and (iii) be used to guide the development life cycle as a whole [2].

Defining requirements is not a simple knowledge transfer process where requirement engineers elicit and document existing client knowledge [3]. Rather, it is a cognitive

---

* Corresponding Author.

D. Zowghi and Z. Jin (Eds.): APRES 2014, CCIS 432, pp. 90–104, 2014.
© Springer-Verlag Berlin Heidelberg 2014

process, in which stakeholders collaboratively find out what has to be done by under-standing problems and domains, learning from other stakeholders by negotiating and discussing different viewpoints [4]. The major challenges of defining requirements for software intensive systems are: (i) lack of adequate communication between users and analysts; (ii) users do not have a clear and detailed expectation about their real needs; (iii) each stakeholder has different expectations and describes his/her needs differently. Thus, the requirements identified are always incomplete, ambiguous, and highly vola-tile. The different communication languages used among stakeholders are prone to misunderstanding.

To meet those challenges, many collaborative RE methods have been proposed. For example, Joint Application Development (JAD), Quality Function Deployment (QFD) and Cooperative Requirements Capture (CRC) have been proposed to rein-force the communication between stakeholders and analysts. But most traditional approaches lack the capabilities to gather requirements clearly and completely in a natural flow [5], as the requirements analysts always dominate the RE process. There-fore, the quality of the elicited requirements heavily depends on the knowledge and the experiences of the requirements analysts.

To reduce the requirements analysts' dominance and promote stakeholders' self-expression and self-improvement, a **B**usiness **P**rocess oriented **C**ollaborative **Re**-quirements **A**cquisition and **R**efining (BPCRAR) method is proposed [6].

This paper reports the results got from a controlled experiment to evaluate the ef-fectiveness and usefulness of the BPCRAR method. We discuss the quantitative and qualitative findings of our empirical study and their potential for improving the BPCRAR method. These findings indicate that BPCRAR could be considered as a promising method to capture and refine business process oriented requirements.

The remainder of this paper is organized as follows: Section 2 introduces related work about collaborative RE. Section 3 outlines BPCRAR. Section 4 presents the empirical work conducted to evaluate BPCRAR. Section 5 discusses possible threats to validity. Section 6 presents our conclusions and further work.

2   Collaborative Requirements Elicitation

Group work is a common way to elicit requirements collaboratively through the pro-motion of stakeholders' cooperation and commitment [7]. Brainstorm, JAD and Focus Group are all typical RE Group meeting methods. Group meeting have two modes: face-to-face mode and online mode. Due to the number of stakeholders that may be involved, face-to-face mode group meeting is difficult to organize and schedule; and online mode group meeting becomes popular. The RE methods such as WinWin[8], EasyWinWin [9], CoREA [10] and Athena [11] all support both modes by electronic tools. In addition, many studies have been proposed to facilitate the communication and participation of distributed stakeholders mainly from the computer supported cooperative work, such as RE-specific wikis [12] and iRequire [13]. Last but not least, some studies are focused on utilizing the stakeholders' profile, the social net-work among stakeholders and data mining technology to generate effective recom-mendation mechanism to promote the collaboration in RE, such as [14] [15].

All these studies concentrate on facilitating the stakeholders' participation. The BPCRAR method is also a collaborative method and mainly focused on the business process oriented requirements' acquisition and refining. It is a solution about how to refine requirements from group stories to formal expression (i.e. business process models) based on progressive refinement.

3   Overview of BPCRAR

The BPCRAR method is proposed to promote stakeholders' self-expression, self-improvement and collaboration. It adopts the group storytelling [11], dialogue game [16], and narrative network modeling (NNM) [17] to facilitate collaboration and communication. The overview of BPCRAR is shown in Figure 1. It consists of four activities: "group storytelling", "create abstraction", "build formal presentation", and "dialog game". The first three activities form a fountain model [18] from concreteness to abstraction and the activity of "dialog game" is a sub activity throughout the three, which provides the interaction rules and acts as a refining wheel to guide stakeholders' expression. The whole process and each activity in the process can be iterated until the final artifacts are gained and validated.

There are three essential roles in BPCRAR: Teller, Facilitator and Modeler.

- **Tellers** are stakeholders whose expectations are crucial to the success of the system, such as customers, users and domain experts. They can tell their expectations, activities or knowledge about the system to be built by a series of stories.
- **Facilitators** are experienced professionals who mediate the processes of telling stories, link facts, and help to produce the first level of abstraction.
- **Modelers** are assigned to qualified requirement analysts who can develop the graphic business models based on the abstractions extracted from stories.

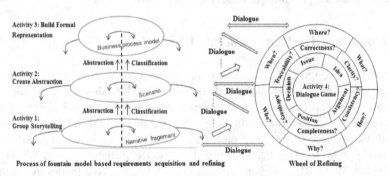

Fig. 1. Overview of BPCRAR Method

The **Activity name, Motivation, Subjects, Objects,** and **Results** of each activity are summarized and based on Activity Theory (AT) [19] in Table 1. The main **Actions** and **Goals** in each activity are further described in Table 2. Due to space limitations, the steps (mainly including **Community, Division of labor,** and the **Rules**) taken by BPCRAR are elaborated using the AT in [6].

Table 1. The Motivation, Subjects, Objects and Results of each activity

Activity	Motivation	Subject	Object	Result
A1: Group Storytelling	Acquire stakeholders' needs	T, F, M	Knowledge, expectations and experiences	Stories
A2: Create abstraction	Identify the scenarios Tellers refer to	F, M, T	Stories	BPEs/NNMs
A3: Build formal presentation	Describe requirement formally by business process model	M, F, T	BPEs/ NNMs	BPM
A4: Dialog game	Provide rule for interaction and refine requirement	M, F, T	Issues in stories, BPEs, BPMs and NNMs	Ideas for solving the issues
Note: Teller (T); Modeler(M); Facilitator(F); Business Process Elements (BPE); Business Process Model(BPM)				

Table 2. The main Actions and Goals in each activity

Activity	Action	Goal
A1:Group Storytelling	Set Theme	Define the scope of the RE process
	Storytelling	Capture stakeholders' needs
	Perform dialogue game	Provide triggers for interaction and refining acquired stories
A2: Create abstraction	Read stories and annotate	Set up traceable annotation for abstraction creation in each story
	Extract BPEs based on stories	Create the first level abstraction of business process
	Build NNMs	Capture actual and potential paths of business process
	Perform dialogue game	Provide triggers for interaction and refining business process
A3:Build formal presentation	Build BPMs	Create formal description of requirements
	Perform dialogue game	Provide triggers for interaction and refining business process
	Validate the BPM	Reach consensus
A4: Dialog game	Raise Issues	Introduce new discussion topics to address issues identified
	Propose of Ideas	Generate solutions to resolve the issues
	Discuss proposed Ideas	Clarify the reasons to support or counter proposed Ideas
	Vote	Evaluate the proposal and reach consensus
	Make decision	Select final Idea(s) to resolve the issue

4   The Controlled Experiment

Before the controlled experiment, we have conducted two case studies to test the usability of BPCRAR in June 2013 with CS graduate students and PHD candidates in Wuhan University. The results of the case studies help us to improve BPCRAR. The controlled experiment was designed to validate the feasibility of BPCRAR.

4.1   Experiment Design

The experiment design refers to the guidelines proposed by Wohlin [20]. According to the Goal-Question-Metric (GQM) [20], the goals of the experiment is to (i) compare the completeness and understandability of the requirements artifacts elicited by BPCRAR and JAD to evaluate their effectiveness; and (ii) evaluate the Perceived Usefulness (PU), Perceived Ease of Learning (PEOL) and Perceived Ease of Use (PEOU) of BPCRAR from the viewpoints of Tellers, Facilitators, and Modelers, (iii) identify issues to be improved in BPCRAR. JAD was chosen as the basis for a comparative measure of effectiveness, because it is one of the most well-known industrial collaborative RE method and can be executed by the CS undergraduate students [21].

The experiment includes 3 independent variables and 5 dependent variables, as showed in Table 3. The chosen dependent variables are based on the requirements engineering process evaluation framework [22] and the collaborative process quality evaluation framework [23].

Table 3. Independent variables and dependent variables in the controlled experiment

Variable name	Type	Description
Role	IV	Teller, Facilitator, and Modeler
Method	IV	BPCRAR and JAD
Object	IV	O1, O2 (as in Section 4.2)
PU	DV	The degree to which participants believe that the technology could improve his/her performance at work
PEOL	DV	The degree to which participants believe that learning a particular RE method is effort-free
PEOU	DV	The degree to which participants believe that using a particular RE method is effort-free
DOC	DV	The ratio of all needs are covered by the specified requirements
DOU	DV	The degree to which the requirements are understandable
Note: Independent Variable (IV); Dependent Variable (DV); Degree of Completeness(DOC); Degree of Understandability (DOU)		

According to the experiments' goals, the research questions and hypothesizes are:

RQ1: Is BPCRAR perceived useful from the viewpoints of Tellers, Facilitators, and Modelers? And the following hypotheses are:

$H1_0$: BPCRAR is perceived not useful from the viewpoints of Tellers.

$H2_0$: BPCRAR is perceived not useful from the viewpoints of Facilitators.

$H3_0$: BPCRAR is perceived not useful from the viewpoints of Modelers.

RQ2: Is BPCRAR perceived easy to learn from the viewpoints of Tellers, Facilitators, and Modelers? And the following hypotheses from the viewpoints of Tellers, Facilitators and Modelers can be assigned as $H4_0$, $H5_0$ and $H6_0$ accordingly.

RQ3: Is BPCRAR perceived as ease to use from the viewpoints of Tellers, Facilitators, and Modelers? And the following hypotheses from the viewpoints of Tellers, Facilitators and Modelers can be assigned as $H7_0$, $H8_0$ and $H9_0$ accordingly.

RQ4: Does BPCRAR produce requirements that are more complete than JAD?

$H10_0$: There is no significant difference between the degrees of completeness of requirements captured by BPCRAR and JAD.

RQ5: Does BPCRAR produce requirements that are more understandable than JAD?

$H11_0$: There is no significant difference between the understandability of the requirements captured by BPCRAR and JAD.

To answer the RQ1, RQ2, and RQ3, the questionnaire includes 3 sets of closed-questions (items) as shown in Table 4, 5 and 6. These closed-questions adopt a 7-point Likert scale (1-Strongly Disagree, 4- Neutral, 7- Strongly Agree). The questions to the same independent variable were randomized to prevent systemic response bias. In addition, in order to ensure the balance of questions in the questionnaire, half of the questions were written in negative sentences to avoid monotonous responses [24]. In this experiment, we deal with Likert scale as interval data. According to Wohlin [20], the Mean should be employed as a measure of central tendency and standard deviation. Each subjective dependent variable was quantified by calculating the arithmetical mean of its closed-question values.

Table 4. Questions about the PU of BPCRAR

Code	Question
PU1	The "Group storytelling" activity is helpful to acquire stakeholders' needs
PU2	The "Create abstraction" activity is helpful to identify the scenarios
PU3	The "Build formal presentation" activity is helpful to formal requirement expressions
PU4	The "Dialog game" activity is helpful to provide rules for interaction and refine requirements

Table 5. Questions about the PEOL of BPCRAR

Code	Question
PEOL1	The rules & DoL of "Group storytelling" activity are easy to learn
PEOL2	The rules & DoL of "Create abstraction" activity are easy to learn
PEOL3	The rules & DoL of "Build formal presentation" activity are easy to learn
PEOL4	The rules & division of labor of "Dialog game" activity are easy to learn
Note: Division of Labor (DOL)	

Table 6. Questions about the perceived ease of use of BPCRAR

Code	Question
PEOU1	The "Group storytelling" activity is easy to participate in
PEOU2	The "Create abstraction" activity is easy to participate in
PEOU3	The "Build formal presentation" activity is easy to participate in
PEOU4	The "Dialog game" activity is easy to participate in

For answering the RQ4 and RQ5, the dependent variables, completeness and understandability, are rated by an expert panel respectively. This panel was formed of three Software Engineering professionals with considerable industry experience in reviewing requirements specifications. For reducing the significant discrepancies based on subjective judgment, they first provided an initial list of requirements on the given topic based on their own expertise as a baseline. In the process of reviewing, the baseline was evolved when new requirements in the artifacts proposed by subjects were confirmed by the panel. And the final version was regarded as the baseline to judge the degree of requirements completeness and understandability delivered by each group. Moreover, the DOC and DOU were not only judged by the final artifacts, BPM models, delivered by the Modeler in each group, but also referred all the artifacts delivered in each step. The evaluation was based on three dimensions, syntactic quality, semantic quality and pragmatic quality independently and rated on 5-Likert scale   (5-Well above average; 3-Average; and 1-Well below average) [25].

Moreover, the questionnaire has 3 open-questions respectively from PEOL, PEOU, and PU to get feedback from participants.

4.2   Experiment Implementation

The experiment was planned as a balanced within-subject design with a confounding effect, signifying that the same subjects use both methods in a different order and with different experimental objects as shown in Table 7. The method in [26] is adopted to design the experiment. 8 group subjects participated in. Due to the participants' availability, the experiment conducted 2 times. The second experiment (EXP. 2) was strict replications of the first experiment (EXP. 1) with the change of subjects. Strictly replicated experiment also increases the confidence of the experiment validity.

Two experimental objects O1 and O2 were selected. O1 is "Online course enrollment in university" and O2 is "Online train tickets booking". Both objects are familiar to the subjects and the subjects can use BPCRAR and JAD to elicit the requirements of O1 and O2 in 120 minutes.

The experiment was conducted in an Advanced Software Engineering course in November 2013 at the Chongqing Technology and Business University. 60 third-year BSc students major in CS participated in the experiment. The participation was voluntary and the participants were awarded bonus points in their software engineering courses in return. We created 8 groups (7 participants per group), and had 4 alternates in case promised subjects did not show. Finally, the 4 alternates were not used. Each group involved 3 Tellers, 1 Facilitator, 1 Modeler, 1 Scribe, and 1 Observer in both BPCRAR and JAD. The Scribes were responsible for documenting the information in the sessions. The Observers took charge of supervising the experiment process complied with the instructions. 56 participants were assigned different roles based on their communication capability, prior modeling knowledge, domain knowledge, speed and clarity of writing, and the participation willingness gathered by background questionnaire. They were randomly assigned to each group based on the role assignment. Several documents were designed as instrumentation for the experiment: training slides, method guidelines, data collection tables and questionnaires. The experimental period of each group was 120 minutes. But the experiment can last a little longer if necessary to avoid ceiling effect [27]. After the experiment done, each participant (except the Scribe and Observer) was asked to fill out the questionnaires. To achieve the effect of single-blind experiment, the JAD groups were also asked to do the similar questionnaire, although the data would not be analyzed.

Table 7. Schedule of the controlled experiment

EXP.1				
	Group A	Group B	Group C	Group D
1st Day (150 min)	1. Introduce Requirements Engineering for all 2. Introduce JAD for all 3. Introduce BPCRAR for all 4. Introduce BPMN for Modeler 5. Train the Scribes to stenograph			
	Questionnaire on PEOL			
2ndDay (20 + 120 min)	Review BPCRAR		Review JAD	
	BPCRAR to O2	BPCRAR to O1	JAD to O2	JAD to O1
	Questionnaire on PU and PEOU			
3rdDay (20 + 120 min)	Review JAD		Review BPCRAR	
	JAD to O1	JAD in O2	BPCRAR to O1	BPCRAR to O2
	Questionnaire about PU and PEOU			
	(A week later)			
	EXP. 2 (Strictly replicated **EXP. 1**)			
	Experts review and rate			
Note: O1: Online train tickets booking; O2:Online course enrollment at university				

The formal JAD protocol consists of five stages: "Project definition", "Background research", "Pre workshop preparation", "The workshop", and "Final documentation", and might execute several days [28]. Due to the time constraints, the subject groups in JAD were required to perform only "The workshop", and "Final documentation" stages. The materials needed in the first three stages have been directly provided.

Significant differences between the executing processes of BPCRAR and JAD in the experiment are (i) JAD uses the structured brainstorming [28], whereas BPCRAR uses group storytelling to capture users' needs; (ii) JAD is mainly organized and dominated by the Facilitator, while BPCRAR uses dialogue games as the negotiation rules to guide the requirements negotiation; (iii) NNM are introduced in the BPCRAR to capture actual and potential paths of business processes.

4.3   Experiment Results

After the whole two experiments execution, the experts reviewed the requirements artifacts submitted from each experimental group. If a requirement not in the initial list given by the experts, the experts will determine whether it can be a "Realizable" or "false-positives". "Realizable" includes several notions: (i) useful for at least one stakeholder, (ii) technically already implemented or implementable, and (iii) socially and legally implementable. A requirement was considered "false-positive", e.g. beyond the target scope of the requirement elicitation or not "Realizable". Repeat requirements are considered only once. Discrepancies in this review were solved by consensus.

In this section, the experimental results, the effect of the orders of experiment methods and objects, and the Grader inter-rater reliability are all analyzed quantitatively and all the hypotheses are tested by SPSS V19, with significance level $\alpha = 0.05$. In addition, qualitative analysis is applied to analyze the answers to the open questions in the questionnaire.

4.3.1   Quantitative and Qualitative Analyses

After the EXP.1 and EXP.2 were performed, the experts reviewed all the artifacts submitted. After thorough consideration and discussion, a total of 53 and 46 requirements are confirmed by experts on the experiment object O1 and O2 respectively.

Table 8. Overall results about the each perceived measure items

Perceived Measures	Question	Teller (n=24)		Facilitator (n=8)		Modeler (n=8)	
		Mean	STD	Mean	STD	Mean	STD
PU	PU1	5.17	1.34	5.13	0.99	5.25	1.28
	PU2	4.96	1.04	5.38	0.92	5.13	1.25
	PU3	4.96	1.04	5.13	0.84	5.25	0.89
	PU4	5.17	0.96	5.25	0.89	5.13	1.36
PEOL	PEOL1	4.96	0.96	4.63	1.06	4.88	0.64
	PEOL2	4.88	0.85	4.75	0.89	4.88	0.84
	PEOL3	4.71	0.86	4.75	0.89	5.00	0.76
	PEOL4	4.54	0.88	4.88	0.84	5.00	1.07
PEOU	PEOU1	5.13	0.95	4.88	1.46	4.88	1.25
	PEOU2	5.13	0.80	4.50	1.31	5.00	0.93
	PEOU3	4.79	0.98	5.38	0.92	5.25	1.17
	PEOU4	4.79	1.02	4.75	0.89	4.13	0.84

In order to enlarge sample size to get hypothesis testing by statistical test method [29], the corresponding data from EXP.1 and EXP.2 are merged.

Table 8 shows the results of descriptive statistics for each perceived items of different roles. The mean scores are all superior to 4 points (neutral score in the 7-point Likert scale), which indicate that Tellers, Facilitators and Molders all showed positive attitude, "slightly Agree", toward the PU, PEOL and PEOU for each activity in BPCRAR. Furthermore, the mean and standard deviation of each perception-based variable from each role is calculated to analyze the whole method respectively as shown in Table 9. The results show that different roles of the subjects showed positive attitude, "slightly agree", toward the PU, PEOL and PEOU for the whole BPCRAR.

The hypotheses H1-H9 were tested by verifying whether the scores that the subjects assign to the PU/PEOL/PEOU are significantly better than the neutral score on the Likert-scale. Shapiro-Wilk test is adopted to test the normality of the data distribution. The data of H1 to H4 and H6 to H9 are normally distributed (p-value ≥ 0.05), therefore, one-tailed one sample t-test are adopted; and the data of H5 are not normally distributed (p-value < 0.05), thus, the Wilcoxon signed-rank test was adopted to test H5. The results in Table 10 state clearly to reject all the hypotheses, namely that the subjects perceived the BPCRAR as easy to learn, easy to use, and useful.

Table 9. Summary of the results of the perceived-based variables

Dependent variable	Teller (n=24)		Facilitator (n=8)		Modeler (n=8)	
	Mean	STD	Mean	STD	Mean	STD
PU	5.06	0.83	5.22	0.73	5.17	1.13
PEOL	4.77	0.75	4.75	0.82	4.94	0.73
PEOU	4.96	0.62	4.88	0.89	4.81	0.86

Table 10. Hypothesis test for perception-based variables

	p-value	Whether to reject null hypothesis
H1	0.000(<0.05)	Yes(BPCRAR is perceived as useful by Tellers)
H2	0.001(<0.05)	Yes(BPCRAR is perceived as useful by Facilitators)
H3	0.011(<0.05)	Yes(BPCRAR is perceived as useful by Modelers)
H4	0.000(<0.05)	Yes(BPCRAR is perceived as ease to learn by Tellers)
H5	0.013(<0.05)[a]	Yes(BPCRAR is perceived as ease to learn by Facilitators)
H6	0.004(<0.05)	Yes(BPCRAR is perceived as ease to learn by Modelers)
H7	0.000(<0.05)	Yes(BPCRAR is perceived as ease to use by Tellers)
H8	0.014(<0.05)	Yes(BPCRAR is perceived as ease to use by Facilitators)
H9	0.016(<0.05)	Yes(BPCRAR is perceived as ease to use by Modelers)
[a] Result obtained with the 1- tailed Wilcoxon signed rank test		

Table 11 shows the descriptive statistics for the performance variables in each experiment. Bold cells indicate that the completeness and understandability of requirements elicited by BPCRAR are higher than those elicited by JAD in both EXP.1 and

EXP.2. As the distribution was normal, the parametric one-tailed t-test was applied to verify the significance of the means. The results in Table 12 state clearly to reject the null hypotheses $H10_0$ and $H11_0$. To guarantee the scorer reliability, the Kendall's coefficient of concordance was adopted to judge the inter-rater reliability of three experts, which validate the reliability (**Completeness**: $W = 0.754$, p =0.003; **Understandability**: $W = 0.718$, p =0.006).

Table 11. Descriptive statistics for the performance variable

	Performance Measures	Method	Min	Max	Mean	STD
EXP.1	Completeness	BPCRAR	2.67	3.67	**3.17**	0.43
		JAD	2.00	3.33	2.58	0.57
EXP.2	Completeness	BPCRAR	3.00	4.00	**3.50**	0.43
		JAD	2.00	3.67	2.83	0.69
EXP.1	Understandability	BPCRAR	2.67	4.00	**3.17**	0.58
		JAD	2.00	3.33	2.50	0.58
EXP.2	Understandability	BPCRAR	2.67	4.00	**3.33**	0.54
		JAD	2.33	3.67	2.92	0.57

Table 12. Hypothesis test for the performance variables

	p-value	Whether to reject null hypothesis
H10	0.016 (<0.05)	Yes (BPCRAR produces requirements more complete than JAD)
H11	0.035 (<0.05)	Yes(BPCRAR produces requirements more understandable than JAD)

To test the effect of the order of both independent variables, RE methods and experimental objects, the method in [26] is adopted.

Suppose difference function $Diff_x$= $observation_x(A)$ – $observation_x(B)$, where x denotes a particular subject group, and A, B are the two possible values of one independent variable. We created Diff variables from each performance dependent variable. And the statistic results show that the orders of the independent variables have no significant influences on the dependent variables as shown in Table 13 (all the p-values obtained are greater than 0.05).

Table 13. The effect of the orders of methods and experimental objects

Orders	Dependent variables	EXP.1	EXP.2
Methods	Completeness	No(0.937)[a]	No(0.394)
	Understandability	No(0.394)[a]	No(0.699)[a]
Experimental objects	Completeness	No(0.818)[a]	No(0.515)
	Understandability	No(0.515)	No(0.687)
[a] Result obtained with the Mann-Whitney non-parametric test			

Finally, a qualitative analysis was performed to analyze the answers to the open-questions in the questionnaire. Most of the subjects confirmed that BPCRAR promoted the discussions by clarifying the DoL and getting people more involved. However, 2 Facilitators indicated that the "Create abstraction" was heavy workload, and 1 Modeler indicated that it was not easy to remember and follow the instructions in "Dialogue Game". The participants suggested that BPCRAR might be more user-friendly if appropriate tools could be adopted to fulfill the tasks like role assignment, story recording and annotation, and group negotiation. Last but not least, participants suggested that more detailed guidelines and typical examples should be provided to facilitate the execution effectively and efficiently.

4.3.2   Summary of Results

For perception-based measurement, the analysis indicates that all the null hypotheses ($H1_0$-$H9_0$) are rejected. Namely, BPCRAR is perceived useful, easy to learn, and easy to use in requirements acquisition and refining from the viewpoint of tellers, facilitators and modelers respectively. However, the relatively high standard deviations existed in the Table 8 indicate that a few participants have different opinions. With regard to PEOL, the mean of tellers' feedbacks on PEOL4 (Dialogue game) and the mean of facilitators' feedbacks on PEOL1 (Group storytelling) are 4.54 and 4.63 respectively, which are relatively low. This implicates that more detailed guidelines and examples should be provided in these activities, which complied with the feedback got from the answers to the open-questions. With regard to PEOU, the mean of facilitators' feedbacks on PEOU2 (Create abstraction) and the mean of modelers' feedbacks on PEOU4 (Dialogue game) are 4.54 and 4.13 respectively, which is relatively low. It suggests that computer-aided functions should be provided to improve the effectiveness and reduce the workload of these activities.

For performance-based measurement, the results of experiments indicate that all the null hypotheses ($H10_0$-$H11_0$) are rejected. Namely, BPCRAR produces requirements more completely and understandably than JAD. In addition, the results from each experiment (as shown in Table 11) indicate that BPCRAR is superior to JAD in terms of minimum, maximum and average. Furthermore, the means of two performance indicators of BPCRAR are greater than 3 (the neutral score), which indicates that the results are superior to the average level. Meanwhile, the standard deviation of BPCRAR in each experiment is smaller than that of JAD, which indicates that BPCRAR is more stable in terms of DOC and DOU.

The discussion above indicates that BPCRAR could be considered a promising method for collaborative requirements acquisition and refining.

5   Threats to Validity

The main threats to the **internal validity** come from: learning effects, subjects' experiences, information exchange among groups, and understandability of the training documents. The differences of learning effects were alleviated by ensuring that each participant applied both method to different experimental objects, and all the possible order combinations were considered. And the effects of the orders of the methods and the experimental objects were evaluated by statistical tests and the results proved its validation. Subjects' experiences may influence the execution of the experiments. To alleviate this threat, the pre-questionnaire was introduced to guide the subjects' assignment. Besides, we conducted sufficient training for both methods. To minimize the information exchange among groups, each group had a separate room to perform the task. But EXP.1 and EXP.2 took place on two different weeks. It is difficult to guarantee no information exchange happened. In order to alleviate this situation, at least to some extent, the participants were asked to return all the material at the end of each experiment. Finally, understanding biases of the training material were alleviated by clearing up all the misunderstandings in the experiment session.

The main threats to the **external validity** are: using students as subjects, and the objects' selection criteria. In our study, the students are acceptable as subjects since nobody has previous experience with any method. To balance the abilities of each group, the pre-questionnaire was conducted and used as the evidence of grouping. The experiments objects "online train tickets booking" and "online course enrollment in university" are selected because both of them are familiar to the undergraduates and have similar sizes and complexity. In future, conducting the experiments in industrial should be highlighted.

The main threats to the **construct validity** are: measures that are applied in the quantitative analysis and the reliability of the questionnaire. Measures adopted in the quantitative analysis are those commonly employed in empirical RE experiments [22]. The reliability of the questionnaire is tested by the Cronbach test. Questions related to PU, PEOL, and PEOU obtained a Cronbach's alpha values that are all higher than the acceptable minimum (0.70) [20]. One limitation of our experiment is that lack of the investigation on other factors (e.g., traceability, verification, accuracy) may influence the method adoption in practice. Another limitation is the lack of use of Technology Acceptance Model (TAM) [30]. In our study, the questionnaire items in "perceived of usefulness of BPCRAR" and "perceived of ease of use of BPCRAR" dimensions mainly based on measurement of each activity in BPCRAR and not based on TAM. Since TAM is one of the most widely applied theoretical model to study user acceptance and usage behavior of emerging information technologies, and it has received extensive empirical support through validations and replications, we plan to design questionnaire according to TAM in the future replicated experiment.

The main threat to the **conclusion validity** is the validity of the statistical tests applied. This was alleviated by applying the most common tests that are employed in the empirical software engineering [20]. However, more replications are preferred to confirm these results.

6   Conclusion and Future Work

This paper presents a controlled experiment to evaluate BPCRAR. The completeness and understandability are evaluated in comparison to JAD and the statistic results show that BPCRAR is superior to JAD in both aspects. Meanwhile, the PU, PEOL, and PEOU of BPCRAR are evaluated from the viewpoint of different roles by questionnaire. The statistic results show that stakeholders recognize its usefulness, ease to learn, and ease to use. According to the validity analysis, more experimentation should be performed to confirm the results.

As future work, we plan to replicate the experiment by considering subjects with different levels of experiences in RE (e.g. industrial practitioners) and objects in other business domains. In addition, implementing the collaborative RE tool based on the Mediawiki and its extensions to support the method is our next step.

Acknowledgements. The research was supported by the National Natural Science Foundation of China under Grant No. 61170026, the National High Technology Research and Development Program of China (863 Program) under Grant No. 2013AA12A206, and the Chongqing Key Lab. of Electronic Commerce & Supply Chain System Special Fund (2012ECSC0210).

References

1. Konaté, J., Sahraoui, A.E.K., Kolfschoten, G.L.: Collaborative Requirements Elicitation: A Process-Centred Approach. Group Decision and Negotiation 1-31 (2013)
2. de Oliveira, M., Viana, D., Conte, T., Vieira, S., Marczak, S.: Evaluating the REMO-EKD technique: A technique for the elicitation of software requirements based on EKD organizational models. In: 2013 IEEE Third International Workshop on Empirical Requirements Engineering, pp. 9–16. IEEE (2013)
3. Grady, J.O.: System requirements analysis. Academic Press (2010)
4. Sutcliffe, A.: User-centred requirements engineering. Springer (2002)
5. Boulila, N., Hoffmann, A., Herrmann, A.: Using Storytelling to record requirements: Elements for an effective requirements elicitation approach. In: Proceedings of the 2011 Fourth International Workshop on Multimedia and Enjoyable Requirements Engineering, pp. 9–16 (2011)
6. Lai, H., Peng, R., Ni, Y.: GDS4RE Report. Technical report, http://www.pengronggroup.org/gds4rereport20140120.pdf
7. Zowghi, D., Coulin, C.: Requirements elicitation: A survey of techniques, approaches, and tools. In: Engineering and Managing Software Requirements, pp. 19–46. Springer (2005)
8. Boehm, B.W., Ross, R.: Theory-W software project management principles and examples. IEEE Transactions on Software Engineering 15(7), 902–916 (1989)
9. Boehm, B., Gr, U., Nbacher, P., Briggs, R.O.: EasyWinWin: A groupware-supported methodology for requirements negotiation, pp. 720–721 (2001)
10. Geisser, M., Hildenbrand, T.: A method for collaborative requirements elicitation and decision-supported requirements analysis. In: Geisser, M., Hildenbrand, T. (eds.) Advanced Software Engineering: Expanding the Frontiers of Software Technology. IFIP, vol. 219, pp. 108–122. Springer, Boston (2006)
11. Laporti, V., Borges, M.R.S., Braganholo, V.: Athena: A collaborative approach to requirements elicitation. Comput. Ind. 60(6), 367–380 (2009)
12. Peng, R., Lai, H.: DRE-specific Wikis for Distributed Requirements Engineering: A Review. In: Proceedings of the 2012 19th Asia-Pacific Software Engineering Conference, pp. 116–126 (2012)
13. Seyff, N., Graf, F., Maiden, N.: End-user requirements blogging with iRequire. In: 2010 ACM/IEEE 32nd International Conference on Software Engineering, vol. 2, pp. 285–288. IEEE (2010)

14. Castro-Herrera, C., Cleland-Huang, J., Mobasher, B.: Enhancing stakeholder profiles to improve recommendations in online requirements elicitation. In: Proceedings of the 17th IEEE International Conference on Requirements Engineering, pp. 37–46 (2009)
15. Lim, S.L., Quercia, D., Finkelstein, A.: StakeSource: harnessing the power of crowdsourcing and social networks in stakeholder analysis. In: Proceedings of the 32nd ACM/IEEE International Conference on Software Engineering, Cape Town, South Africa, pp. 239–242. ACM (2010)
16. Ravenscroft, A., McAlister, S.: Designing interaction as a dialogue game: Linking social and conceptual dimensions of the learning process. In: Interactions in Online Education: Implications for Theory and Practice, pp. 73–90 (2006)
17. Pentland, B.T., Feldman, M.S.: Narrative networks: Patterns of technology and organization. Organization Science 18(5), 781–795 (2007)
18. Henderson-Sellers, B., Edwards, J.M.: The object-oriented systems life cycle. Commun. Acm. 33(9), 142–159 (1990)
19. Kuutti, K.: Activity theory as a potential framework for human-computer interaction research. In: Context and Consciousness: Activity Theory and Human-Computer Interaction, pp. 17–44 (1996)
20. Wohlin, C., Runeson, P., Hst, M., Ohlsson, M.C., Regnell, B., Wessln, A.: Experimentation in software engineering. Springer (2012)
21. Costain, G., McKenna, B.: Experiencing the Elicitation of User Requirements and Recording Them in Use Case Diagrams through Role-Play. Journal of Information Systems Education 22(4), 367–380 (2011)
22. Emam, K., Madhavji, N.H.: An instrument for measuring the success of the requirements engineering process in information systems development, vol. 1, pp. 201–240. Springer, Netherlands (1996)
23. den Hengst, M., Dean, D.L., Kolfschoten, G., Chakrapani, A.: Assessing the quality of collaborative processes, vol. 1, p. 16b (2006)
24. Hu, P.J., Chau, P.Y., Sheng, O.R.L., Tam, K.Y.: Examining the technology acceptance model using physician acceptance of telemedicine technology. J. Manage. Inform. Syst. 16(2), 91–112 (1999)
25. Gemino, A., Wand, Y.: A framework for empirical evaluation of conceptual modeling techniques. Requirements Engineering 9(4), 248–260 (2004)
26. Briand, L.C., Labiche, Y., Di Penta, M., Yan-Bondoc, H.: An experimental investigation of formality in UML-based development. Ieee. T. Software Eng. 31(10), 833–849 (2005)
27. Dag, I.K., Sjøberg, A.B., Arisholm, E., Dybå, T.: Challenges and recommendations when increasing the realism of controlled software engineering experiments. In: Conradi, R., Wang, A.I. (eds.) ESERNET 2001. LNCS, vol. 2765, pp. 24–38. Springer, Heidelberg (2003)
28. Duggan, E., Thachenkary, C.: Higher Quality Requirements: Supporting Joint Application Development with the Nominal Group Technique. Information Technology and Management 4(4), 391–408 (2003)
29. Dyb Aa, T., Kampenes, V.B., Sj, O., Berg, D.I.K.: A systematic review of statistical power in software engineering experiments. Inform. Software Tech. 48(8), 745–755 (2006)
30. Davis, F.D.: Perceived usefulness, perceived ease of use, and user acceptance of information technology. Mis. Quart. 319-340 (1989)

Modeling and Specifying Parametric Adaptation Mechanism for Self-Adaptive Systems[*]

Zhuoqun Yang[1] and Zhi Jin[2]

[1] Institute of Mathematics, Academy of Math. and Syst. Sci., Chinese Academy of Sciences
Haidian Dstr., Beijing 100190, P.R. China
zhuoqun.y@gmail.com
[2] Key Laboratory of High Confidence Software Technologies (MoE), Peking University
Haidian Dstr., Beijing 100871, P.R. China
zhijin@pku.edu.cn

Abstract. Self-adaptive system (SAS) is capable of adjusting its behavior to cope with changes in the deployed environment. Parametric adaptation is an important fashion for achieving adaptation. Context can be defined as the reification of the environment. It may influence the decisions on how to adjust the system behavior. Thus, how to incorporate context into the parametric adaptation mechanism becomes a challenging issue. This paper provides solutions to this issue from a requirements engineering perspective. We develop the goal-oriented requirements model for SASs and build the context model for the environment, and then integrate these two models via defined relations. Adaptation goal model is derived by refining the adaptation goal with adaptation tasks which are underpinned by MAPE loop. Finally, we show how to utilize the specifications to design parametric adaptation algorithms. Our approach is illustrated with an example from the intelligent transportation application.

Keywords: requirements model, context model, parametric adaptation, specification, adaptation algorithm.

1 Introduction

Self-adaptive system (SAS) is a novel computing paradigm in which the software is capable of adjusting its behavior in response to meaningful changes in the environment and itself [1]. The ability of adaptation is characterized by self-* properties, including self-healing, self-configuration, self-optimizing and self-protecting [2]. Innovative technologies and methodologies inspired by these characteristics have already created avenues for many promising applications, such as intelligent transportation, mobile computing, ambient intelligence, ubiquitous computing, etc.

Software-intensive systems are systems in which software interacts with other software, systems, devices, sensors and with people intensively. Such environmental

---

[*] This research is supported by the National Natural Science Foundation of China under Grant Nos. 61232015 and 91318301.

D. Zowghi and Z. Jin (Eds.): APRES 2014, CCIS 432, pp. 105–119, 2014.

entities may be inherently changeable, which makes self-adaptiveness become an essential feature. Context can be defined as the reification of the environment [3] that is whatever provides as a surrounding of a system at a time. Context is essential for the deployment of self-adaptive systems. It provides a manageable and computable description of the environment. As the environment is changeable, the context is unstable and ever changing and the system is desired to perform different behaviors for interacting with different contexts. Therefore, engineers need to build effective adaptation mechanisms to deal with context changes caused by the environmental changes.

Requirements Engineering (RE) for self-adaptive systems primarily aims to identify adaptive requirements, specify adaptation logic and build adaptation mechanisms [4]. Conducting context analysis at the requirements phase will be worthwhile at the design and development phases, because context may influence the decisions about what to build and how to build them.

Recently, RE community have made great strides in providing methodologies and technologies for building adaptation mechanisms of SASs [5]. [6] proposed FLAGS by extending the KAOS model with fuzzy goals and provided adaptation countermeasures when the goal is dissatisfied. [7] investigated requirements for adaptation models that specify the analysis, decision-making, and planning of adaptation as part of a feedback loop. Requirements-aware approaches [8, 9] considered requirements of self-adaptive systems as run-time entities that can be monitored and reasoned over to diagnose violations. [10] proposed RELAX, a formal requirements specification language, to specify the behavior of dynamically adaptive systems. [11] introduced threat modeling to identify context uncertainty with RELAX specification. [12] proposed an autonomic architecture to allow adaptive systems to achieve structural adaptation.

However, specifying adaptation mechanism while considering context changes is lacking in investigation, especially for the parametric adaptation. This issue is important because parametric adaptation is another adaptation type except for structural adaptation [13] and engineers can design more reasonable adaptation logic and adaptation mechanisms via explicitly specifying how to achieve parametric adaptation.

This paper focuses on modeling and specifying parametric adaptation mechanisms for SASs. Firstly, we introduce the conceptual model consisting of the entities in the system and the environment, and define new model elements and then describes how to build the requirements model for the SAS and develop the context model for the environment. The adaptation goal model is derived by incorporating context into the requirements model and refining the adaptation goal with adaptation mechanisms consisting of adaptation tasks that are underpinned with control loop. We adopt and extend the specification grammar of Tropos [14] to specify the adaptation mechanisms. Then we design the parametric adaptation algorithms of control loop tasks from the specifications. The approach is illustrated with an example from the intelligent transportation applications.

The rest of the paper is organized as follows. Section 2 introduces the goal-oriented modeling method, followed by the approach overview in Section 3. Section 4 describes how to build adaptation goal model, followed by the specifications and algorithms in Section 5. Section 6 discusses the proposed approach, followed by related work in Section 7. Section 8 concludes the paper and describes the future work.

2   Goal-Oriented Requirements Modeling

Goal model and the goal-oriented analysis have been widely used in RE literature to present the rationale of both humans and systems. A goal model describes the stake-holder's needs and expectations for the target system.

Figure 1 presents a simple KAOS model [15]. The goals model stakeholders' intentions while the tasks model the functional requirements that can be used to achieve the goals. Goals can be refined through AND/OR decompositions into sub-goals or can be achieved by sub-tasks. For AND decomposition (e.g., $t_1 \wedge t_2 \rightarrow g_2$), the parent goal will be satisfied when all its sub-elements are achieved, while for OR decomposition (e.g., $g_3 \vee g_4 \rightarrow g_1$), the parent goal can be satisfied by achieving at least one of its sub-elements. OR-decompositions incorporate and provide sets of alternatives which can be chosen flexibly to meet goals. Softgoals model the NFRs, which have no clear-cut criteria for their satisfaction and can be used to evaluate different choices of alternative tasks. Tasks can contribute to softgoals through the help or hurt contribution relation.

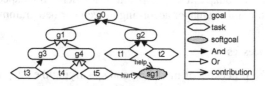

Fig. 1. An Example of Goal Model

3   Approach Overview

This section presents the mechanism underpinning our modeling and analysis approach, describes the processes to achieve adaptation and briefs the motivating example that is used to illustrate the model and specification.

3.1   Framework

Figure 2 depicts the framework of our approach, which is composed of three basic layers: Problem Layer, Model Layer and Adaptation Layer.

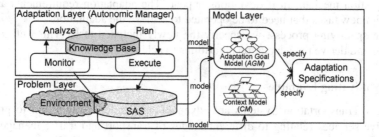

Fig. 2. Framework for Modeling and Specifying

The Problem Layer consists of the self-adaptive system itself and its operational environment. A SAS can interact with the environment through some shared phenomena (denoted by the overlap part) where the system captures kinds of computable contexts provided in the environment.

The Adaptation Layer is built with the MAPE-K control loop [4]. The delta-arrows refer to the control flow. In the *Monitor* process, the autonomic manager uses some sensors to monitor the context variables from the deployed environment which refers to the related context in the shared phenomena. The monitored data are delivered to the *Analyze* process. The manager detects whether there are requirements deviations and delivers the results to the *Plan* process. Autonomic manager makes adaptation decisions and re-detect the requirements. If the deviated requirements are held again, the *Execute* process implements the new configuration through some actuators.

The Model Layer consists of the adaptation goal model (AGM), the context model (CM) and the adaptation specifications. An AGM is a requirements model derived by incorporating the M-A-P-E processes into the traditional goal model of the system. The context model describes the explicit inner structures of the operational environment of the system. The adaptation specifications are derived by specifying the M-A-P-E tasks of the autonomic manager according to well-formed grammar.

3.2   Overall Processes

Figure 3 presents the processes of modeling and specifying the adaptation mechanism for self-adaptive systems.

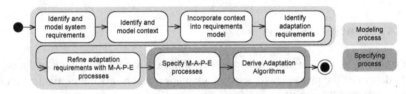

Fig. 3. Processes of Modeling and Specifying Adaptation Mechanism

In the modeling process, we first identify and model the requirements of the target system, and identify and model the related context from the shared phenomena. Then, the relationship between the requirements model and the context model will be built. According to the relationship, we identify which requirements should be held through the adaptation mechanism if deviations appear. The adaptation requirements are refined with new tasks that need to be operated to achieve the adaptation.

In the specifying process, we specify the newly included tasks with well-formed grammar and derive the adaptation algorithms to achieve these tasks.

3.3   Motivating Example

Intelligent Transportation Systems are advanced applications which aim to provide innovative services relating to different modes of transport and traffic management. Highway-Rail Crossing Control System is a fundamental concern [16].

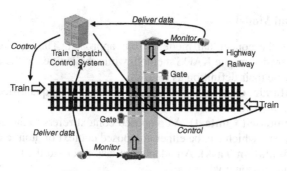

Fig. 4. The Train Dispatch System

We take the Train Dispatch System (TDS) as the motivating example, which is presented in Figure 4. Rails are built across a highway for freight trains' passing across. At the crossing, gates are built on both sides of the highway for blocking the vehicle when a train is coming. However, when vehicle flow on the highway gets increased, if the train dispatch time interval is a certain constant, it may cause the traffic jam. To deal with this problem and prevent the overcrossing, the system needs the adaptation ability of adjusting the dispatch time interval at runtime. Thus, the objective of TDS is determining the appropriate dispatch time interval according to vehicle flow on the highway. To illustrate what the expected traffic situations are, we assume that the system should achieve two requirements, which are described in Table 1. These two requirements can function as Awareness Requirements (AwReq) [8].

Table 1. Awareness Requirements

AwReq	Meaning
AwReq 1	More than 50% of the vehicles can pass through the entire highway within 400sec.
AwReq 2	The amount of vehicles on the highway is always under 300.

For the convenience of illustrating the approach, we use some named symbols to denote variables or parameters. Table 2 presents the symbols and their meanings.

Table 2. Symbol Meaning

Symbol	Meaning
V	Velocity of a vehicle on the highway
$t_{dispatch}$	Dispatch time interval
p	Percentage of vehicles whose pass through time is under 400sec
n	Number of vehicles on the highway

4   Modeling Requirements and Context

In this section, we first provide the conceptual model of our approach, and then describe how to derive the adaptation goal model.

4.1   Conceptual Model

Figure 4 presents the conceptual model of our approach. The entities in the white rectangle are adopted from the KAOS method, while the entities in the dark are newly defined. We provide their definition as follows.

Definition 1 (Atomic Context). An atomic context is a quantified context that doesn't consist of any sub-contexts.

Definition 2 (Composed Context). A composed context refers to the context consists of some sub-contexts, which can be either composed context or atomic context.

Definition 3 (Adaptation Task). An adaptation task refers to the task that should be done to achieve adaptation goal.

Definition 4 (Adaptation Goal). An adaptation goal refers to the goal that is related to adaptation requirements and should be refined with adaptation tasks.

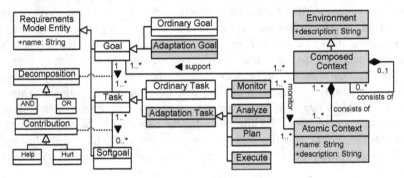

Fig. 5. Conceptual Model

According to the conceptual model we define the adaptation goal model as a triple: $AGM = (RM, CM, SUP)$. RM refers to the requirements model of a self-adaptive system, which can be defined as a septuple: $RM = (G, AG, T, AT, SG, DEC, CON)$. $G = \{g_1 \dots g_n\}$ is a set of ordinary goals. $AG = \{Ag_1 \dots Ag_n\}$ is a set of adaptation goals. $T = \{t_1 \dots t_n\}$ is a set of ordinary tasks. $AT = \{At_1 \dots At_n\}$ is a set of adaptation tasks. $SG = \{sg_1 \dots sg_n\}$ is a set of softgoals. $DEC: G \times G \cup G \times T$ is the Decomposition relation and $DEC = \{And, Or\}$. $CON: T \times SG$ is the Contribution relation and $CON = \{Help, Hurt\}$. Context model CM is defined as $CM = (CC, AC, CON)$, where $CC = \{cc_1 \dots cc_n\}$ is a set of composed contexts; $AC = \{ac_1 \dots ac_n\}$ is a set of atomic contexts; $CON: CC \times CC \cup CC \times AC$ is the Consists-of relation. $SUP: AC \times AG$ refers to the atomic context support the adaptation with the contextual values.

4.2   Modeling Requirements and Context

The partial requirements model of Train Dispatch System is presented in Figure 6. The root goal is Prevent traffic jam while dispatching train (g), which can be satisfied by achieving its two sub-tasks: Dispatch train with time interval of $t_{dispatch}$ ($t1$) and Determine $t_{dispatch}$ to maintain $p>50\%$ and $n<300$ ($t2$). $t2$ is built to achieve the awareness requirements which are described in Table 1.

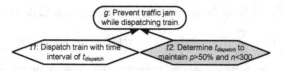

Fig. 6. Partial Requirements Model of Train Dispatch System

Actually, there are many contexts that can be elicited from the operational environment of an Intelligent Transportation System, such as weather, vehicle flow, velocity, etc. However, we only concern the context which may influence the awareness requirements and the determination of the train dispatch time interval. Figure 7 presents the context model of the motivating example. The composed context is Contexts related to vehicle on the highway (cc), which consists of three atomic contexts, including Number of vehicle enter the highway every minute (N^E) ($ac1$), Number of vehicle leave the highway every minute (N^L) ($ac2$), Velocity (V) of the vehicle on the highway ($ac3$). The atomic contexts can be directly gauged by sensors, e.g., camera.

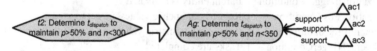

Fig. 7. Context Model of Train Dispatch System

4.3   Deriving Adaptation Goal Model

Due to the atomic contexts support the determination of $t_{dispatch}$, $t2$ is transformed into an adaptation goal (Ag) with *Support* relation from $ac1$, $ac2$ and $ac3$ (Figure8).

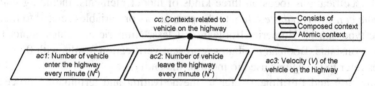

Fig. 8. Transform Ordinary Task into Adaptation Goal

The adaptation goal is refined with adaptation tasks that can represent the M-A-P-E processes. Accordingly, we add four adaptation tasks to the goal model. The adaptation goal model (AGM) after refinement is depicted in Figure 9.

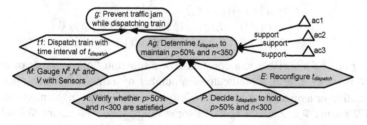

Fig. 9. Refine the Adaptation Goal with Adaptation Tasks

The number of vehicle on the highway (n) at k minute can be derived with

$$n_k = \sum_{i=0}^{k} |N_i^E - N_i^L|, \text{where } i \text{ refers to the } i\text{th minute}$$

The percentage of vehicles whose pass through time is under 400sec (p) at k minute can be computed with

$$p = \frac{n(V)}{n_k}, \text{where } V \geq \frac{\text{Length of the highway}}{400sec}$$

5   Specifying Adaptation Mechanism

5.1   Specification Grammar

To specify the model elements, we adopt the specification grammar of Tropos and extend the entity with atomic context, which is depicted in Figure 10.

AGM specifications focus on three kinds of model elements, including *goal, task* and *atomic context. Attribute* refers to the parameters or variables related to the entity. Attribute-type can be Numeric, Boolean or Class. Numeric attributes depict the variables or constants. Boolean attributes represent verification results with 0 or 1. Class attributes refer to the agents used to monitor the entity.

Initialization and fulfillment refer to the activating and terminating process of a goal or a task. *Condition-type* consists of PreCondition, TriggerCondition and Post-Condition. The description of each condition is provided in Table 3.

Table 3. Description of Initializaiton and Fulfillment Conditions

Condition	Refer to
Initialization PreCondition	Parent entity is dissatisfied.
Initialization TriggerCondition	Parent entity is activated.
Initialization PostCondition	Related parametric values are set to void.
Fulfillment PreCondition	Required parametric values are received.
Fulfillment TriggerCondition	Tasks are completed.
Fulfillment PostCondition	Properties are held or parametric values are delivered.

Invariant refers to the property that should be held all the time while variant refers to the property that can swing sometimes. The formulas in the specifications are derived with first-order linear temporal logic. The syntax is given by:

$$t ::= x \mid c \mid f(t_1, ..., t_n)$$
$$\phi ::= t \mid P(t_1, ..., t_n) \mid \neg\phi \mid \phi \wedge \phi \mid \phi \vee \phi \mid \phi \rightarrow \phi \mid$$
$$X\phi \mid F\phi \mid G\phi \mid \phi U \phi \mid \forall x \cdot \phi \mid \exists x \cdot \phi$$

A term t can be a variable x, a constant c or a function f of a number of terms. A formula Φ is either a term, a predicate of a number of terms, a Boolean operation, a timed operation or a quantifiers operation. $X\Phi$ refers to Φ holds in the next state of the system. $F\Phi$ means Φ eventually holds in some future state. $G\Phi$ means Φ holds in all states of the system. $\Phi_1 U \Phi_2$ refers to Φ_1 holds until Φ_2 holds.

```
                          /*Elements*/
entity := goal | task | atomic context
goal := goal-type mode name [attributes] [invariant] [variant] [initialization] [fulfillment]
task := task-type name From goal.name input output [attributes] [initialization] [fulfillment]
atomic context := name Support goal.name [attribute] violation
goal-type := Ordinary Goal | Adaptive Goal
mode := achieve | maintain
task-type := Ordinary Task | Monitor | Analyze | Plan | Execute
input := Input name
output := Output name
                          /*Attributes*/
attribute := Attribute attribute⁺
attribute := attribute-type : name
attribute-type := Numeric | Boolean | Class
                /*Invariant, Variant, Initialization, Fulfillment*/
invariant := Invariant invar-property⁺
invar-property := Constraint formula
variant := Variant var-property⁺
var-property := Possibility formula
initialization := Initialization conditional-type formula
fulfillment := Fulfillment conditional-type formula
condition-type := PreCondition | TriggerCondition | PostCondition
```

Fig. 10. Adaptation Goal Model Specification Grammar

5.2 Specifying Adaptation Control Loop

Figure 11 depicts the specification of adaptation task M. The attributes of task M consist of Numeric attributes N^E, N^L, V and a Class attribute Camera that has the structure of {select, N^E, N^L, V}. It has no input, while the outputs are the monitored values of N^E, N^L and V. The Initialization PreCondition is the disfulfillment of parent goal Ag and the Initialization TriggerCondition is the activation of Ag. The Initialization PostCondition is setting the values of numeric variable void. The Fulfillment PreCondition is that some instances of camera class are selected as sensors. The Fulfillment TriggerCondition is achieving the related monitored value. The Fulfillment PostCondiation is outputting the numeric values.

Monitor M: Gauge N^E, N^L *and* V with Sensors
From Adaptation Goal
Ag: Determine $t_{dispatch}$ to maintain p>50% and n<300
Attribute
Numeric N^E, N^L, V
Class Camera {select, N^E, N^L, V}
Input atomic contexts
Output values of N^E, N^L, V
Initialization PreCondition $\neg Fulfill\ (Ag)$
Initialization TriggerCondition $Activate\ (Ag)$
Initialization PostCondition
set $Camera.\{N^E, N^L, V\} = void$
Fulfillment PreCondition
$Camera.select = TRUE$
Fulfillment TriggerCondition
$Camera.\{N^E, N^L, V\} \neq void$
Fulfillment PostCondition $Output\ (N^E, N^L, V)$

Fig. 11. Specification of Adaptation Task: M

Analyze A: Verify whether p>50% and n<300 are satisfied
From Adaptive Goal
Ag: Determine $t_{dispatch}$ to maintain p>50% and n<300
Attribute
Numeric N^E, N^L, V, $t_{dispatch}$
Boolean sat
Input N^E, N^L, V, $t_{dispatch}$
Output sat
Initialization PreCondition $\neg Fulfill\ (Ag)$
Initialization TriggerCondition $Activate\ (Ag)$
Initialization PostCondition set sat = void
Fulfillment PreCondition input $(N^E, N^L, V, t_{dispatch})$
Fulfillment TriggerCondition
$verify\ (p(N^E, N^L, V, t_{dispatch}) > 50\% \wedge$
$n(N^E, N^L, V, t_{dispatch}) < 300)$
Fulfillment PostCondition
$sat = verify()\ \wedge output(sat)$

Fig. 12. Specification of Adaptation Task: A

Figure 12 provides the specification of adaptation task A. It contains four numeric attributes where N^E, N^L, V are the output of task M and $t_{dispatich}$ is the current dispatch time interval. In addition, the Boolean attribute *sat* is used to represent the satisfaction of the verified awareness requirements. When a violation is detected, *sat* is assigned to 0, otherwise, it is assigned to 1. The Initialization Postcondition is setting the value of *sat* to void. The Fulfillment PreCondition is inputting the values of numeric attributes of previous task M. The Fulfillment TriggerCondition is conducting the verification of awareness requirements. The PostCondition is outputting the value of *sat*.

Figure 13 describes the specification of adaptation task P. It contains the Numeric attributes and Boolean attribute of task A while $t^{new}_{dispatch}$ refers to the new determined dispatch time interval. The Initialization PostConditition is setting the new parametric value with current parametric value. The Fulfillment PreCondition is inputting the values of *sat*, N^E, N^L, V and $t_{dispatch}$. The Fulfillment TriggerCondition is the process of decision making. The Fulfillment PostCondition is outputting the value of $t^{new}_{dispatch}$.

Plan P: Decide $t_{dispatch}$ to hold $p>50\%$ and $n<300$
From Adaptive Goal
$\quad$ Ag: Determine $t_{dispatch}$ to maintain $p>50\%$ and $n<300$
$\quad$ **Attribute**
$\qquad$ **Numeric** N^E, N^L, V, $t_{dispatch}$, $t^{new}_{dispatch}$
$\qquad$ **Boolean** *sat*
$\quad$ **Input** *sat*, N^E, N^L, V, $t_{dispatch}$
$\quad$ **Output** $t^{new}_{dispatch}$
$\quad$ **Initialization PreCondition** $\neg Fulfill\ (Ag)$
$\quad$ **Initialization TriggerCondition** *Activate* (Ag)
$\quad$ **Initialization PostCondition** set $t^{new}_{dispatch} = t_{dispatch}$
$\quad$ **Fulfillment PreCondition** *input* $(sat, N^E, N^L, V, t_{dispatch})$
$\quad$ **Fulfillment TriggerCondition**
$\qquad$ while $(sat \neq 1)\{\ t^{new}_{dispatch} = t^{new}_{dispatch} + \Delta;$
$\qquad$ $sat = verifyp((t^{new}_{dispatch}, N^E, N^L, V) > 50\% \wedge$
$\qquad\qquad$ $n(t^{new}_{dispatch}, N^E, N^L, V) < 300;)$
$\qquad$ return $t^{new}_{dispatch}\ \}$
$\quad$ **Fulfillment PostCondition** *output* $(t^{new}_{dispatch})$

Fig. 13. Specification of Adaptation Task: P

Execute E: Refoncigure $t_{dispatch}$
From Adaptive Goal
$\quad$ Ag: Determine $t_{dispatch}$ to maintain $p>50\%$ and $n<300$
$\quad$ **Attribute**
$\qquad$ **Numeric** $t_{dispatch}$, $t^{new}_{dispatch}$
$\quad$ **Input** $t^{new}_{dispatch}$
$\quad$ **Output** $t_{dispatch}$
$\quad$ **Initialization PreCondition** $\neg Fulfill\ (Ag)$
$\quad$ **Initialization TriggerCondition** *activate* (Ag)
$\quad$ **Initialization PostCondition** set $t_{dispatch} = void$
$\quad$ **Fulfillment PreCondition** *input* $(t^{new}_{dispatch})$
$\quad$ **Fulfillment TriggerCondition** $t_{dispatch} = t^{new}_{dispatch}$
$\quad$ **Fulfillment PostCondition**
$\qquad$ $F(p(t_{dispatch}, N^E, N^L, V) > 50\% \wedge n(t_{dispatch}, N^E, N^L, V) < 300)$

Fig. 14. Specification of Adaptation Task: E

Figure 14 presents the specification of adaptation task E. It contains two Numeric attributes: the configuration dispatch time interval $t_{dispatch}$ and newly determined parametric time interval $t^{new}_{dispatch}$. The initialization PostCondition is setting the configuration of time interval void. The Fulfillment PreCondition is inputting the new parametric value of dispatch time interval. The Fulfillment TriggerCondition is assigning the value to the configuration, while the Fulfillment PostCondition is achieving the invariant of adaptation goal Ag.

5.3   Specification-Based Adaptation Algorithms

According to the specifications of adaptation tasks, we can derive corresponding algorithms by integrating with these specifications. This section provides the algorithms of adaptation tasks. The texts in bold in the algorithms are adopted from segments of the specifications. These algorithms present how to use the specifications and can be generally utilized to design parametric adaptation code for any SASs whose adaptation mechanism is modeled and specified with our approach.

Monitoring Atomic Contexts. Algorithm 1 is designed for monitoring atomic contexts. The monitored variables (line 3) and monitoring agents (line 4) are already defined in the specifications of task M. The structure of agents (line 5 and 6) is defined based on the Class attribute in the specification of task M. Before monitoring, the system should select instances of the monitoring agent (line 7). After monitoring, the monitored value gauged by agent instances should be sent to the following analyzing process (line 8 and 9).

Algorithm 1 Monitoring Atomic Contexts

Input: *atomic contexts*: the atomic contexts that have support relation to adaptation goal
Output: *monitoredValues*: the monitored values of the atomic contexts

1:     **AtomicContextMonitoring** (*atomic contexts*)
2:        **for** each **Monitor** task M **do**
3:            *monitoredVariables* ← *M_Specification.Numeric_Attribute*
4:            *monitoring_AgentClass* ← *M_Specification.Class_Attribute*
5:            struct *monitoring_AgentClass*
6:                {Boolean *select*; float *monitoredValues*} instance 1, instance 2......
7:            **if** (instance i.*select* = **TRUE**)
8:                instance i.*monitoredValues*← gaugedValues
9:                **return** instance i.*monitoredValues*
10:           **else** select other instance
11:           **end if**
12:      **end for**

Analyzing Requirements Violations. Analyzing algorithm is used for detecting whether awareness requirements are violated. Before verification, Fulfillment Pre-Condition of adaptation task A should be checked (line 3). If the Fulfillment PreCondition is true, the awareness requirements are verified with the monitored values and the current system parametric configuration (line 3 to 5). When requirements are satisfied, the Boolean attribute is assigned to 1 (line 6 and 7). Otherwise, the Boolean attribute is assigned to 0 (line 8). Thereafter, the Boolean is delivered to the next process (line 9). If the Fulfillment PreCondition is not satisfied, the monitoring agents should redo the monitoring task (line 11)

Algorithm 2 Analyzing Requirements Violations

Input: *monitoredValues*: the monitored value of the atomic contexts
        currentParametricConfiguration: the values of system parameters before adaptation
Output: *sat*: a Boolean attribute representing the results of requirements verification

1:     **violationAnalyzing** (*monitoredValues, currentParametricConfiguration*)
2:        **for** each **Analyze** task A **do**
3:            **if** (*A*.**FulfillmentPreCondition=TRUE**)
4:                *verificationInput* ← *monitoredValues, currentParametricConfiguration*
5:                verify *A*.**FromAdaptationGoal.Invariant**
6:                **if** (*A*.**FromAdaptationGoal.Invariant=TRUE**)
7:                    **Boolean** *sat* ← 1
8:                **else Boolean** *sat* ← 0
9:                **return** *sat*
10:               **end if**
11:           **else goto AtomicContextMonitoring( )**
12:           **end if**
13:      **end for**

Deciding New Parametric Values. Algorithm 3 is designed for determining how to adjust system parameters to maintain the awareness requirements. If the Fulfillment PreCondition is true (line 3) and the awareness requirements are still satisfied (line 4), no decision needs to be made. Monitoring agent should continuously monitor the atomic context (line 5). If awareness requirements are violated, current values of parameters should be adjusted and iterative verification should be performed to check whether the adjusted value is appropriate (line 6 to 9). Then new parametric values are delivered to the executing process (line 10). If the Fulfillment PreCondition is false, the analyzing process needs to be redone for capturing the value of *sat* (line 12).

Algorithm 3 Deciding New Parametric Values

Input: *monitoredValues*: the monitored value of the atomic contexts
    currentParametricConfiguration: the values of system parameters before adaptation
    sat: a Boolean attribute representing the results of requirements verification
Output: *newParametricValues*: the values of system parameters after decision making

1:	**newParameterDeciding** (*monitoredValues, currentParametricConfiguration, sat*)
2:	**for** each **Plan** task *P* **do**
3:	**if** (*P*.**FulfillmentPreCondition**=TRUE)
4:	**if** (*sat*=1) **goto AtomicContextMonitoring**( )
5:	**else** *newParametricValues* ← *currentParametricConfiguration*
6:	**while** (*sat*≠1) **do**
7:	*newParametricValues* ← *newParametricValues*+Δ
8:	**violationAnalyzing**(*monitoredValues, newParametricValues*)
9:	**end while**
10:	**return** *newParametricValues*
11:	**end if**
12:	**else goto violationAnalyzing**( )
13:	**end if**
14:	**end for**

Executing Parametric Configuration. Executing algorithm focuses on carrying out the parametric reconfiguration. If the Fulfillment PreCondition is true, the parametric values of the system configuration are assigned to the adjusted parametric values (line 3 to 5). If the Fulfillment PreCondition is not true, the planning task should be redone for deriving the adjusted values (line 6).

Algorithm 4 Executing Parametric Configuration

Input: *newParametricValues*: the values of system parameters after decision making
Output: *currentParametricConfiguration*: the values of system parameters before adaptation

1:	**configurationExecuting** (*newParametricValues*)
2:	**for** each **Execute** task *E* **do**
3:	**if** *E*.**FulfillmentPreCondition**=TRUE
4:	*currentParametricConfiguration* ← *newParametricValues*
5:	**return** *currentParametricConfiguration*
6:	**else goto newParameterDeciding** ( )
7:	**end if**
8:	**end for**

---

6   Discussion

By integrating the requirements model and the context model, the modeling method can clearly define the relationships between the requirements and the context (environment). With our modeling method, each awareness requirement of a self-adaptive system is transformed into an adaptation goal that can be further refined into adaptation tasks underpinned by the MAPE-K control loop.

The specification grammar is designed for describing model elements. It contains both static aspects including name, attribute, invariant, etc. and dynamic aspects including input, output, initialization conditions and fulfillment conditions. With these explicit descriptions, engineers can design more reasonable adaptation logic.

Adaptation algorithms are derived from corresponding segments of the specifications. The derivation method can be utilized to any self-adaptive systems that are modeled and specified with our method. It shows how the specifications can be used to build the adaptation mechanisms and presents how the adaptation tasks incorporate with each other.

7   Related Work

Modeling Adaptation Mechanisms. [6] extended the KAOS model with fuzzy goals and provided adaptation countermeasures when the goal is dissatisfied. [7] investigated requirements for adaptation models that specify the analysis, decision-making, and planning of adaptation as part of a feedback loop. To monitor requirements, [8] argued that requirements for self-adaptive systems should be run-time entities that can be reasoned over in order to understand the extent to which they are being satisfied. [9] proposed a way to elicit and formalize the awareness requirement. [17] proposed adaptation mechanisms for repairing deviations caused by unsatisfied domain assumptions. [18] introduced how to monitor and diagnose requirements violations based on reasoning over the KAOS model. Compared with these works, this paper proposed the adaptation mechanism by building the adaptation goal model in an incremental way. The MAPE-based adaptation processes are considered as additional tasks that are used to refine and transform the initial requirements model.

Specifying Adaptation Mechanisms. [6] specified the fuzzy goal by using fuzzy linear temporal logic. [10] proposed RELAX to specify the adaptation behavior of dynamically adaptive systems when. [19] introduced an approach to formally specifying adaptation requirements and used this logic to specify three commonly used adaptation semantics. [20] presented goal-oriented specifications of adaptation semantics. Different from them, our specification can not only describe the model elements themselves, but also connect each element together with six conditions (Table 3). We also investigated how these specifications can be utilized by engineers. To this end, we introduced the corresponding pseudo code of the adaptation tasks to illustrate the use of the specifications. Thus, for different adaptation scenarios, engineers may just modify the algorithm code according to the specifications of the system.

Modeling Context. [11] leveraged the threat model to identify context uncertainty with RELAX specification and integrated the context model with the requirements model. [21] proposed a goal-oriented RE modeling and reasoning framework for systems operating in varying contexts, introduced contextual goal models to relate goals and contexts, presented context analysis to refine contexts and identify ways to verify them. [22] used contexts to model domain variability in goal models and discussed the modeling of contexts, the specification of their effects on system goals and the analysis of goal models with contextual variability. Inspired by these works, we went a step further by incorporating the context model into the adaptation mechanism.

8   Conclusion

This paper aims to model and specify parametric adaptation mechanisms for self-adaptive systems. We modeled both the requirements and the context, introduced the adaptation goal model, refined the adaptation with MAPE loop as adaptation tasks, specified the adaptation tasks with well-formed grammar, and derived parametric adaptation algorithms from the specifications.

The principles of modeling can serve as general guidance for requirements engineers to clearly identify and model requirements and context for self-adaptive systems. Modeling MAPE loop as adaptation tasks of adaptation goal provides an access to visual modeling and specifying control loops in the requirements model. The specifications can be generally adopted to describe the parametric adaptation mechanism. Furthermore, the adaptation algorithms are derived from corresponding segments of the specifications of M-A-P-E tasks. The algorithms present the use of the specification of the adaptation mechanism. In conclusion, the derived models, specifications and algorithms can be utilized to achieve the parametric adaptation in self-adaptive systems and help engineers better understand how to design the parametric adaptation mechanisms and how to achieve the parametric adaptation.

Our future work continuously focuses on investigating incorporating the context into the requirements model for achieving the parametric adaptation. In addition, we will explore how to apply these parametric adaptation mechanisms and adaptation algorithms to some real applications. We also intend to provide innovative adaptation mechanisms by integrating the parametric adaptation with the structural adaptation.

References

1. Cheng, B.H.C., et al.: Software Engineering for Self-Adaptive Systems: A Research Roadmap. In: Cheng, B.H.C., de Lemos, R., Giese, H., Inverardi, P., Magee, J. (eds.) Self-Adaptive Systems. LNCS, vol. 5525, pp. 1–26. Springer, Heidelberg (2009)
2. Salehie, M., Tahvildari, L.: Self-adaptive software: Landscape and research challenges. ACM Trans. Auton. Adapt. Syst. 2, 1–42 (2009)
3. Andrea, A.F., Savigni, A.: A Framework for Requirements Engineering for Context-Aware Services. In: 1st International Workshop From Software Requirements to Architectures (2001)
4. Brun, Y., Di Marzo Serugendo, G., Gacek, C., Giese, H., Kienle, H., Litoiu, M., Müller, H., Pezzè, M., Shaw, M.: Engineering Self-Adaptive Systems through Feedback Loops. In: Cheng, B.H.C., de Lemos, R., Giese, H., Inverardi, P., Magee, J. (eds.) Software Engineering for Self-Adaptive Systems. LNCS, vol. 5525, pp. 48–70. Springer, Heidelberg (2009)

5. Yang, Z., Li, Z., Jin, Z., Chen, Y.: A Systematic Literature Review of Requirements Modeling and Analysis for Self-adaptive Systems. In: Salinesi, C., van de Weerd, I. (eds.) REFSQ 2014. LNCS, vol. 8396, pp. 55–71. Springer, Heidelberg (2014)
6. Baresi, L., Pasquale, L., Spoletini, P.: Fuzzy Goals for Requirements-Driven Adaptation. In: 18th IEEE International Conference on Requirements Engineering, pp. 125–134 (2010)
7. Vogel, T., Giese, H.: Requirements and assessment of languages and frameworks for adaptation models. In: Kienzle, J. (ed.) MODELS 2011 Workshops. LNCS, vol. 7167, pp. 167–182. Springer, Heidelberg (2012)
8. Sawyer, P., Bencomo, N., Whittle, J., Letier, E., Finkelstein, A.: Requirements-Aware Systems: A Research Agenda for RE for Self-adaptive Systems. In: 18th IEEE International Conference on Requirements Engineering, pp. 95–103 (2010)
9. Souza, V.E.S., Lapouchnian, A., Robinson, W.N., Mylopoulos, J.: Awareness requirements for adaptive systems. In: 6th International Symposium on Software Engineering for Adaptive and Self-Managing Systems, pp. 60–69 (2011)
10. Whittle, J., Sawyer, P., Bencomo, N., Cheng, B.H.C., Bruel, J.M.: RELAX: Incorporating Uncertainty into the Specification of Self-Adaptive Systems. In: 17th IEEE International Conference on Requirements Engineering, pp. 79–88 (2009)
11. Cheng, B.H.C., Sawyer, P., Bencomo, N., Whittle, J.: Goal-Based Modeling Approach to Develop Requirements of an Adaptive System with Environmental Uncertainty. In: Schürr, A., Selic, B. (eds.) MODELS 2009. LNCS, vol. 5795, pp. 468–483. Springer, Heidelberg (2009)
12. Yiqiao, W., Mylopoulos, J.: Self-Repair through Reconfiguration: A Requirements Engineering Approach. In: 24th IEEE/ACM International Conference on Automated Software Engineerin, pp. 257–268 (2009)
13. McKinley, P.K., Sadjadi, S.M., Kasten, E.P., Cheng, B.H.C.: Composing Adaptive Software. Computer 37, 56–64 (2004)
14. Fuxman, A., Liu, L., Mylopoulos, J., Pistore, M., Roveri, M., Traverso, P.: Specifying and analyzing early requirements in Tropos. Requir. Eng. 9, 132–150 (2004)
15. Dardenne, A., Lamsweerde, A.V., Fickas, S.: Goal-directed requirements acquisition. Sci. Comput. Program. 20, 3–50 (1993)
16. Bell, C.A., Hunter, K.M.: Low Volume Highway-rail Grade Crossing Treatments for the Oregon High Speed Rail Corridor, technical report, Transportation Research Institute, Oregon State University (1997)
17. Feather, M.S., Fickas, S., van Lamsweerde, A., Ponsard, C.: Reconciling system requirements and runtime behavior. In: 9th International Workshop on Software Specification and Design, pp. 50–59 (1998)
18. Wang, Y., Mcilraith, S.A., Yu, Y., Mylopoulos, J.: Monitoring and diagnosing software requirements. Automated Software Engg. 16, 3–35 (2009)
19. Zhang, J., Cheng, B.H.C.: Using temporal logic to specify adaptive program semantics. Journal of Systems and Software 79, 1361–1369 (2006)
20. Brown, G., Cheng, B.H.C., Goldsby, H., Zhang, J.: Goal-oriented specification of adaptation requirements engineering in adaptive systems. In: 1st International Workshop on Self-Adaptation and Self-Managing Systems, pp. 23–29 (2006)
21. Ali, R., Dalpiaz, F., Giorgini, P.: A goal-based framework for contextual requirements modeling and analysis. Requir. Eng. 15, 439–458 (2010)
22. Lapouchnian, A., Mylopoulos, J.: Modeling Domain Variability in Requirements Engineering with Contexts. In: Laender, A.H.F., Castano, S., Dayal, U., Casati, F., de Oliveira, J.P.M. (eds.) ER 2009. LNCS, vol. 5829, pp. 115–130. Springer, Heidelberg (2009)

Evaluating Presentation of Requirements Documents: Results of an Experiment

Yu-Cheng Tu, Ewan Tempero, and Clark Thomborson

Department of Computer Science, University of Auckland, Auckland, New Zealand

Abstract. There are diverse stakeholders for requirements documents in many development environments, and yet these requirements documents should be presented in such a way that all stakeholders will be able to engage them successfully. In order to produce effective requirements documents, analysts need guidance when developing new documents. They also need a convenient and accurate way to evaluate the effectiveness of existing documents. We have been exploring whether our three-factor measurement of document "transparency" would be useful in these ways. Our experimental results, presented in this article, support the hypothesis that transparency can be usefully characterised by accessibility, understandability, and relevance.

1 Introduction

There are many stakeholders for requirements documents, meaning presenting these documents in such a way that all will be able to engage them successfully is a challenge. We have been exploring how the concept of "transparency" can be used to evaluate the effectiveness of documents (or any artefacts) for a given set of stakeholders. We have developed a definition of transparency, and identified specific properties of a document that support or interfere with its transparency. We are now evaluating how well these ideas help assess the effectiveness of document. We have performed an experiment to answer two main questions — whether the general concept of transparency is useful for evaluating the effectiveness of documents, and whether our particular characterisation of transparency is useful. The first question has been answered in other discussions [1,2][1]. We present the results regarding the second question in this paper.

Our experiment compared two requirements documents that presented functional requirements to 10 software developers and 48 university students of computer science or software engineering. According to our definition (discussed in section 2.3), one of the documents was more transparent than the other. Our overall goal of the experiment was to determine which document was more effective. Our overall results (the first question above, and discussed in more detail in section 2.4) provided support that the document we had assessed as being more transparent was also the more effective. We also asked participants to comment on properties of transparency that we had identified, and more generally on what

---

[1] These are available from http://goo.gl/sWgW2Q

D. Zowghi and Z. Jin (Eds.): APRES 2014, CCIS 432, pp. 120–134, 2014.
© Springer-Verlag Berlin Heidelberg 2014

they found helped or hindered engaging with the documents. It is the responses to these questions that we discuss in this paper.

The remainder of the paper is organised as follows. In the next section, we discuss the background and related work. In particular, we discuss issues with communication as they relate to documentation, and provide more details on our view of transparency. In section 3, we present the methodology used in our experiment, including detailing aspects of the requirements documents examined by the participants. Section 4 presents the results of the experiment. Finally section 5 presents our conclusions and discusses future work.

2   Background and Related Work

2.1   Communication through Documents

One challenge in requirements engineering is poor communication between users and developers. According to Bubenko [3], problems in communication are due to users not fully understanding the implications of the requirements presented to them by developers. Bubenko further says that current modelling methods for recording requirements are difficult for users to understand. He also says that developers have problems in analysing and determining the quality of a requirements specification. Similarly, Al-Rawas and Easterbrook [4] say that it is difficult to resolve misunderstanding of requirements between stakeholders using documentation, which is a one-way communication channel. One reason for misunderstanding is the unfamiliarity of the notations used to model requirements. Another reason is the use of terminology to communicate technical matters where one party cannot understand [5].

Poor communication can be a consequence of the presentation of requirements which in turn affects users' ability in comprehending requirements. For example, formal notations are useful for verifying the completeness of requirements, but they are often difficult for non-expert stakeholders to understand. Bubenko [3] mentions in the methodology challenges in requirements engineering that users often sign-off requirements specifications without fully understanding them.

We are interested in understanding how to evaluate presentation of requirements that affect communication in requirements engineering. Much focus in requirements engineering is on formal and semi-formal requirements specifications, however, Bubenko mentions that one of the challenges is "to improve user – developer communication, much more than to expand the use of formal methods". Although the challenge of improving user – developer communication was raised almost 20 years ago, there seems to be little advice on the effect of different requirements presentations on user – developer communication. If we better understand how requirements presentation affected users and developers, then we will be able to produce more effective requirements documents with fewer communication problems.

2.2   Documentation in Requirements Engineering

In software engineering, documents are used as a medium to communicate information, ideas or feedback about a software system to stakeholders. Forward and Lethbridge [6] say that "documentation is an important tool for communication and should always serve a purpose". Likewise, requirements documents such as requirements specifications are also important to successful requirements engineering.

A requirements specification is a basis of communication among all stakeholders [7]. It is being used through the software life cycle, from systems procurement, development, and to implementation of a software system [3]. According to SWEBOK [8], requirements documentation is one key to the success of any requirements process. To be successful, requirements are examined by stakeholders to ensure that software engineers have defined the right system. The requirements for a software system should be understandable and usable by experts and non-expert stakeholders. Therefore, it is important that requirements notations and processes are appropriate for different stakeholders [9].

However, it is not easy to produce effective requirements documents for all stakeholders. According to Al-Rawas and Easterbrook [4], requirements documents are "poor substitute for interpersonal communication". This is mainly due to the fact that there are many stakeholders for requirements documents and they usually prefer using different notations. Not every stakeholder will be familiar with different notations. Al-Rawas and Easterbrook discover in their interviews with various software developers that 86% of their participants said their customers need additional explanation to understand the notations used for the requirements. They also discover that developer's time is wasted in interpreting raw natural language requirements where a diagram or a formal notation could be used to represent the requirements. Similarly, one challenge faced in requirements validation is the review of requirements documentation as stakeholders cannot review the document thoroughly and sign-off due to time pressure [10].

The effectiveness of requirements documents in helping stakeholders achieving their goals can be affected by different factors. For example, according to Davis et al. [11], there are 24 qualities of a quality software requirements specification (SRS). A quality SRS "contributes to successful, cost-effective creation of software that solves real user needs". Example qualities include unambiguous, complete, and correct information. Similarly, an SRS document can be evaluated with indicators such as size, readability, depth and text structure [8]. However, current research focuses on methodology and notations used for representing requirements [9]. There seems to be little advice as to how to evaluate how effective a document is, other than to have potential stakeholders to try to use it, and little advice as to how to create a document that stakeholders will be able to successfully engage with. We believe that the concept of transparency can help with both goals, and we discuss this concept in the next section.

2.3 Transparency in Software Engineering

The term "transparency" in many areas has the notion of information being visible or open to those with a stake in that information. This concept is important, especially, to organisations as it has effects on the success, reputation, and credibility of organisations [12]. Transparency can also be one of the criteria for evaluating the effectiveness of public participation because it enables the public to see the outcome of such participation [13,14]. In business ethics, transparency is an ethical principle which aims to enhance public acceptance as well as to demonstrate fairness of organisations in decision-making [15].

Similarly, transparency refers to the visibility of a product or a development process to stakeholders. Stakeholders can evaluate a software system or to make decisions based on the visible information. This term is used in many areas of software engineering [2]. These areas include information privacy [16,17], computer ethics [18,19,20], and agile development [21,22,23]. However, the different uses appear inconsistent and there is no clear definition.

Based on our literature review [2], we define transparency in software engineering as *the degree to which stakeholders can answer their questions by using the information they obtain about a software system during its life cycle.* In this definition, stakeholders refer to anyone involved in the development of a software system. Example stakeholders are software developers, project managers, clients, and end users.

While our definition explains what transparency means, it does not provide an easy means to establish what transparency there is. To this end, we have identified three characteristics that apply to transparency: to answer stakeholders' questions, information needs to be *accessible, understandable,* and *relevant*. Accessibility concerns the ability of stakeholders in obtaining information. We define accessibility as *the degree to which stakeholders can obtain information that they believe is likely to answer their questions easily.*

To decide if the information answers their questions, stakeholders must understand the meaning of the information. This characteristic of transparency, understandability, we define as *the degree to which the information obtained by stakeholders can be comprehended with prior knowledge.*

Relevance is concerned with how well stakeholders can answer their questions using the information. Relevance is defined as *the degree to which the information obtained by stakeholders answers their questions.*

As noted in the introduction, we performed the experiment to help answer the questions as to whether our overall definition of transparency is useful, and whether the characteristics we have identified help determine transparency as we have defined it. In this paper we present the results relating to the second question. First, we summarise the results of the first question.

2.4 Usefulness of Transparency

Our experiment presented two documents that we had assessed as having different levels of transparency to participants, and asked questions relating to participants' ability to engage with them. Section 3 provides an overview of the experimental design and the materials. Regarding our first question, the usefulness of the concept of transparency, indicated that the document we evaluated as having better transparency was also the document that our participants were better able to engage with them. Participants spent less time and were able to answer more questions correctly with the document that we evaluated to be more transparent. Participants who used the more transparent document were also more confident about their answers. Full details of these results, their analysis and discussion, are available in discussions by Tu et al. [1,2] (see footnote 1).

3   Methodology

3.1   Experimental Design

The main research questions for this paper are:

1. Are the properties of accessibility, understandability, and relevance useful to reasoning about transparency?
   This question directly addresses our main goal of determining whether these characteristics are useful to establishing transparency.
2. What elements in requirements documents affect participants' ability in understanding requirements?
   This question helps us determine whether we have missed anything that may be relevant to determining the transparency of documents.

The experiment involves the use of two different types of requirements documents and a questionnaire (see footnote 1). The first requirements document is an actual requirements document (ReqSpec) which describes an integration of an accommodation management system and an identity management system for a particular organisation. The second document is a use case model (UCM), which we created using the information from the ReqSpec document. A questionnaire is also constructed for participants to answer questions about the documents.

The ReqSpec document was originally the requirements document for a system that has been implemented. The only modifications we have made are to anonymise it. It is written in natural language and in free text format. It does not follow any specific formats or standards.

The UCM document is created by extracting information from the ReqSpec document. We chose the use case model as the second requirements document type because it is used to capture functional requirements of a software system [24]. To construct use cases for our experiment, we follow the template guidelines by Anda et al. [25]. The template guidelines include a template for describing an actor and a template for describing a use case. Information is extracted from the ReqSpec document with minimal changes to the original text. All use cases are based on the original text of the ReqSpec document.

The questionnaire for our experiment contains 23 questions for participants from software industry and 26 questions in total for student participants. Some of the questions are optional. The questionnaire is divided into three sections: Demographics, Part 1. Reviewing Functionality of a Software System, and Part 2. Overview of the Software Document. In the Demographics section, participants are asked to answer questions about themselves such as their roles in a software project, their degree and major.

The purpose of Part 1 is to help us to compare the effectiveness of the two requirements documents. In this section each of the participants are given one of the two documents described above and asked to answer questions based on the information provided in the document. They are also asked to write down problems if they could not answer the question rather than leave it blank. This section contains eight questions in total. The first question asks participants to write down the type of requirements documents that they receive at the start of the experimental session. Participants are then asked to record the time they start answering this section. The questions are organised in the order of ease in locating answers in the ReqSpec document. All questions, except for one, have specific answers found in the ReqSpec document and the UCM document. The last question asks participants to record the time when they finish answering this section of the questionnaire. There was a 40-minute time limit to this section.

In Part 2, we ask participants nine questions about their opinions on the requirements documents. We ask participants questions relating to the three attributes of transparency. These attributes are not explicitly stated in the questions, but rather are described in general terms.

Experimental Hypotheses. Our assessment of transparency suggests that the UCM document is better than the ReqSpec document [2]. On the basis of our assessment, we have the following hypotheses:

1. Accessibility
   - H_0 : There is no difference between the accessibility of UCM document and the accessibility of ReqSpec document.
   - H_a : UCM document has better accessibility than ReqSpec document.
2. Relevance
   - H_0 : There is no difference between the understandability of UCM document and the understandability of ReqSpec document.
   - H_a : UCM document has better understandability than ReqSpec document.
3. Understandability
   - H_0 : There is no difference between the relevance of UCM document and the relevance of ReqSpec document.
   - H_a : UCM document has better relevance than ReqSpec document.

3.2   Execution

We used convenience sampling for selecting potential participants in our experiment. Our experiment was a between-subject design in which each participant was subject to only one treatment. Each participant read only one type of the requirements documents, either a ReqSpec document or a UCM document.

Participants' main tasks were to answer the questionnaire and to read the requirements documents given to them at the beginning of the experimental session. Participants were not required to read everything provided in the documents. They need to read only the parts that they think could help them to answer questions in Part 1 of the questionnaire.

Participants in our experiment could choose to participate either in-person or on-line. For the in-person experiment, the researcher handed participants the materials in printed copies. The researcher was present at all times during the experiment session to answer any questions. For the on-line experiment, the questionnaire was self-administered. Participants received the materials in PDF format as well a link to the web-based questionnaire via email. Participants completed the web-based questionnaire on their own.

4   Results

The responses were transcribed into spreadsheets. To perform statistical analysis, Likert scale responses were transformed into numerical values. For example, Likert items such as "Very poor, Poor, Satisfactory, Good, and Very Good" were transformed into 1, 2, 3, 4, and 5 respectively. We used the transformed values in parametric statistical tests such as t-tests, which according to Norman [26], could be used for Likert data without "coming to the wrong conclusion".

We labelled the comments made by participants in the questionnaire with codes. The codes were based on our definition of transparency as well as any interesting points that arose in the comments. We then identified themes from the codes and grouped the codes according to themes. Coding enabled us to identify any common patterns relating to transparency from the experiment.

4.1   Demographics

We recruited 10 software practitioners and 48 university students. There were 29 participants for each type of document. Of the 10 industry participants, four people have zero to four years of experience and six have five to nine years of experience working in the software industry. All industry participants reported that they held the role as developers in a software project at the time of the experiment. Some participants were also architects or requirements engineers.

47 student participants came from the University of Auckland. Of the 48 student participants, there were 21 graduate students and 27 undergraduate students. Of the 27 undergraduate students, 16 were specialising in Software Engineering. All of the undergraduate student participants were in their second year of study or above at the time of the experiment.

4.2   Transparency of Requirements Documents

Accessibility. In question P2Q5a (see footnote 1), we ask our participants about the accessibility of the requirements documents. We ask them how helpful

Fig. 1. Participants' assessments on how well the ReqSpec document and the UCM document were in helping participants to identify the desired information to answer questions in Part 1 (Accessibility)

the given document is to identify the information that they might need to answer questions in Part 1. Figure 1 shows participants' assessment of how well the documents were in helping participants to identify information. 10/29 participants using the ReqSpec document rated it good or very good whereas 21/29 participants using the UCM document rated it good or very good. Some participants also commented on how the documents helped them to identify information. For example, one of the comments from participants using the UCM document is "Contents & Use case diagram helped to identify the sections".

The mean values for the two treatments are 3.03 and 3.90 with standard deviations of 0.94 and 0.77 for the ReqSpec document and the UCM document respectively. The mean values suggest that the ReqSpec document and the UCM document were more than satisfactory for our participants on average.

To test whether the difference is statistically significant, we perform an independent-samples t-test. The t-test ($t = -3.81$, $df = 56$) indicates that the difference is statistically significant (0.000) at the 0.05 level of significance. The mean difference is -0.86, and the 95% confidence interval of the difference is -1.32 and -0.41. Further, Cohen's effect size value ($d = 1.01$) suggests a high practical significance.

The analysis shows that there is a difference in the accessibility of information using different requirements documents. Since the UCM document mean is greater than the ReqSpec document mean, the UCM document is better than the ReqSpec document in terms of helping participants to identify the desired information.

Understandability. In P2Q5c, we ask participants how helpful they think that the documents are to understand information and how well they think that they have understood the information in the documents. Figure 2 shows participants' assessments on the ReqSpec document and the UCM document in helping them to understand the functionality of the software system.

More than 60% of our participants reported that both documents were good or very good in helping them to understand the functionality of the software system. Two out of the 58 participants reported that the documents were poor.

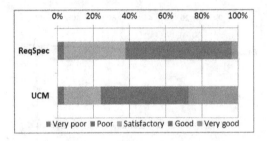

Fig. 2. Participants' assessments of the helpfulness of the ReqSpec document and the UCM document to understand the functionality of the software system (Understandability)

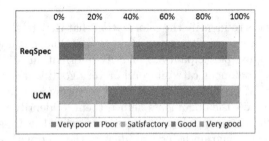

Fig. 3. Participants' self-assessments on how well they have understood the information provided in the ReqSpec document and the UCM document (Understandability)

The mean values for treatment ReqSpec and treatment UCM are 3.62 and 4.00 with standard deviations 0.62 and 0.80 respectively. The t-test gives some evidence against the existence of no difference between the means ($p = 0.049$). The t-value is -2.01 with 56 degrees of freedom. The mean difference is -0.38, and the 95% confidence interval of the difference is -0.76 and -0.002. Moreover, Cohen's effect value ($d = 0.53$) suggests a moderate practical significance. Since the mean for the UCM document is greater than the mean for the ReqSpec document, the UCM document is more helpful than the ReqSpec document in participants' understanding of the functionality of the software system.

In P2Q6a, we ask a similar question about how well participants think that they have understood the information provided in the documents. As shown in Figure 3, more than half of the 58 participants reported that they have a good or very good understanding of the documents. No participants who used the UCM document reported that they understood the information poorly. Four participants who used the ReqSpec document reported that they understood the information poorly.

The means are 3.52 and 3.83 with standard deviations 0.83 and 0.60 for treatment ReqSpec and treatment UCM respectively. The t-test shows a two-tailed p-value of 0.109 which suggests that there is no significant difference at the 0.05 level of significance ($t = -1.63$, $df = 51.09$, mean difference $= -0.31$, 95%

Table 1. Number of participants who either went through different parts of the requirements document to answer P1Q6 or not (Relevance)

	ReqSpec	UCM	Total
Yes	20	11	31
No	9	18	27
Total	29	29	58

confidence interval of difference $= -0.69, 0.07$). Cohen's effect value is 0.43 which suggests a low to moderate practical significance.

The statistical analysis shows that there is some evidence against the null hypothesis. The UCM document seems better than the ReqSpec document for the understandability of functional requirements. However, the statistical analysis for P2Q6a shows no significant difference in the understandability of information using the ReqSpec document and the UCM document by our participants. The mean values from P2Q5c and P2Q6a indicate that both documents were more than satisfactory in helping participants to understand information.

Relevance. In Part 2 of the questionnaire, we ask two questions about the relevance of information. We first ask participants in P2Q4 whether they have to go through different parts of the requirements documents in order to answer P1Q6. P2Q4 enables us to evaluate the sufficiency of the information at a particular location to answer the questions. If the information is insufficient, participants are likely to try and look for another location in the document.

Table 1 shows the number of participants who either went through different parts of the document or not. It appears that there were more participants who went through different parts of the ReqSpec document than participants who went through the UCM document to answer P1Q6. The observed proportion of yes to no for participants using the ReqSpec document is 0.69:0.31, whereas the proportion of yes to no for participants using the UCM document is 0.38:0.62. We compare the two proportions by using Fisher's exact test. The null hypothesis for the test is that there is no difference between the two proportions. We get a two-tailed p-value of 0.03 which is significant at the 0.05 level. Therefore, we reject the null hypothesis. This supports the existence of a difference between participants using different documents to answer P1Q6. In addition, the Phi coefficient of association ($\phi = -0.31$) suggests a weak negative association.

We also ask participants in P2Q5b to rate how helpful they think that the documents are to read only the relevant information to answer questions in Part 1. Figure 4 shows the distribution of participants' assessments on the requirements documents in P2Q5b. Participants using the ReqSpec document seem to have varied opinions about the document. Approximately 80% of participants using the UCM document reported the UCM document was good or very good in reading relevant information.

The means for the responses by participants using the ReqSpec document and participants using the UCM document are 2.97 and 3.76 with standard

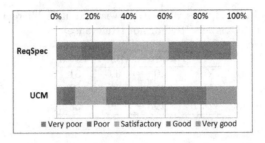

Fig. 4. Participants' assessments on how well the ReqSpec document and the UCM document were in helping participants to read only the relevant information that they needed to answer each question in Part 1 (Relevance)

deviations of 1.12 and 0.95 respectively. We find that the two-tailed p-value is 0.005 from the t-test which is less than the 0.05 level of significance ($t = -2.91$, $df = 56$, mean difference $= -0.79$, 95% confidence interval $= -1.34, -0.25$). Hence, we reject the null hypothesis. This indicates that there is a significant difference in the relevance of information in the ReqSpec document and the UCM document. Furthermore, Cohen's effect value ($d = 0.76$) suggests a moderate to high practical significance.

The analysis shows that the UCM document provides more relevant information than the ReqSpec document. Fewer participants who used the UCM document went through different parts of the document than participants who used the ReqSpec document. Participants who used the UCM document tended to be more satisfied with the relevant information than participants who used the ReqSpec document.

4.3   Elements that Affect Transparency of Requirements Documents

Accessibility. We find several themes that affect the accessibility of requirements documents. We find that the organisations of the ReqSpec document and the UCM document have positive and negative effects on the accessibility of information. For example, participants found the use case diagram, the document structure, and the table of contents in the UCM document helpful in locating information. On the other hand, participants using the ReqSpec document commented that headings and sections of the document needed to be improved. An index and an appendix could be included in the ReqSpec document to improve participants' locating information.

Another theme that arises is the format of the document. 55 participants were given physical copies of the ReqSpec document and the UCM document in the experiment. Participants were required to find information in the document manually, which in turn could take more effort than searching for information electronically. A few of our participants made that observation. One participant also commented that his or her "ability to manually search text has diminished" because he or she became used to finding information on a computer. This suggests that information in electronic format could help to improve accessibility of information.

We also find different factors that hinder participants in locating information within the ReqSpec document or the UCM document. For example, participants using the ReqSpec document found similar information was distributed throughout the document, and as a result they were confused when trying to locate specific information. Some participants using the ReqSpec document also commented that the table of contents was not helpful for finding information or that the navigation of the document was not easy. Similarly, one participant using the UCM document mentioned that he or she needed to "... refer back and forth..."

Among the comments made by participants using the ReqSpec document, there is a common theme regarding time. Out of all 58 participants, five participants who used the ReqSpec document noted that they could not locate the information after spending 10 minutes or a long time on each question of Part 1 of the questionnaire. However, we did not find any participants who used the UCM document commenting that they spent more than 10 minutes on each question. Similarly, at least 10 of the 29 participants using the ReqSpec document mentioned that they needed to look through the document to answer questions whereas no participants using the UCM document made that comment.

Understandability. We identify two main themes that are related to the understandability. The first is related to how the ReqSpec document and the UCM document affect the understandability of information. Participants who used the UCM document said, the use case diagram was useful in helping them to understand the functionality of the system. However, a few of the participants who used the UCM document suggested that the use case diagram was insufficient. More diagrams such as workflow diagrams could improve understanding of the system's functionality. Participants using the ReqSpec document also suggested including use case diagrams as well as diagrams such as sequence diagrams in the document to help readers understand the system. Similarly, participants using the ReqSpec document and participants using the UCM document suggested that using pictures or illustrations helps in understanding.

The second theme is related to different factors that hinder participants' understanding of the information. A few of our participants commented that they needed more time to understand the information presented, particularly in the ReqSpec document. Similarly, the terminology and abbreviations used in the ReqSpec document and the UCM document were not easy for two of our participants. Another factor that hindered the participants' understanding of information is the confusing nature of the information in the ReqSpec document. Of the 58 participants, 4 participants commented that the information was confusing.

Relevance. We find three main themes that affect how relevant receivers thought the information was to answer the questions. 26 participants commented that they could not answer questions sufficiently using the requirements documents.

Participants commented on problems such as missing detailed information in the documents. Participants also commented on the information in the documents being unclear which also affected their ability in understanding information.

The second theme that we find is related to participants having too much information which might affect the time that they spend on answering their questions. Several participants using the ReqSpec document reported that there was too much text to read in the document. There were also two participants using the UCM document who reported that the use cases were long. Furthermore, there were concerns about over-documentation and long documents which could cause participants to spend too much time on documenting or reading irrelevant information.

Another theme is related to the problem of finding relevant information by our participants. This theme comes mainly from the responses made by participants to P1Q7. There was no clear or specific information in either document to answer P1Q7. 23 participants commented that they could not find the information at the expected location to answer P1Q7. For example, one of the participants who used the ReqSpec document reported that he or she "looked in section 3 page 27 because contents suggested data requirements but did not find relevant information." Similarly, a participant who used the UCM document answered P1Q7 with the comment: "... not seen relevant information on page 17. Neither for the Use Case Diagram on page 4." Based on such comments, we find that the information presented in the documents could be irrelevant for answering questions.

4.4 Limitations

This experiment is limited with respect to generalisation of the results to other types of requirements documents. The experiment only compares two types of requirements documents for presenting functional requirements of a software system. The results might be different if the questions for the requirements documents were different. For example, the UCM document could be less relevant to participants than the ReqSpec document if we asked questions relating to non-functional requirements of the software system.

This experiment is also limited to the type of participants we recruited. For the purpose of the experiment, we limited our participants to software developers and university students who have some experience using different software artefacts. The results might be different if non-expert stakeholders were involved in the experiment. Non-expert stakeholders such as clients might be unfamiliar with notations or language used in the requirements documents. They might also engage with the documents differently to expert stakeholders.

There are also threats to validity of this experiment. For example, the questionnaire might favour the UCM document. The questions might contain keywords that only appeared in the UCM document. To mitigate this threat, we first created the UCM document using the information provided in the ReqSpec document. We then created the questions based on the ReqSpec document. Full details of the threats and mitigations are available in other discussions [1,2].

Although there are limitations in our experiment, we have made progress towards answering our research questions. We have collected evidence to support our hypotheses about the usefulness of accessibility, understandability, and relevance to characterise transparency. We present our conclusions and discuss future work in the following section.

5   Conclusions

From the first part of our experiment we knew that the UCM document was to be the more effective document. In the second part of the experiment which we reported on here, we are interested in establishing why. The results of the experiment suggest that our characterisation of transparency with the properties of accessibility, understandability, and relevance provides a useful means to determine the transparency of requirements documents. We are able to identify the differences in the presentation of requirements documents with the three properties of transparency. In the experiment, we find that the UCM document is better than the ReqSpec document in terms of accessibility and relevance. We find that both documents are more than satisfactory for our participants to understand information about the functional requirements of a software system.

We also discover different elements in the requirements documents that have affected our participants' ability in understanding requirements. Elements such as document organisations, table of contents, and diagrams have both positive and negative effects on the transparency of information in requirements documents.

The results of the experiment give us confidence to continue investigating the concept of transparency, that it is a fruitful area for future research in software engineering. In this paper, we demonstrate the evaluation of two types of requirements documents with software developers and university students. As future work, we can apply the three properties of transparency to compare other types of documents as well as diagramming notations with different types of stakeholders.

References

1. Tu, Y., Tempero, E., Thomborson, C.: Evaluating transparency of requirements documents (March 2014) (unpublished manuscript)
2. Tu, Y.: Transparency in Software Engineering. PhD thesis, University of Auckland, New Zealand, Thesis under examination (2013)
3. Bubenko, J.A.: Challenges in requirements engineering. In: Second IEEE International Symposium on Requirements Engineering (1995)
4. Al-Rawas, A., Easterbrook, S.: Communication problems in requirements engineering: A field study. In: Professional Awareness in Software Engineering (1996)
5. Saiedian, H., Dale, R.: Requirements engineering: Making the connection between the software developer and customer. Inform. Software Tech. 42(6) (2000)
6. Forward, A., Lethbridge, T.C.: The relevance of software documentation, tools and technologies: A survey. In: ACM Symposium on Document Engineering (2002)

7. Leffingwell, D., Widrig, D.: Managing Software Requirements: A Unified Approach. Addison-Wesley Professional (2000)
8. Abran, A., Bourque, P.: SWEBOK: Guide to the Software Engineering Body of Knowledge. IEEE Computer Society (2004)
9. Cheng, B.H.C., Atlee, J.M.: Current and future research directions in requirements engineering. In: Lyytinen, K., Loucopoulos, P., Mylopoulos, J., Robinson, B. (eds.) Design Requirements Engineering. LNBIP, vol. 14, pp. 11–43. Springer, Heidelberg (2009)
10. Hansen, S., Berente, N., Lyytinen, K.: Requirements in the 21st century: Current practice and emerging trends. In: Lyytinen, K., Loucopoulos, P., Mylopoulos, J., Robinson, B. (eds.) Design Requirements Engineering. LNBIP, vol. 14, pp. 44–87. Springer, Heidelberg (2009)
11. Davis, A., Overmyer, S., Jordan, K., Caruso, J., Dandashi, F., Dinh, A., Kincaid, G., Ledeboer, G., Reynolds, P., Sitaram, P., Ta, A., Theofanos, M.: Identifying and measuring quality in a software requirements specification. In: IEEE First International Software Metrics Symposium (1993)
12. Oliver, R.: What is transparency?. McGraw-Hill (2004)
13. Bickerstaff, K., Tolley, R., Walker, G.: Transport planning and participation: The rhetoric and realities of public involvement. J. Transp. Geogr. 10(1) (2002)
14. Rowe, G., Frewer, L.: Public participation methods: A framework for evaluation. Science, Technology, & Human Values 25(1) (2000)
15. Vaccaro, A., Madsen, P.: Transparency in business and society: Introduction to the special issue. Ethics and Information Technology 11(2), 101–103 (2009)
16. Clarke, R.: Internet privacy concerns confirm the case for intervention. Communications of the ACM 42(2) (February 1999)
17. Awad, N., Krishnan, M.: The personalization privacy paradox: An empirical evaluation of information transparency and the willingness to be profiled online for personalization. MIS Quarterly 30(1) (2006)
18. Santana, A., Wood, D.: Transparency and social responsibility issues for wikipedia. Ethics and Information Technology 11 (2009)
19. Fleischmann, K., Wallace, W.: A covenant with transparency: Opening the black box of models. Communications of the ACM 48(5) (May 2005)
20. Fleischmann, K., Wallace, W.: Ensuring transparency in computational modeling. Communications of the ACM 52(3) (March 2009)
21. Ingalls, P., Frever, T.: Growing an agile culture from value seeds. In: Agile Conference, AGILE 2009 (August 2009)
22. Bird, C.: Top 10 tips for better agile. Information Professional 2(6) (2005)
23. Schwaber, K., Sutherland, J.: The scrum guide (July 2012),
    http://www.scrum.org/Portals/0/Documents/Scrum%20Guides/Scrum_Guide.pdf
24. Fowler, M.: UML distilled: A brief guide to the standard object modeling language. Addison-Wesley Professional (2004)
25. Anda, B., Sjøberg, D., Jørgensen, M.: Quality and understandability of use case models. In: Lindskov Knudsen, J. (ed.) ECOOP 2001. LNCS, vol. 2072, pp. 402–428. Springer, Heidelberg (2001)
26. Norman, G.: Likert scales, levels of measurement and the "laws" of statistics. Advances in Health Sciences Education 15(5) (2010)

Impact Analysis of Granularity Levels
on Feature Location Technique

Chakkrit Tantithamthavorn, Akinori Ihara, Hideaki Hata, and Kenichi Matsumoto

Software Engineering Laboratory,
Graduate School of Information Science,
Nara Institute of Science and Technology, Japan
{chakkrit-t,akinori-i,hata,matumoto}@is.naist.jp
http://www.se-naist.jp

Abstract. Due to the increasing of software requirements and software features, modern software systems continue to grow in size and complexity. Locating source code entities that required to implement a feature in millions lines of code is labor and cost intensive for developers. To this end, several studies have proposed the use of Information Retrieval (IR) to rank source code entities based on their textual similarity to an issue report. The ranked source code entities could be at a class or function granularity level. Source code entities at the class-level are usually large in size and might contain a lot of functions that are not implemented for the feature. Hence, we conjecture that the class-level feature location technique requires more effort than function-level feature location technique. In this paper, we investigate the impact of granularity levels on a feature location technique. We also presented a new evaluation method using effort-based evaluation. The results indicated that function-level feature location technique outperforms class-level feature location technique. Moreover, function-level feature location technique also required 7 times less effort than class-level feature location technique to localize the first relevant source code entity. Therefore, we conclude that feature location technique at the function-level of program elements is effective in practice.

Keywords: Feature Location, Granularity Level, Effort-Based Evaluation.

1 Introduction

In modern software development, software systems continue to grow in size and complexity due to the increasing of software requirements. The early version of the Eclipse Platform project[1], which was released in May 2001, consists of 283,229 lines of code, while the latest version released in January 2014, consists of 2,674,685 lines of code. In thirteen years, the size of the Eclipse Platform project has grown almost 10 folds. This explosive growth of software size has increased more rapidly than the ability of human to maintain them. As a result, identifying where and how a feature is implemented in the source code based on a given requirement in order to implement new features, enhance existing features, or fix bugs is painstaking and time-consuming for developers.

---

[1] http://www.ohloh.net/p/eclipse

D. Zowghi and Z. Jin (Eds.): APRES 2014, CCIS 432, pp. 135–149, 2014.
© Springer-Verlag Berlin Heidelberg 2014

To help developers locate the implementation of a given feature quickly, software engineering research has paid attention to the creation of fully automated feature location techniques. These techniques suggest the source code entities where a feature request will most likely be modified based on the description of the feature request. Current research uses Information Retrieval (IR) models to locate source code entities that are textually similar to a given feature request. These source code entities can be at various levels of granularity in the program elements e.g., *the class or file level* [1,2], and *the function or method level* [3,4].

Prior work reports that developers need to investigate most of the non-related functions in a class file, if the class is suggested to be modified based on a given feature request [5]. Dit et al. also stated that the more fine-grained the program elements located by a technique, the more specific and accurate the technique is [6]. Thus, this paper conjectures that *feature location technique at the function-level is effective in practice.*

In this paper, we investigate the impact of granularity levels in program element on a feature location technique. We compare the results of feature location techniques at the class-level and the function-level. We use the Vector Space Model (VSM) as a baseline model for feature location technique. We evaluate the techniques on 1,968 issue reports based on three large open-source software projects. In particular, we explore the following research questions:

RQ1: Does function-level feature location technique outperform class-level feature location technique?

Function-level feature location technique outperforms class-level feature location technique.

RQ2: How much effort does function-level feature location technique actually save over class-level feature location technique?

Function-level feature location technique requires 7 times less effort than class-level feature location technique to localize the first relevant source code entity.

Without a strong understanding of which granularity levels of feature location technique is practical for developers, the impact of feature location technique will be minimal, software quality assurance resources may not be properly allocated and software releases may be delivered late and over-budget.

2   Background and Motivation

In this section, we first present the motivation behind our research hypothesis. First, we discuss some of the common findings from previous studies. We then use an issue report from Eclipse project as a typical example and discuss the implication from our observation. Finally, we discuss the challenges of our study.

2.1   Common Findings

While feature location technique research at the class-level and the function-level has been well-studied so far, we raise a question that need to be investigated whether function-level feature location technique is more practical than class-level feature location technique. We discuss some common findings to support our research hypothesis as follows:

Long Documents are Not Suitable for Feature Location Technique. Previous research reported that the Vector Space Model (VSM) is the best generic IR model for feature location technique [1]. However, VSM is far from perfect because this model prefers small documents during ranking [2,7,8,9]. Source code entities at the class-level is often a long document, which decreases the similarity value of VSM. Zhou et al., [2] pointed out that long documents are poorly represented in the characterization of VSM because most of a given class commonly contains words that are not relevant to the issue report i.e., *noise*. An implication is that function-level feature location technique may be able to locate source code entities more accurate than class-level feature location technique.

Class-Level Feature Location Requires a Large Amount of Extra Effort to Locate the Implementation of Features. Class-level feature location technique often leaves developers with a large amount of extra effort needed to examine all instructions in a class until a function is located, which is not practical for developers. Hata et al., [5] noticed that developers need to investigate most of the non-related functions in a class file, if the class file is suggested to be modified. Giger et al., [10] also noticed that narrowing down the location of source code entities can save manual inspection steps. Dit et al., [6] also stated that the more fine-grained the program elements located by a technique, the more specific and accurate the technique is. An implication is that a function-level feature location technique could save human effort needed to locate source code entities that implemented the feature.

Traditional Evaluation Techniques are Not Appropriate for Granularity Level Comparison. Hata et al., [5] reported that the function sizes are nearly 10 times smaller than the class sizes. Since Arisholm et al. reported that the cost of such quality assurance activities on a source code is roughly proportional to the size of the source code entity [11], the effort required to read top k ranked classes and top k ranked functions are different. Therefore, traditional evaluation metrics cannot be used for a fair comparison at different granularities. An implication is that a new evaluation technique considering effort required to read top ranked entities are desirable to study the impact of granularity level in the program element on feature location technique.

2.2 Observation

We use an already-fixed issue report in Eclipse Platform's project as a typical example (see Figure 1). This issue report has ID 137088[2] and was reported on April 17, 2006 for Eclipse v3.2 under Ant component. It says that there is a bug of *StringIndex-OutOfBoundsException* in the function *AntLaunchDelegate.appendProperty()* when a developer tried to launch an Ant script.

---

[2] https://bugs.eclipse.org/bugs/show_bug.cgi?id=137088

Issue ID: 137088	Related class file: ant/org.eclipse.ant.ui/Ant Tools Support/org/eclipse/ant/internal/ui/launchConfigurations/ AntLaunchDelegate.java
Product Platform	
Comp. Ant Ver 3.2	
Summary: *StringIndexOutOfBoundsException in AntLaunchDelegate.appendProperty()*	
Description: *Im getting the following crash when I try to launch an Ant script and one of my user properties is an empty string.*	
For example, AntLaunchDelegate.appendProperty(..., "myName","")	
Here's the offending line of code...	

`if (value.charAt(value.length() - 1)`
`   == class.separatorChar) {`
`   commandLine.append(`
`      class.separatorChar);`
`}`	

The content of the related class file code:

```
private void appendProperty(...) {
    commandLine.append(" \"-D"); //$NON-NLS-1$
    commandLine.append(name);
    commandLine.append('=');
    commandLine.append(value);
-   if (value.charAt(value.length() - 1)
                == class.separatorChar) {
+   if (value.length() > 0 &&
                value.charAt(value.length() - 1)
                == class.separatorChar) {
      commandLine.append(class.separatorChar);
    }
    commandLine.append("\""); //$NON-NLS-1$
}
private void appendTaskAndTypes(...) {}
private AntRunner configureAntRunner(....){}
private StringBuffer generateCommandLine(...){}
private StringBuffer generateVMArguments(...){}
protected IBreakpoint[] getBreakpoints(...){}
private String getSWTLibraryLocation(){}
private void handleException(...){}
public void launch(...){}
private void runInSameVM(...){}
private void runInSeparateVM(...){}
private void setDefaultVM(...){}
private void setProcessAttributes(...){}
private String stripUnescapedQuotes(...){}
```

Fig. 1. The issue report ID #137088 in Eclipse project and one changed line of their related class

To identify the corresponding class file, we look into a snippet of commit logs[3] related to this issue. We found that there is only one class file (i.e., *AntLaunchDele-gate.java*) that is changed to fix this issue. Without comments and headers, the size of the class file is 619 lines of code. We also found that there is only one changed line i.e., the *if* statement in the function *appendProperty()* (see Figure 1). We can imply from this observation that even if class-level feature location technique can successfully identify the relevant class file, it requires a huge amount of effort to locate the specific location of the source code that implement this feature. The observation of this example is consistent with previous findings [5,10].

2.3 Challenges

Lack of Availability of Baseline Datasets. Current research has built their ground-truth datasets at only one granularity level. This did not allow us to investigate the comparative results at different granularity levels. To get around this problem, we built a collection of 1,968 issue reports from three large open source software projects of the Eclipse software. These issue reports were linked to actual relevant classes and functions based on a given issue report.

---

[3] We used the command "git show -U0 f89a9e717db328f421432a7890b58bd656adc242" to identify changed files.

Lack of Practical Grounding with Current Evaluation Methods. Current research often evaluates their approach using common IR evaluation metrics such as top-k accuracy, precision and recall. However, these metrics only focus on the performance of ranking models without considering the human effort to read the top-k suggested source code entities. These metrics also do not provide a practical comparison because they ignore the different sizes of classes and functions. To tackle this challenge, we introduce a new evaluation metric which take into consideration effort. We assume that developers will inspect all the returned suggested source code entities. Therefore, we represent the term "effort" with lines of code (LOC). This allowed us to compare the performance at different granularity levels.

3   Study Design

We first present the studied projects that we used in our experiment. Second, we provide data preparation procedure. Third, we present the workflow of feature location technique using the Vector Space Model (VSM). Finally, we present the effort-based evaluation.

3.1   Studied Projects

In this study, we study three large open source software projects under Eclipse Platform, Eclipse PDE, and Eclipse JDT. All subject systems were written in Java. There are two reasons to choose these three projects. First, these projects are large, active and real-world systems, which allow us to perform a realistic evaluation of our model under their testing system. Second, each software project carefully maintains issue tracking system and source code version control repositories, which allow us to build our *ground-truth* datasets to evaluate our approach. Table 1 describes the statistics summary of dataset in more details.

Table 1. Statistics summary of studied projects

Project Name	Study Period	Issues	# of classes	# of functions	# LOC
Eclipse Platform	May 2, 2001 - Dec 31, 2012	744	1,758	7,121	165,404
Eclipse PDE	June 5, 2001 - Dec 31, 2012	756	4,979	26,339	271,002
Eclipse JDT	May 24, 2001 - Dec 31, 2012	468	4,222	49,486	1,076,985
	Total	1,968	10,959	82,946	1,513,391

3.2   Data Preparation Procedure

We first obtain the source code information from version control system (VCS) and the issue report information from the issue tracking system. We then create the ground-truth dataset to test the studied projects.

Source Code Information. Generally, most of popular version control systems such as Git or Subversion keep track of source code entities only in class-level. Obtaining source code information at the function-level from existing large software project is challenging. We have to keep track source code histories at the function-level form an entire software project. To do this, it is a painstaking and time-consuming activity. In this study, we used *Historage* [12] – a fine-grained version control system (VCS), which allow us to analyze source code histories at the function and class-levels from an entire software project.

Issue Report Information. We obtain issue report information from the Eclipse issue tracking system[4]. We select only already-fixed issue reports which labeled as "FIXED". We also exclude issue reports where we could not establish a link to the source code entities.

Creating the Ground-Truth Data. We identify changes from commit logs using the SZZ algorithm [13]. This algorithm parses the commit log messages from the source code repository Historage, looking for messages such as "Fixed issue #137088" or similar variations. If found, the algorithm establishes a link between all the source code entities in the commit transaction with the identified issue report ID. The result is a set of links between issue reports and source code entities, which we use to evaluate our approach under test.

3.3   Workflow of Feature Location Technique Using the Vector Space Model

This section provides a brief overview of the workflow for IR-based feature location technique using the Vector Space Model (VSM). First, we perform data preprocessing on the source code and issue reports. Second, we perform indexing. When a new issue report is received, we treat the issue report as a query and source code entities as a document corpus. Third, we calculate the degree of relevancy using VSM to find the most relevant source code entities based on textual features. Fourth, and Finally, we return the top k search results to the developers. We describe the details of this processing in the following steps.

Step 1: Data Preprocessing. This step extracts semantic words from source code entities and issue reports. For each source code entity, we perform data preprocessing on both the class and function-levels. We remove all punctuation signs and digits. We then

---

[4] https://bugs.eclipse.org/bugs/

split all words into tokens and normalize them by transforming them to lower case. For multiple-word identifiers such as *GetInitialValue()*, we do not separate them into single words. The study by Sinha et al. [14] claimed that "Doing any pre-processing of the code to split identifiers into words did not yield benefits." We also do not perform any stemming process retaining the original meaning. The experiment by Hill et al. [15] concludes that "Stemming has relatively little effect." Finally, we remove common English words (e.g. a, an, the) and general programming language words (e.g. int, double, char)

Step 2: Indexing. In this step, weights calculated from similarity scores represent the importance of individual words. In this study, we use *tf.idf* weighting, a combination of the frequency of the index term occurrences in a document (the *term frequency*, or *tf*) and the frequency of index term occurrences over the entire collection of documents (*inverse document frequency*, or *idf*). The *idf* aims to give high weights to terms that occur in very few documents. Among many variations of weights, the *logarithm variant* was used because it can lead to better performance [16,7]. A typical formula for *tf* and *idf* is shown in Equation 1.

$$tf(t, d) = log(f_{td}) + 1, \, idf(t) = log(\frac{N}{1 + n_t}) \tag{1}$$

where t represents an index term, d represents a particular document, f_{td} is the number of term t occurrences in document d, N is the total number of documents, and n_t is the number of documents in which term t occurs. Finally, each term weight $w_{t \in d}$ in the document vector $\vec{V_d}$ and its norm $|\vec{V_d}|$ is calculated as follows:

$$w_{t \in d} = tf_{td} \times idf_t = (log(f_{td}) + 1) \times log\left(\frac{N}{n_t}\right) \tag{2}$$

$$|\vec{V_d}| = \sqrt{\sum_{t \in d} \left((log(f_{td}) + 1) \times log\left(\frac{N}{n_t}\right)\right)} \tag{3}$$

Likewise, we also obtain the vector of term weights for the query $\vec{V_q}$ and its norm $|\vec{V_q}|$.

Step 3: Similarity Function. In this step, we calculate the degree of similarity between an issue report and source code entities using *cosine similarity* as shown in Equation 4. With this equation, source code entities with the highest scores are considered as the most similar to a given issue report.

$$SimilarityFunction(q, d) = \frac{\vec{V_q} \bullet \vec{V_d}}{|\vec{V_q}||\vec{V_d}|} \tag{4}$$

Step 4: Retrieval & Ranking. Suggested source code entities are retrieved by the model. Such a model assigns a relevant score to each source code entity that is textually similar to an issue report. This score is then used to order the entities, and a developer can select the entities with the highest score to implement new features, enhance existing features, or fix bugs.

3.4 Effort-Based Evaluation

We used source lines of code (LOC) as a proxy to measure the effort required to inspect a code. Arisholm et al., [11] pointed out that the cost of such quality assurance activities on a source code is roughly proportional to the size of the source code entity. This metric represent "effort size" with lines of code (LOC). After the classes and functions are ranked, we take all the top classes and functions whose the cumulative sum of LOC is less than or equal to a window.

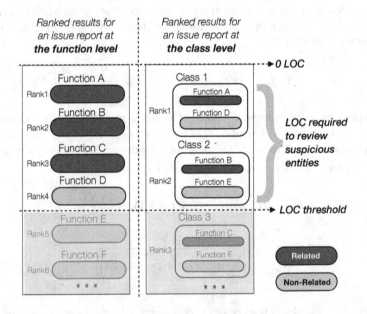

Fig. 2. Overview of effort-based evaluation

Figure 2 shows an example of suggested source code entities at the function and class levels based on a given issue report. These entities are ranked by their relevant scores calculated from Equation 4, so the entities most likely related to an issue report are at the top. A dark gray label refers to an entity related to an issue report, while a light grey label refers to a entity which is not related to an issue report. We determine a baseline LOC threshold as the effort available for review. This LOC threshold allows us to measure the performance at different granularity levels for a fair comparison, which is appropriate for a granularity level comparison study.

4   Results

4.1   Performance

RQ1: Does function-level feature location technique outperform class-level feature location technique?

Analysis Method. To answer RQ1, we performed two experiments. First, we used the *LOC-based performance* to assess the performance of feature location technique at the function and class levels. In the evaluation, for each issue report, we first obtained the rank of relevant functions and classes by calculation from Equation 4. We then checked the ranks of these locations from the search results. We performed this evaluation for all issue reports and calculated the percentage of successfully localized issue reports. For the comparison, we set the LOC threshold size ranging from 500 to 5,000 LOC with the idea that 5,000 is a reasonable number of LOC for a developer to search through before growing impatient and resorting to other means of feature location technique.

Second, we performed paired-statistical tests to measure the performance improvements brought by function-level feature location technique. In the paired-statistical tests, two chosen approaches must have the same number of data points. We formulated a one-tailed null hypothesis and the related alternative hypothesis as follows:

H_{01}: *There is no statistical difference in terms of accuracy between function-level feature location technique and class-level feature location technique.*

H_{a1}: *The LOC-based performance of function-level feature location technique is greater than the LOC-based performance of class-level feature location technique.*

We used the Wilcoxon Signed-Rank test to reject the null hypotheses H_{01} using the 1% confident level (i.e., $p - value < 0.01$).

Evaluation Metric. To assess the performance, we define a metric called the *LOC-based performance* designed to measure the performance of feature location technique by taking into consideration effort. This metric will measure the percentage of successfully localized issue reports. We consider an issue report to be successfully localized if at least one suggested entity in the baseline ground-truth dataset was returned below a baseline LOC threshold. If none of the suggested entities was returned, the issue report cannot be localized. We denote the number of issue reports as N_C if the issue report is successfully localized, or N_{IC} if the issue report is not successfully localized. The following formula computes the percentage of issue reports for which are successfully localized:

$$\text{LOC-based Performance} = \frac{N_C}{N_C + N_{IC}} \qquad (5)$$

To illustration, suppose that source code is selected for inspection using a feature location technique that orders source code entities (e.g., classes or functions) in terms of their similarity measure. Then, if an inspection budget allows inspection of 5,000 LOC of the source code, the higher the number of successfully localized issue reports, the better the technique is.

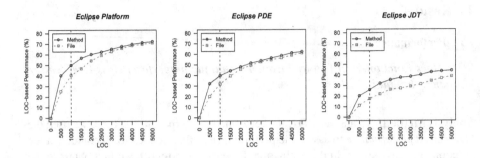

Fig. 3. The performance of function-level feature location technique compared to class-level feature location technique using LOC-based performance

Results. Figure 3 shows the performance of function-level feature location technique compared to class-level feature location technique using LOC-based performance. The x-axis denotes the total LOC to be examined. The y-axis represents the LOC-based performance values. For every studied project, we used a comparative size at 1,000 LOC threshold. It is apparent from this figure that function-level feature location technique correctly identifies the location of source code entities for a larger number of issue reports than class-level feature location technique. For the Eclipse Platform project, function-level feature location technique can successfully identify 49.86%, while class-level feature location technique can identify 40.45% of the issue reports. For the Eclipse PDE project, function-level feature location technique can identify 39.81%, while class-level feature location technique can identify 31.87% of the issue reports. For the Eclipse JDT project, function-level feature location technique can identify 26.07%, while class-level feature location technique can identify 17.74% of the issue reports. Furthermore, we also have statistical significant evidence to reject the null hypothesis H_{01}. The p-values for all studied systems are below the standard significant value, $p-value < 0.01$.

Summary. For these three studied projects, we can confidently conclude that function-level feature location technique is significantly achieves better performance than class-level feature location technique.

4.2 Efficiency

RQ2: How much effort does function-level feature location technique actually save over class-level feature location technique?

Analysis Method. To answer RQ2, we consider efficiency in two dimensions: (1) effort required to find the first relevant source code entity; and (2) effort required to find 80% of the relevant source code entities. We performed this experiment for all issue reports and represented the results by box-plots of the distribution of LOC that needed to be examined. Intuitively, the less effort required to review, the more efficient the technique is.

Then, we assess whether the differences in the amount of LOC to be reviewed to find the first relevant source code entity and 80% of the relevant source code entities are statistically significant between function-level feature location technique and class-level feature location technique. To select an appropriate statistical test, we use the Shapiro-Wilk test to analyze the distributions of our data points. We observe that these distributions do not follow a normal distribution. Thus, we use a nonparametric test, i.e., Wilcoxon-Mann-Whitney test, to test our null hypotheses to answer **RQ2**. We reject the null hypotheses H_{02}, H_{03} using the 1% confident level (i.e., $p - value < 0.01$). We formulate one-tailed null hypotheses and the related alternative hypotheses as follows:

H_{02}: *There is no statistical difference in terms of the amount of LOC to be reviewed to find the first relevant source code entity between function-level feature location technique and class-level feature location technique.*

H_{a2}: *The amount of LOC to be reviewed to find the first relevant source code entity of function-level feature location technique is less than class-level feature location technique.*

H_{03}: *There is no statistical difference in terms of the amount of LOC to review to find 80% of the relevant source code entities between function-level feature location technique and class-level feature location technique.*

H_{a3}: *The amount of LOC to be reviewed to find 80% of the relevant source code entities of function-level feature location technique is less than class-level feature location technique.*

Result
(1) Effort Required to Find The First Relevant Source Code Entity. For each studied project, as shown in Figure 4, we plotted a quartile box plot to show the distribution of the amount of LOC that must be reviewed to identify the first relevant source code entities. The x-axis represents the level of granularity, either function-level or class-level. The y-axis represents the total LOC to be examined. From this figure, it is apparent that, function-level feature location technique required less effort than class-level feature location technique to identify the first feature request location. For the Eclipse Platform, function-level feature location technique required 113 LOC (median), while class-level feature location technique required 906 LOC (median) to find the first feature request location. This means function-level feature location technique requires less effort than class-level feature location technique to find the first feature request location. For the Eclipse PDE, function-level feature location technique requires 154 LOC, while class-level feature location technique requires 861 LOC to find the first feature request location. For the Eclipse JDT, function-level feature location technique requires 248 LOC, while class-level feature location technique requires 1,839 LOC to find the first feature request location.

These results indicate that for these projects, function-level feature location technique required less effort than class-level feature location technique to find the first relevant source code entity. Interestingly, for those issue reports with function-level feature location technique, the maximum LOC to identify the first relevant source code entity ranged from 1,633 LOC to 2,026 LOC, while the maximum LOC for class-level feature location technique ranged from 10,789 LOC to 51,775 LOC. These results help

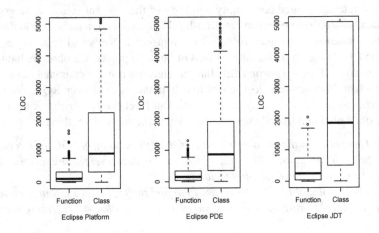

Fig. 4. Distribution of LOC that need to be examined to identify the first relevant source code entity

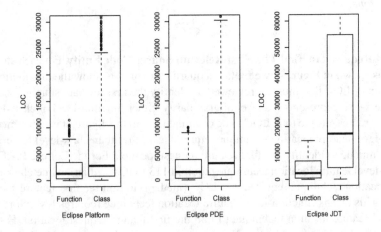

Fig. 5. Distribution of LOC that need to be examined to localized 80% of relevant source code entities

us confirm that function-level feature location technique required less effort than class-level feature location technique to find the first relevant source code entity. We also found that the difference in terms of the amount of LOC to be reviewed to find the first relevant source code entity are statistically significant ($p - value < 0.01$) to reject the null hypothesis H_{02}.

(2) Effort Required to Find 80% of The Relevant Source Code Entities. Figure 5 shows the distributions of the amount of LOC that needed review to localize 80% of the relevant source code entities. The x-axis represents the level of granularity, either function-level or class-level. The y-axis represents the total LOC to be examined. For the Eclipse Platform, function-level feature location technique required 1,309 LOC (median) to find 80% of the relevant source code entities, while class-level feature location technique required 2,744 LOC (median). For the Eclipse PDE, function-level feature location technique required 1,522 LOC and class-level feature location technique required 3,132 LOC to find 80% of the relevant source code entities. For the Eclipse JDT, function-level feature location technique required 2,354 LOC and class-level feature location technique required 17,176 LOC to find 80% of the relevant source code entities. We also found that the difference in terms of the amount of LOC to review to find 80% of the relevant source code entities are statistically significant ($p - value < 0.01$) to reject the null hypothesis H_{03}.

Summary. The results indicate for these projects, function-level feature location technique required 7 times less effort than class-level feature location technique to localize the first relevant source code entity and 4.4 times less effort to localize 80% of the relevant source code entities. We can conclude that function-level feature location technique can effectively save human effort in identifying relevant source code entities.

5 Threats to Validity

The Main Threats to Internal Validity lies in our truth data collection technique, which relies on the SZZ algorithm [13]. Although the SZZ algorithm is a commonly used technique for linking feature request reports to source code entities, Bird et al. reported that there is a linking bias in identifying feature requests with revision logs and feature request reports [17]. Recently, Nguyen et al. has been proposed a novel linking algorithm [18], which may alleviate this threat.

Threats to External Validity. These are concerned with the generalization of our findings. In this paper, we used three large open source software under the Eclipse Project to conduct our case study. All these projects were written in Java. Although these are large real-world software projects, our results may not generalize to other open source or commercial software projects, especially in other programing languages.

Threats to Construct Validity. The main threat refers to the effort-based evaluation. In our comparative study between function-level and class-level feature location technique, we used effort-based evaluation. However, the effort used here (LOC) may not reflect actual efforts. As a first approximation, it seems acceptable to represent the term effort using LOC because developers may consider much more complex relations or other deep dependencies. In future research, we may need to consider complexity and dependency metrics.

6 Conclusions and Future Works

In this research, we addressed the question of practical feature location technique. We investigated whether function-level feature location technique is more practical than class-level feature location technique by conducting a large-scale empirical study to compare the results of IR-based feature location technique at class and function levels. Our main findings are.

- For the same amount of inspection effort, function-level feature location technique outperforms class-level feature location technique. Especially at lower levels of inspection effort, function-level feature location technique correctly identifies the relevant source code entities for a larger number of issue reports than class-level feature location technique.
- Function-level feature location technique required 7 times less effort than class-level feature location technique to localize the first relevant source code entity. We also found that Function-level feature location technique required 4.4 times less effort than class-level feature location technique to find 80% of the relevant source code entities. These results indicate that function-level feature location technique can help developers locate a larger percentage of issue reports with less inspection efforts.

From these results, we conclude that feature location technique at the function-level of program elements is effective in practice. Using function-level feature location technique should help developers reduce the level of inspection effort needed to find feature requests, increase the number of relevant source code entities, and improve the overall handling of feature location technique.

Based on this study, future research will focus on empirical studies of actual efforts, and conduct experiments to confirm the results and functions with other open-source and commercial software projects, and other programing languages.

Acknowledgement. We would like to thank the anonymous reviewers for their very constructive feedback on early drafts of this work. This research is conducted as part of Grant-in-Aid for Young Scientists (B), 25730045, Grant-in-Aid for Young Scientists (Start-up), 25880015, and for Exploratory Research 2554002 by Japan Society for the Promotion of Science (JSPS).

References

1. Canfora, G., Cimitile, A., Garcia, F., Piattini, M., Visaggio, C.A.: Evaluating performances of pair designing in industry. Journal of Systems and Software 80(8), 1317–1327 (2007)
2. Zhou, J., Zhang, H., Lo, D.: Where Should the Bugs Be Fixed? In: Proceedings of the 34th International Conference on Software Engineering (ICSE 2012), pp. 14–24 (2012)
3. Lukins, S.K., Kraft, N.A., Etzkorn, L.H.: Bug Localization Using Latent Dirichlet Allocation. Information and Software Technology 52(9), 972–990 (2010)
4. Wang, S., Khomh, F., Zou, Y.: Improving Bug Localization using Correlations in Crash Reports. In: Proceedings of the 10th Working Conference on Mining Software Repositories, MSR 2013 (2013)
5. Hata, H., Mizuno, O., Kikuno, T.: Bug Prediction Based on Fine-Grained Module Histories. In: Proceedings of the 34th International Conference on Software Engineering (ICSE 2012), pp. 200–210 (June 2012)

6. Dit, B., Revelle, M., Gethers, M., Poshyvanyk, D.: Feature Location in Source Code: A Taxonomy and Survey. Journal of Software: Evolution and Process 25(1), 53–95 (2013)
7. Manning, C.D., Raghavan, P., Schütze, H.: Introduction to Information Retrieval, vol. c. Cambridge Unviersity Press, New York (2008)
8. Tantithamthavorn, C., Teekavanich, R., Ihara, A., Matsumoto, K.: Mining A Change History to Quickly Identify Bug Locations: A Case Study of the Eclipse Project. In: Proceedings of the 2013 IEEE International Symposium on Software Reliability Engineering Workshops (ISSREW 2013), pp. 108–113 (2013)
9. Tantithamthavorn, C., Ihara, A., Matsumoto, K.: Using Co-change Histories to Improve Bug Localization Performance. In: Proceedings of the 14th IEEE/ACIS International Conference on Software Engineering, Artificial Intelligence, Networking and Parallel/Distributed Computing (SNPD 2013), pp. 543–548 (July 2013)
10. Giger, E., D'Ambros, M., Pinzger, M., Gall, H.C.: Method-Level Bug Prediction. In: Proceedings of the ACM-IEEE International Symposium on Empirical Software Engineering and Measurement (ESEM 2012), pp. 171–180 (2012)
11. Arisholm, E., Briand, L.C., Johannessen, E.B.: A Systematic and Comprehensive Investigation of Methods to Build and Evaluate Fault Prediction Models. Journal of Systems and Software 83(1), 2–17 (2010)
12. Hata, H., Mizuno, O., Kikuno, T.: Historage: Fine-grained Version Control System for Java. In: Proceedings of the 12th International Workshop on Principles of Software Evolution (IWPSE 2011), pp. 96–100 (2011)
13. Zimmermann, T., Zeller, A.: When Do Changes Induce Fixes? ACM SIGSOFT Software Engineering Notes 30(4), 1–5 (2005)
14. Sinha, V.S., Mani, S., Mukherjee, D.: Is Text Search an Effective Approach for Fault Localization: A Practitioners Perspective. In: Proceedings of the 3rd Annual Conference on Systems, Programming, and Applications: Software for Humanity (SPLASH 2012), pp. 159–170 (2012)
15. Hill, E.: On the Use of Stemming for Concern Location and Bug Localization in Java. In: Proceedings of the 12th International Working Conference on Source Code Analysis and Manipulation (SCAM 2012), pp. 184–193 (2012)
16. Croft, B., Metzler, D., Strohman, T.: Search Engines: Information Retrieval in Practice. Addison-Wesley (2010)
17. Bird, C., Bachmann, A., Aune, E., Duffy, J., Bernstein, A., Filkov, V., Devanbu, P.: Fair and Balanced? Bias in Bug-Fix Datasets Categories and Subject Descriptors. In: Proceedings of the the 7th Joint Meeting of the European Software Engineering Conference and the ACM SIGSOFT Symposium on the Foundations of Software Engineering (FSE 2009), pp. 121–130 (2009)
18. Nguyen, A.T., Nguyen, T.T., Nguyen, H.A., Nguyen, T.N.: Multi-Layered Approach for Recovering Links Between Bug Reports and Fixes. In: Proceedings of the ACM SIGSOFT 20th International Symposium on the Foundations of Software Engineering (FSE 2012), pp. 1–11 (2012)

A Pair-Oriented Requirements Engineering Approach for Analysing Multi-lingual Requirements

Massila Kamalrudin[1,*], Safiah Sidek[1], Norsaremah Salleh[2],
John Hosking[3], and John Grundy[4]

[1] Innovative Software System & Services Group, Universiti Teknikal Malaysia Melaka,
Melaka, Malaysia
(massila,safiahsidek)@utem.edu.my
[2] Department of Computer Science, International Islamic University Malaysia, 50728
Kuala Lumpur, Malaysia
norsaremah@iium.edu.my
[3] College of Engineering & Computer Science, Australian National University, Canberra, ACT
0200, Australia
john.hosking@anu.edu.au
[4] Centre for Computing and Engineering Software Systems, Swinburne,
University of Technology, PO Box 218, Hawthorn, Victoria 3122, Australia
jgrundy@swin.edu.au

Abstract. Requirements written in multiple languages can lead to error-proneness, inconsistency and incorrectness. In a Malaysian setting, software engineers are exposed to both Malay and English requirements. This can be a challenging task for them especially when capturing and analyzing requirements. Further, they face difficulties to model requirements using semi-formal or formal models. This paper introduces a new approach, Pair-Oriented Requirements Engineering (PORE) that uses an Essential Use Case (EUC) model to capture and analyze multi-lingual requirements. This approach is intended to assist practitioners in developing correct and consistent requirements as well as developing teamwork skills. Two quasi-experiment studies involving 80 participants in the first study and 38 participants in a subsequent study were conducted to evaluate the effectiveness of this approach with respect to correctness and time spent in capturing multi-lingual requirements. It was found that PORE improves accuracy and hence helps users perform better in developing high quality requirements models.

Keywords: Pair-Oriented, Analysing Requirements, Multi-lingual requirements.

1 Introduction

Multi-lingual communication is common in countries that have a mother-tongue other than the pervasive English language. In Malaysia, whose primary language is the Malay language, "code-switching" between English and Malay has become a common

---

* Corresponding Author.

D. Zowghi and Z. Jin (Eds.): APRES 2014, CCIS 432, pp. 150–164, 2014.

practice of communication [1]. Code-switching has also become a common practice in the Malaysian IT industry. Considering that the Malay language is the official language of Malaysia, this language is commonly used in the government IT sector, especially in writing the requirements of a system, and when eliciting or capturing requirements from clients or stakeholders who are not fluent in English. Meanwhile, the English language is commonly used in the business IT sector. This situation leads to a plethora of multi-lingual requirements – those expressed in both Malay and English languages, or a mixture of both [1]. Working with multi-lingual requirements, software engineers need to be proficient in both languages to be able to capture quality requirements that meet the needs of the stakeholders.

There are a wide variety of methods for modelling and analysing software requirements. These include goal-oriented, viewpoint-oriented, agent-oriented and object-oriented approaches [2-4]. Although the benefits of these methods are widely recognised, software engineers need a high level of understanding and skill to be able to capture and analyse requirements. As such, besides dealing with multi-lingual issues, software engineers also face difficulties to handling various tools for analysing requirements used in the IT industry.

Considering the use of both Malay and English language in the Malaysian IT industry, students of software engineering in the Malaysian institutions of higher education are exposed to multi-lingual requirements. These students need to be familiar with IT terms and scenarios in both languages so that when they enter the IT industry, they will be able to function effectively in this environment. Further, it has been reported that many students have trouble in capturing requirements using semi-formal or formal models such as UML, tabular models, algebra or mathematics [5].

Motivated by these issues, we propose a new approach for requirements capture and analysis, Pair-oriented Requirements Engineering (PORE). We expect this approach to be suitable for novice users who in this case face two main issues in software development. The first issue relates to knowledge and skills of the various methods to analyse requirements, and the second issue relates to the analysis of multi-language requirements. The PORE approach builds on our earlier work to support the development and analysis of multi-lingual requirements using the EUC modelling approach [1]. In our earlier work, we have developed a new toolset for developing and evaluating EUCs in the English language 0,0 only. In that body of work, we adopted the EUCs approach due to its simplicity and understandability by stakeholders, findings that were supported by our evaluations. As a result, we were keen to investigate whether the advantages we had observed with EUCs could be extended to multi-lingual requirements, namely requirements in English and Malay language

In this paper, we introduce our new Pair-Oriented Requirements Engineering (PORE) approach using the Essential Use Cases (EUCs) modeling approach to capture and analyse multi-lingual requirements. Considering students as novice practitioners (software engineers), we investigated its application with two cohorts of students, each cohort taking one of two software engineering related courses, Requirements Engineering and Software Testing, at the Universiti Teknikal Malaysia Melaka, a public university in Malaysia. Specifically, we were interested to investigate whether a pair analysis approach using EUCs leads to better results in comparison to individual analysis undertaken by students. The focus of this study is to investigate the outcome of working as a pair rather than how the students work together. Therefore, our key research question is:

"Do students working in pairs perform better than students working individually in analysing multi-lingual requirements using an Essential Use Case modelling approach?"

In this paper, we report the outcomes of the two experiments to determine the effectiveness of the PORE method for capturing and analysing multi-lingual requirements. In each experiment, the time taken and the accuracy (score) of the students' EUCs analysis of requirements expressed in both Malay and English languages are evaluated. Based on the correlation between time taken and the correctness of both languages, the results of this research indicate a positive result when PORE is used.

2   Background and Motivation

2.1   Essential Use Cases (EUCs)

The EUC approach is defined by its creators, Constantine and Lockwood, as a "structured narrative, expressed in a language of the application domain and of users, comprising a simplified, generalized, abstract, technology free and independent description of one task or interaction that is complete, meaningful, and well-defined from the point of view of users in some role or roles in relation to a system and that embodies the purpose or intentions underlying the interaction" [6]. An EUC takes the form of a dialogue between the user and the system. The aim is to support better communication between developers and stakeholders via a technology-free model and to assist better requirements capture. This is achieved by allowing only specific detail that is relevant to the intended design to be captured [7].

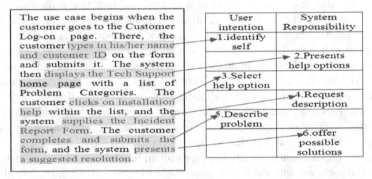

Fig. 1. Example of Natural Language Requirements and Essential Use Case model [10][8]

An EUC description is generally shorter and simpler than other requirements descriptions as it only comprises the essential steps (core requirements) of intrinsic user interest. It comprises user intentions and system responsibilities to document the user/system interaction without the need to describe a user interface in detail. The abstractions used, abstract interactions are more focused towards the steps of the use case rather than narrating the use case as a whole. The essential interactions between user and system are organised into an interaction sequence, the EUC. Figure 1 shows an example of natural language requirements (left hand side) and an EUC (right hand side) capturing these requirements (adapted from [8]). A set of essential interactions (highlighted), are extracted from the requirements. From each of these, a specific key phrase (the essential requirement of the target system it captures), called an abstract interaction, is abstracted and shown in the Essential Use case on the right as user intentions (left column) and system responsibilities (right column).

2.2   EUC Tool Support

We have developed a range of tools to support the use of EUCs. MaramaAI supports automatic extraction of EUCs from textual requirements, together with the comparison of those EUCs against the best practice EUC patterns [9] . It also supports generation of user interface models and prototypes to assist communication with stakeholders [10] and was extended to include support for multi-lingual requirements [1]. More recently, we developed a web-based tool, MEReq, which supports multi-lingual requirements capture and EUCs extraction [11] with consistency management between the multi-lingual requirements and models. For the purpose of the study presented here, the two tools described above were not used since the focus of this study is to investigate the effect of pair work on requirements capture and analysis in a multi-lingual context using EUCs.

2.3   Pair Analysis and PORE

In pair-programming, two developers sit together to work on the same code using a single computer [12],[13]. There are two roles used in pair programming: the "Driver" who types the code and the "Navigator" who observes the activity of the driver [14]. Motivated by the popularity and success of pair programming, we adapted the pairing concept to the capture and analysis of multi-lingual requirements. Essentially, the concept of driver and navigator can be used for effective requirements capture and analysis, when both users are actively communicating and discussing the task given. Thus in PORE, the same pairing approach is applied with, two roles identified: the "Codifier' who captures and analyses the requirements as EUCs and the "Navigator" who observes and checks the capture and analysis activities of the codifier.

2.4   PORE and EUCs

We considered the adoption of PORE combined with the use of EUCs for requirements analysis. Our postulation was that the accessibility of EUCs and the quality enhancements provided by pairing would result in improved quality of analyzing and capturing multi-lingual requirements, as exhibited by measures, such as the correctness of analysis and the time spent by users to complete the task.

3   Related Work

There has been much research examining pairing in the software development process that shows significant benefits to the development process and output. The most common is pair-programming. Silliti et al. [15] investigated the effects of pair-programming on developers' attention and productivity by looking at the influences of pair programming on their code writing style and their   interaction with the development machine. They found that pair-programming allows the developers to stay more focussed and spend a longer time on task and switch less often between tools. However, more data is needed to support these preliminary findings.

There has been some research on pair-designing. Canfora et al. [16] implemented pair-programming in the design phase in an industry setting by having two designers work together on the same task, at the same time and on the same machine. They provided textual requirements and used the use cases and class diagram as analysis and design documents for the experiments. They found that pair-designing improved the quality but it increased the time required to complete the task [16]. Further experiments including qualitative study are in need to ensure the accuracy of the findings.

Bellini et al. [12], also conducted an experiment and its replica in both Italian and Spanish academic settings to understand the capability of pair-designing in diffusing and enforcing design knowledge when a system design is evolved. They used formalised system design documentation in UML including textual system requirements specification, use cases and class diagram. They found that pair-designing helps to increase the diffusion of the knowledge among the project team as well as providing a good level of predictability on the enforcement of knowledge compared to the traditional designing setting [12]. However, a similar experiment in industry and application of this approach to more complex systems is needed.

Albakry and Kamalrudin [5] implemented pair-analysis by adapting pair-programming to the requirements analysis process in an academic setting. They conducted a preliminary study to compare the outcomes of pair and single participants by evaluating the performance and correctness of the answers as well as the students' satisfaction and confidence [5]. Their findings were positive but require more experiments with larger groups of participants for further confirmation. Additionally, a better way to pair the students for analysis work by considering the differences of course background and culture is needed.

In summary, prior work demonstrates the benefits of pairing in software development. However, there has been a limited work on pairing in requirements engineering. No research using pairing to solve multi-lingual requirements and the Essential Use Cases as a semi-formalised way to capture requirements has been documented.

4   Research Methodology

This study was conducted to investigate the effect of pairing on the correctness and time spent of novice users working on analysing multi-lingual requirements using

EUCs. In this study, students are considered as novice users. As such, throughout this paper, the term students will be used to refer to novice users. The formulation of hypothesis, the sample, the instruments and the study procedure used in this study are described below. To address the objective of this study, a quasi-experimental study has been employed and the research design is as shown in Figure 3.

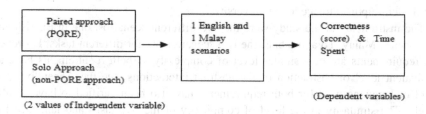

Fig. 2. Research Design

Using our PORE approach we had students capture and analyse multi-lingual requirements in both Malay and English languages. EUCs are used to model the captured requirements as they have proven to be useful to capture and analyse multi-lingual requirements [1]. In this respect, the effectiveness of PORE with EUCs was measured based on the correctness of the students' EUC models (score out of 6) and the time they took to capture and analyse the multi-lingual requirements. Hence, students' scores and time spent were our dependent variables, and pairing and solo approaches the independent variable. The following two hypotheses were used:

H1: There will be a significant difference in   correctness between paired and solo students when analyzing multi-lingual requirements using an Essential Use Case modeling approach.

H2: There will be a significant difference in   time spent between paired and solo students when analyzing multi-lingual requirements using an Essential Use Case modeling approach.

To test the reliability of our results, the quasi experiment was performed on two different cohorts. Both studies were conducted at UTeM, a Malaysian public university, but at a different time frame. The first study was done during semester II, 2011/2012, while the second was conducted during semester I, 2012/2013.

A different sample of participants was selected for the two studies: the first study involved 80 participants from a Requirements Engineering course, comprising 75 Malaysian students and 5 international students. Due to the structure of the study group, they were divided into two study sections: 40 participants per section, allowing each section to be assigned to one treatment of the independent variable. The replica study involved 38 students from a Software Testing course, comprising 36 Malaysian students and 2 international students. The structure of this study group divided the cohort into 2 sections, 28 participants in one and 10 participants in the second.

All of the participants in the two studies were proficient in both languages. The Malaysian students' level of English language proficiency was approximately equal across the cohort as all of them had achieved between Band 3 and Band 4 in the Malaysian English Language Entrance Examination (MUET), a national English language examination undertaken by Malaysian students. For the international students, they had achieved at least Band 6.5 for IELTS (International English Language Testing System) upon entrance to the university.

The instruments of the study were the two different scenarios, one in English and the other in Malay. To avoid bias, the two scenarios are for different tasks. However, the requirements are of a similar level of complexity as both requirements have an equivalent level of abstraction of the abstract interactions (see the Appendix). The level of language used for both requirements has also been verified to have similar level. The similarity in the level of complexity of the two tasks and language has been verified by an expert in requirements who is proficient in both languages.

Participants were required to capture and analyze requirements manually, using two different sets of simple requirements: one in English language and the other in Malay language. They were instructed to attempt the task manually rather than using any of the EUC support tools we had developed. This is because our main concern was to assess whether they have an understanding of capturing and analyzing requirements manually using the EUC concept, without the assistance of any tools. This is crucial, as the participants should have a strong understanding of the modeling concept in "pen and paper" rather than being dependent on any specific tool. We also wanted them to be familiar with the manual PORE approach before starting to use the supporting tools. We will explore their experiences using MEReq in a subsequent study.

4.1 Study Procedures

At the start of the academic semesters for each of the two studies, one of the authors provided the subjects with an overview of the experiment (including the pairing concept) in one of the course lectures. Prior to the conduct of the experiments, participants were given three similar exercises in both languages. This allows the participants to gain familiarity with working with EUCs and pair work.

During the experiment, two scenarios were given (refer to appendix) to the participants: reserving a vehicle (with requirements expressed in the Malay language) and Getting Cash (expressed in English). We asked them to capture these requirements in Malay and English EUCs respectively (i.e. Malay EUC model for Malay requirements and English EUC model for English requirements). The participants had to model requirements in EUCs by extracting the correct essential requirements and then model the right sequencing and responsibilities in the EUCs. The need to model both English and Malay requirements simulated the "code-switching" typical in Malay multilingual settings. Participants were given 60 minutes to complete the task.

5   Results

5.1   Study 1

A total of 80 students participated in our study. Subjects were final year Computer Science students enrolled in a Requirements Engineering course at UTeM. Participants were divided into two study groups consisting of 40 subjects per group. 40 participants attempted the tasks individually, while the other 40 participants attempted the tasks in pairs, resulting in 20 pair works. In this study, the international students were instructed to work in pairs with the Malay speakers. Table 1 shows the results of applying a bivariate Pearson correlation test to measure the association between scores and the time spent by both pair and solo students. Results show the strongest correlations between Malay and English scores ($r(60) = 0.59$, $p = .000$).

Table 1. Correlation (Scores and Time Spent) (N=60)

	EScore	ETime	MScore	MTime
EScore				
ETime	.222*	1		
MScore	.590**	.078	1	
MTime	.233*	.347**	.211	1

*. Correlation is significant at the 0.05 level (1-tailed)
**. Correlation is significant at the 0.01 level (1-tailed)

Table 2. Descriptive Statistic (Solo and Pair)

		N	Mean	SD
EScore	Solo	40	2.23	1.143
(range: 0 to 6)	Pair	20	3.10	1.252
	Total	60	2.52	1.242
ETime	Solo	40	10.83	4.494
(range:0 to 60)	Pair	20	12.95	6.083
	Total	60	11.53	5.127
MScore	Solo	40	2.88	.992
(range: 0 to 6)	Pair	20	3.55	1.276
	Total	60	3.10	1.130
MTime	Solo	40	10.10	3.761
(range:0 to 60)	Pair	20	11.30	5.686
	Total	60	10.50	4.482

Hypothesis Testing

Table 2 shows the sample size, values for mean scores and standard deviations for each group. The mean scores for the pair group are greater than the solo group. In terms of the time spent, on average solo students spent less time than paired students in both types of requirements. Hypothesis H1 and H2 were tested using an independent sample *t*-test. This test is appropriate to be used when investigating the difference between two unrelated groups on approximately normal dependent variables [23]. In our case the two groups are pair and solo, while our dependent variables are students' scores. The results from the Levene test indicate that the assumption of homogeneity of variances of each variable was not violated (i.e. F=0.142, $p = 0.708$ for Escore; F= 2.301, $p=0.135$ for ETime; F=3.266, $p=0.076$ for MScore; F=3.388; $p=0.071$ for MTime). Hence we assume that the variances of scores in the two groups are equal.

The *t*-test results (see Table 3) showed that paired groups were significantly different from solo participants on English based scores ($p = 0.009$). Inspection of the two group means indicates that the average score for English-based requirements for paired groups (3.10) is significantly higher than the scores for solo students (2.23). The difference between the means is 0.87 point on a 6-point test. Similarly the pair group outperformed the solo group for Malay based requirements task. Thus, based on our data we found strong support for the alternate hypothesis for H1 i.e. that there is a significant different in correctness between pair and solo students. Our results showed that the pair group performed better than the solo group.

In terms of the time spent, although the pair group in general tended to spend more time during the exercise, we could not find a statistically significant difference between the groups. The time taken by pair group in completing the exercise did not differ significantly from the solo group ($p = 0.13$ for English requirements; $p = 0.33$ for Malay requirements). Hence the null hypothesis for H2 was supported. Increasing sample size for future studies will help to increase the statistical power value, hence would give us more discrimination.

Table 3. Comparison of Pair and Solo Group on Scores and Time Spent   ($N_1 = 40$ solo $N_2=20$ pairs)

	t-test for Equality of Means			
	t	df	Sig.	Mean difference
EScore	-2.71	58	0.009	-0.875
ETime	-1.53	58	0.131	-2.125
MScore	-2.26	58	0.028	-0.675
MTime	-0.98	58	0.332	-1.200

5.2   Study 2: Replication

A total of 38 students participated in the replicated study. Subjects were final year Computer Science students enrolled in a Software Testing course in Universiti Teknikal Malaysia Melaka (UTeM) and they did not participate in the earlier study. The participants had enough experience and knowledge in requirements engineering and EUC modeling specifically as they had already taken requirements engineering and software engineering subjects before. As in the first study, the research is organised in two Sections of the course. Twenty eight (28) participants in Section 1 were required to solve the task in solo, while 10 participants in Section 2 worked in pairs, resulting in 5 paired works. In this study, international students were instructed to work in pairs since Malay is not their primary language.

Table 4 shows results from applying a bivariate Pearson correlation test to measure the association between scores and the time spent by both pair and solo students. Results show positive and significant correlation between the time spent for the Malay and English requirements. ($r(38) = 0.32, p = .001$).

Hypothesis Testing

Table 5 shows the sample size, values for mean scores and standard deviations for each group. Our data shows that mean scores for pair groups are greater than the solo groups for both Malay and English requirements. In terms of time spent, on average solo groups spent less time than paired students for Malay requirements. However, for English requirements, the paired groups spent less time than solo students. We think that this is due to a few subjects in the paired group being international students. They needed more time for discussion with their partner who was a native Malay speaker.

Table 4. Correlations between Scores and Time Spent (N=38)

	EScore	ETime	MScore	MTime
EScore	1			
ETime	.174	1		
MScore	-.093	.133	1	
MTime	.147	.323*	.089	1

*. Correlation is significant at the 0.05 level (2-tailed)

Table 5. Descriptive Statistic (Solo and Pair)

		N	Mean	SD
EScore	Solo	28	1.64	0.911
(range: 0 to 6)	Pair	10	1.80	0.919
	Total	38	1.68	0.904
ETime	Solo	28	14.07	5.741
(range:0 to 60)	Pair	10	13.60	4.575
	Total	38	13.95	5.402
MScore	Solo	28	2.50	0.577
(range: 0 to 6)	Pair	10	3.60	0.843
	Total	38	2.79	0.811
MTime	Solo	28	14.89	5.705
(range:0 to 60)	Pair	10	18.50	11.816
	Total	38	15.84	7.765

Table 6. Comparison of Pair and Solo Group on Scores and Time Spent (N1= 28 solo, N2=10 pairs)

	t-test for Equality of Means			
	t	df	Sig.	Mean difference
EScore	-.467	36	0.643	-0.157
ETime	-.260	36	0.816	0.471
MScore	-1.747	36	0.000	-1.100
MTime	-1.271	36	0.212	-3.607

The hypothesis was also tested using an independent sample t-test and the Levene test. The Levene test indicates that the assumption of homogeneity of variances of each variable was not violated (i.e. F=0.38, p = 0.847 for Escore; F= 0.26, p=0.613 for ETime; F=2.015, p=0.164 for MScore; F=1.423; p=0.241 for MTime). Hence we assume that the variances of scores in two groups are equal.

The t-test results (see Table 6) showed that there were no significant differences in correctness between paired students and solo students (ρ = 0.643) for English requirements. Similarly, there were no significant differences on the time taken to solve the requirements in English (ρ =0.816). However, for the Malay requirements, we found that there is a significant difference in correctness between paired and solo students (ρ = 0.00), thus supporting our hypothesis. However, we could not find a statistically significant difference between paired and solo students in terms of the time spent to solve a task written in Malay. Based on these results, we found evidence that pairing work has benefited students when analysing Malay requirements. This was consistent with the results from our previous study.

6   Discussions

Based on the results presented in the previous section, we found evidence that PORE is able to help novice users perform better in requirements engineering in captured requirements quality score. This was particularly useful when analysing requirements written in the Malay language. However, our results showed only partial support for users working in pairs on English requirements having improved captured requirements quality scores. In terms of the time spent, we found that there was no evidence to differentiate the time taken to solve the task between pair and solo group for both languages. The aggregation of the hypothesis testing results of each study is presented in Table 7.

Table 7. Summary of Findings

Study	Supported Hypothesis - pair group outperform solo? (YES/NO)			
	H1: Correctness (scores)		H2: Time Spent	
	Malay	English	Malay	English
Study 1	YES	YES	NO	NO
Study 2	YES	NO	NO	NO

There are some uncontrolled variables that may have affected the validity of these experimental results. One of these was the language that is the mother tongue of our subjects. In this study, most of our subjects were Malay native speakers and only a few were international students who came from other countries, such as China and the Middle East. The ability of these students to comprehend and analyse requirements written in Malay may be limited as compared to requirements written in English. Other uncontrollable variable that may affect the findings of this study are the level of knowledge of each individual, their cultural background and personality.

There is also a possibility that the level of difficulty or complexity of the task may have influenced the results and students may have spent more time working on the more difficult requirements set. We believe that further work is needed in order to investigate the impact that task complexity has upon PORE's effectiveness.In terms of the time taken to analyse English requirements, we found from both studies that the pair group spent a little longer than the solo group; however the results were not statistically significant. We speculate that there is be a greater amount of communication and discussion among paired group when compared to solo group but that this discussion leads to a solution as quickly as with individuals and with some evidence that this is typically a better solution. This is because two heads can have different understanding, thus they might suggest different ideas and solutions exploring the solution space more efficiently. Similar findings appear for both groups of students working on Malay requirements. We suggest future work should include a larger sample size to confirm or refute current findings.

7   Conclusions and Future Work

We have described our newly developed requirements engineering method called PORE. PORE is used together with the Essential Use Case model (EUC) to analyse multi-lingual requirements (i.e. those using English and Malay language). In this paper, we presented a study and its replication analysing a set of multi-lingual requirements using undergraduate students as subjects. The results obtained partially support our proposition that novice users exhibit better performance in term of correctness and time spent in analyzing multi-lingual requirements when working in pairs. We found that in both studies, the pair group outperformed the solo group for the Malay-based requirements task. For the English-based requirements, we found such supporting evidence in Study 1 only. Our results showed that there was no significant difference in terms of the time spent to analyze the tasks between pair and solo groups. We speculate that task complexity might play a role in influencing this result. We also anticipate that the study will give different findings if users are asked to extract an EUC model in a different language from the provided requirements language.

For future work, we plan to conduct more replications of our study with a larger number of students in Requirements Engineering and Software Engineering. We also plan to explore this approach with other modeling languages such as UML use case, sequence and class diagrams and then compare them with our findings. We also plan to use other languages to support our proposition that PORE is able to improve the quality of requirements models in analysing requirements in a multi-lingual context. We also intend to explore PORE usage in industry to identify the benefits of implementing this method in analysing requirements in real business activity. However, practitioners are more experienced as they have had professional training. Hence, we will use more complex requirements for this study. Finally, we plan to embark on a PORE study using our developed support tools, such as MEReq [1], contrasting it with the study reported here which has focused on a paper-based capture and analysis of multi-lingual requirements.

Acknowledgments. This research is funded by the Ministry of Higher Education Malaysia (MOHE), Universiti Teknikal Malaysia Melaka (UTeM) and Swinburne University of Technology. We also would like to acknowledge Pn. Nor Haslinda Ismail for allowing us to conduct the experiments in her class.

References

1. Kamalrudin, M., Grundy, J., Hosking, J.: Supporting requirements modelling in the Malay language using essential use cases. In: 2012 IEEE Symposium on Visual Languages and Human-Centric Computing (VL/HCC), pp. 153–156. IEEE (2012)
2. Regev, G., Wegmann, A.: Where do goals come from: The underlying principles of goal-oriented requirements engineering. In: Proceedings of the 13th IEEE International Conference on Requirements Engineering, pp. 353–362. IEEE (2005)
3. Goedicke, M., Herrmann, T.: A case for viewpoints and documents. In: Paech, B., Martell, C. (eds.) Monterey Workshop 2007. LNCS, vol. 5320, pp. 62–84. Springer, Heidelberg (2008)
4. Chen, Z., Ghose, A.: Web agents for requirements consistency management. In: Proceedings of the IEEE/WIC International Conference on Web Intelligence, WI 2003, pp. 710–713. IEEE (2003)
5. Albakry, K., Kamalrudin, M.: Pair analysis of requirements in software engineering education. In: 2011 5th Malaysian Conference in Software Engineering (MySEC), pp. 43–47. IEEE (2011)
6. Constantine, L.L., Lockwood, L.A.: Software for use: A practical guide to the models and methods of usage-centered design. Pearson Education (1999)
7. Biddle, R., Noble, J., Tempero, E.: Essential use cases and responsibility in object-oriented development. In: Australian Computer Science Communications, vol. 24(1), pp. 7–16. Australian Computer Society, Inc., Chicago (2002)
8. Constantine, L.L., Lockwood, L.A.: Structure and style in use cases for user interface design. Object Modeling and User Interface Design, 245–280 (2001)
9. Kamalrudin, M., Hosking, J., Grundy, J.: Improving requirements quality using essential use case interaction patterns. In: Proceedings of the 33rd International Conference on Software Engineering, pp. 531–540. ACM (2011)
10. Kamalrudin, M., Grundy, J.: Generating essential user interface prototypes to validate requirements. In: Proceedings of the 2011 26th IEEE/ACM International Conference on Automated Software Engineering, pp. 564–567. IEEE Computer Society (2011)
11. Kamalrudin, M., Grundy, J.: MaramaAI: Tool support for capturing requirement and checking the inconsistency. In: 21st Australian Software Engineering Conference. IEEE Computer society, Auckland (2010)
12. Bellini, E., Canfora, G., García, F., Piattini, M., Visaggio, C.A.: Pair designing as practice for enforcing and diffusing design knowledge. Journal of Software Maintenance and Evolution: Research and Practice 17(6), 401–423
13. Braught, G., Eby, L.M., Wahls, T.: The effects of pair-programming on individual programming skill. ACM SIGCSE Bulletin 40(1), 200–204 (2008)
14. Gehringer, E.F.: A pair-programming experiment in a non-programming course. In: Companion of the 18th Annual ACM SIGPLAN Conference on Object-Oriented Programming, Systems, Languages, and Applications, pp. 187–190. ACM (2003)

15. Sillitti, A., Succi, G., Vlasenko, J.: Understanding the impact of pair programming on developers attention: A case study on a large industrial experimentation. In: 2012 34th International Conference on Software Engineering (ICSE), pp. 1094–1101. IEEE (2012)
16. Canfora, G., Cimitile, A., Garcia, F., Piattini, M., Visaggio, C.A.: Evaluating performances of pair designing in industry. Journal of Systems and Software 80(8), 1317–1327 (2007)

8   Appendix: Requirements Used

Malay requirements:

1. *"Use Case"* bermula apabila pengguna menyatakan hasrat utk membuat tempahan untuk menyewa kereta.
2. Sistem bertanyakan tempat untuk mengambil dan menghantar tempahan besertakan tarikh dan masa untuk mengambil tempahan. Pengguna menyatakan tempat dan tarikh yang dikehendaki.
3. Sistem bertanyakan jenis kenderaan yang dikehendaki oleh pengguna. Pengguna menyatakan jenis kenderaan yang dikehendaki.
4. Sistem memaparkan semua kenderaan yang sesuai dengan tempat untuk mengambil kenderaan berdasarkan tarikh dan masa yang dikehendaki. Sekiranya, pengguna mengkehendaki maklumat lanjut tentang kenderaan yang spesifik, sistem memaparkan maklumat tersebut kepada pengguna.
5. Sekiranya pengguna memilih sebuah kenderaan untuk tempahan, sistem pun meminta maklumat untuk mengenalpasti pengguna (nama penuh, nombor telefon, alamat emel, alamat untuk kenalpasti,dll). Pengguna memberi maklumat yang dikehendaki.
6. Sistem memaparkan maklumat untuk keselamatan (cthnya,perlindungan kebinassan,insuran kemalangan peribadi) dan bertanyakan samada pengguna menerima atau menolak setiap produk. Pengguna menyatakan pilihannya.
7. Sekiranya, pengguna menyatakan hasratnya untuk "menerima tempahan", sistem akan memberitahu pengguna bahawa tempahannya sudah selesai dan memaparkan pengesahan tempahan kepada pengguna. *"Use case"* ini tamat apabila pengesahan tempahan telah ditunjukan kepada pengguna.

User Intention	System Responsibility
1. membuat pilihan	
	2. memberi pilihan
	2. memaparkan maklumat
	4. meminta pengesahan
5. memberi maklumat	
	6. mengesahkan tempahan

Fig. 3. The EUC Requirements model in the Malay language

English requirements:

1. The use case begin when the Client insert an ATM card. The system reads and validates the information on the card.
2. System prompts for pin. The client enters PIN. The system validates the PIN.
3. System asks which operation the client wishes to perform. Client selects "Cash withdrawal."
4. System request amounts. Client enters amount.
5. System request type. Client selects account type (checking, saving, credits)
6. The system communicates with the ATM network to validate account ID, PIN and availability of the amount requested.
7. The system asks the client whether he or she wants receipt. This step is performed only if there is paper left to print the receipt.
8. System asks the client to withdraw the card. Client withdraws card. (This is security measure to ensure that clients do not leave their cards in the machine.)
9. System dispenses the requested amount of cash.
10. System prints receipt.
11. Client receives cash
12. The use case ends.

User Intention	System Responsibility
1. Identify self	
	2. verify identity
	3. offer choices
4. choose	
	5. Dispense Cash
6. Take Cash	

Fig. 4. The EUC Requirements model in English language

An Empirical Cognitive Model of the Development
of Shared Understanding of Requirements

Jim Buchan

SERL, School of Computer & Mathematical Sciences, Auckland University of Technology,
Private Bag 92006, Auckland 1142, New Zealand
jim.buchan@aut.ac.nz

Abstract. It is well documented that customers and software development teams need to share and refine understanding of the requirements throughout the software development lifecycle. The development of this shared understanding is complex and error-prone however. Techniques and tools to support the development of a shared understanding of requirements (SUR) should be based on a clear conceptualization of the phenomenon, with a basis on relevant theory and analysis of observed practice. This study contributes to this with a detailed conceptualization of SUR development as sequence of group-level state transitions based on specializing the Team Mental Model construct. Furthermore it proposes a novel group-level cognitive model as the main result of an analysis of data collected from the observation of an Agile software development team over a period of several months. The initial high-level application of the model shows it has promise for providing new insights into supporting SUR development.

Keywords: Requirements understanding. Distributed cognition, Team Mental Model, shared cognition.

1   Introduction

There is a clear need for customers and software development teams to share and refine understanding of the client's requirements. Although activities related to this are most intense in the early phase of requirements discovery and validation, they continue throughout the software development lifecycle. Inadequate shared understanding of these requirements, or breakdowns in sharing this understanding from miscommunications and misunderstandings, can have a very high impact on requirements quality, project costs, development productivity, and application quality [1].

In software development, the development of shared understanding of requirements is most closely associated with Requirements Engineering (RE) activities. In [2], Sutcliffe describes RE as about "doing the right thing", as opposed to "doing things right" (the domain of software engineering). He points out that there is little value to a client in expertly implementing a software solution that does not address the right application domain problem. The challenge of RE is how to effectively and efficiently develop a consistent view of what the "right thing" is. In [3], Bubenko

D. Zowghi and Z. Jin (Eds.): APRES 2014, CCIS 432, pp. 165–179, 2014.
© Springer-Verlag Berlin Heidelberg 2014

emphasizes the importance of the interactions between the system production team with organizational actors (clients) to understand their "visions, intentions, and activities regarding their need for computer support." Development of high quality shared understanding of these needs and requirements will (iteratively) lead to a high quality solution design. It will provide solid foundation for reasoning and negotiating with clients about the characteristics of the desired system to be implemented.

In practice this is an inherently complex and challenging process, relying on a complex network of interactions and information flows. It involves people with divergent backgrounds and world-views, as well as the manipulation of a multitude of artifacts [4]. A consequence of this is that development of this shared understanding of the stakeholder requirements and the requirements of the goal software solution is often very time consuming, difficult to monitor, and prone to misunderstandings and miscommunications [4]. Some of the barriers and enablers related to the development of shared understanding of stakeholder requirements have been reported in our earlier work, confirming its complexity and challenge [5].

Given that (1) the development of a shared understanding of requirements (SUR) is a major aim of RE, (2) it is an enduring challenge and error-prone, due to its inherent complexity, and (3) it has a high impact on RE quality (and subsequent project success), there is a clear case for continuing empirical research in this area in order to understand the problems to address. Taking the lead from [6], in which it is observed that not enough research effort has been put into "advancing a theoretical or empirical understanding" of RE activities in practice and why they are so challenging, this paper advances a theory of SUR development in the context of RE based on an empirical study of practice. The aim is to deepen understanding of the practitioner's problem so that the challenges of SUR development can be explained. This provides a defendable basis for deciding on how to address them. In addition, such an empirically informed theory provides a foundation for evaluating existing and new techniques and tools.

This paper takes a cognitive view of SUR and develops an empirical model of the cognitive activities involved in the development of SUR. Reframing the challenges of SUR development from the perspective of this cognitive framework provides a mechanism for applying principles from cognition theory to SUR development. Analyzing the empirical cognitive model using theories of cognition provides a cognitive explanation of the challenges (and enablers) of SUR development. Application of cognitive principles leads to new (cognitively-based) strategies for addressing these challenges. This paper reports the development of the empirical cognitive model of SUR evolution that is based on the analysis of field data gathered from an extended, non-participatory observational case study of a team developing software in a commercial setting. The application of principles from cognition theory to this new cognitive model is introduced in this paper, but the detailed analysis and implications are to be reported in a future publication.

The next section introduces the notion of SUR as a (dynamic) state of shared cognition with group-level properties appropriated from the Team Mental Model construct. This idea is extended in section 3 to develop a high-level cognitive view of SUR development that identifies two phases of cognition: monitoring for gaps in

SUR, and addressing any gaps uncovered. This perspective shapes the subsequent data collection and the content and interaction analyses of the field data, which are described in section 4. The detailed model of the cognitive activities involved in SUR development that emerges from the data analyses is described and discussed in section 5. The conclusion and future work are presented in section 6.

2   SUR as Requirements-Focused Team Mental Models

In order to know what data to collect and how to analyze this data to understand the challenges of SUR development, the SUR construct needs to be clearly defined. The idea of a "shared" understanding implies that the understanding is inherently a group-level property, since it cannot be a property of an individual alone, but it is an ambiguous and contentious term. What cognitive structure is it that is shared between the individuals in a state of shared understanding? What is it that changes when shared understanding evolves? What does "shared" mean in this cognitive context? Identical? Consistent? Overlapping? Compatible? Following the lead of [7], who argue for the importance of being explicit about the meaning of "shared understanding" being adopted in related research, this section provides a working definition of the SUR construct before applying it to develop a high level model of SUR development in the next section.

A well-established construct from studies of team work is the Team Mental Model (TMM) [8], a form of shared cognition. In literature the TMM construct emerged to help understand how teams work in complex, dynamic and uncertain contexts. Empirical studies of team work have shown that high levels of convergence of team members' mental models are causally linked to high levels of team performance. The same goal and contextual characteristics apply to the study of collaborative software development. It is therefore reasonable to view SUR as a specialized form of TMM, with a requirements focus. Taking this view, a state of SUR (at some point in time) is attributed with the same properties as a TMM and so, adapting the description in [8], can be conceptualized in the following way.

(1) SUR is viewed as structured mental representations of knowledge and understanding about relevant aspects of requirements, that are similar in each team member [9].

(2) SUR is considered an enabler of a team's effectiveness by providing a mechanism for team members to be on the same page in the sense of describing, predicting and explaining requirements in a similar way [9].

(3) SUR is conceptualized as emerging states of the team with group-level properties shaped by the cognitive contribution of team members, but more than an aggregation of their individual requirements understanding [10].

(4) The content of SUR is shared knowledge structures that include declarative (what), procedural (how) and strategic (why) knowledge about requirements [9].

(5) The property of "sharedness" in SUR is conceptualized as cognitive similarity and is the degree to which team members' understanding of requirements are similar in the sense of having some common or overlapping (but not identical) knowledge structures that are consistent [11].

(6) SUR has the property of "accuracy", which refers to how closely the SUR aligns with the "true state of the world" [12].

The notion of a snapshot of SUR at some point in time as a state of shared cognition (similar mental models) with the specific group-level properties of content, "sharedness" and accuracy provides a useful conceptualization of the SUR construct. The question now is how is new SUR created? What is the mechanism that results in the team developing successively higher levels of useful shared understanding of the stakeholders' requirements? With the view of SUR as a state (set of properties) of the group at some point in time, it is natural to consider the emergence and development of shared understanding of requirements as a dynamic move through a sequence of states in "shared requirements understanding" space. Taking this view, a group's shared understanding of a requirement changes from one state to another as the group work jointly on improving and sharing this understanding. This idea is discussed in the next section to provide a high-level framework of SUR development that shapes the subsequent fieldwork and data analysis to develop a more detailed empirical model.

3   SUR Development as Dynamic State Transitions

Figure 1 presents model of SUR development based on the notion of SUR evolving in time from one state of SUR to another. Framing SUR development in this way highlights the notion of a gap between the two states of SUR and suggests that a mechanism is needed to address this gap. This identifies two main high-level activities in SUR development: (1) the collaborative uncovering of a gap (i.e. a level of insufficiency) in SUR, and (2) collaboratively addressing this gap to achieve a new state of SUR. The constant uncertainty in sufficiency of shared understanding discussed in literature is depicted by a constant gap in the current state of shared understanding and some idealized (unknowable) optimal state of shared understanding, where all necessary, sufficient understanding is shared and accurate for the tasks in hand at that point in time. Uncovering a gap in SUR is conceptualized as collaboratively designing a new goal state of SUR that highlights the shortcomings of the current state of SUR. Addressing this gap in SUR involves undertaking appropriate activities to achieve this new goal state. The model shows that the team may end up in a state of SUR (at time T2) with different properties to the envisioned goal state. The degree of change of SUR may vary depending on the time frame (T1 to T2).

In this specialized TMM model, the properties of a state of SUR that may change from one state to the next include: (1) content, such as the relevant application domain knowledge structures and level of detail that is similar across team members, (2) the level of consistency of the content between team members ("sharedness"), (3) the accuracy of the content (it's consistency with structure in the world). In this view, a gap in SUR could be relevant knowledge about a requirement that is: missing, lacks sufficient detail, is not adequately shared between team members, is inconsistent between team member, or is an error (inconsistent with the world).

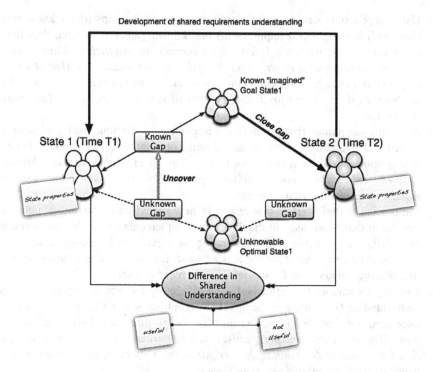

Fig. 1. SUR development as group-level state transitions

The model also captures the idea that the actual change in understanding transitioning from one state to the next may be useful to the team or not, in the sense that the new shared understanding of a requirement in state2 may end up being unimportant for the tasks at hand.

The model incorporates the notion of the constant pressure of the team to uncover "what they don't know they don't know" about the requirements and transform it into a known gap in their shared understanding. Then to address this gap through further collaborative effort to converge on a new negotiated state of shared understanding about a requirement.

In this model, ideal development of shared understanding would be a set of transitions where the imagined goal state, the idealized optimal state and the actual new state 2 (at time T2) are congruent, and the effort to develop shared understanding would be sufficient and necessary to transition to (ideal) state2.

Framing the development of SUR in the perspective of this model provides some new insights into potential high-level strategies for supporting the development of SUR and improving RE. These are listed below together with (in italics) related activities observed in the case study team.

(1) Creating sufficient opportunities to check for gaps in current shared understanding of a requirement. *Using an Agile RE process where these opportunities happen frequently as part of the way work is done without unacceptable extra cost.*

(2) Using appropriate strategies for transforming unknown gaps (don't know what they don't know about a requirement) into known gaps (know what they don't know about a requirement). *Uncovering assumptions, insufficient detail or missing knowledge about a requirement. Verifying representations of shared knowledge about a requirement against the real-world context of that requirement. Describing, explaining and predicting aspects of requirements in a collaborative team context.*

(3) Applying techniques that promote the alignment of the imagined goal state of shared understanding with the idealised actual optimal states. *Taking time to analyse options in framing a requirement, switching views of a requirement between problem and solution space, maintaining "memory" of previous shared understanding negotiations and outcomes.*

(4) Minimising wasteful effort that results in new shared understanding about a requirement that is not used in the design and implementation of that requirement. *Identifying and focusing on understanding the significant knowledge about a requirement and its context for the task at hand (and not wasting time on refining and sharing unimportant knowledge about a requirement).*

(5) Utilising techniques that effectively and efficiently recover from gaps in shared understanding (i.e. evolve to the next known optimal state). *Collaborative knowledge creation, knowledge seeking and knowledge filtering related to a requirement. Discussing multiple perspectives on a requirement to converge on a negotiated common understanding of a requirement. Observing or measuring real-world phenomena related to a requirement.*

In summary, the model in Figure 1 provides a high-level view of the mechanism of the development of SUR as a collaborative effort firstly to uncover gaps in SUR and then to recover from these gaps. In this TMM perspective states of SUR are distinguished by having different group-level properties of content, "sharedness" and accuracy, and gaps in SUR can be thought of as inadequacies in these for the tasks at hand. The TMM view of SUR suggests that collaborative activities such describing, explaining, and predicting aspects of requirements may uncover gaps in SUR and, by addressing these, create a new state of SUR. Finally the model suggests some high-level strategies for supporting the development of SUR, supported by observation of practitioners at work.

These initial insights are used to analyze the data gathered from the in-depth case study by focusing on identifying patterns of interaction during collaborative RE activities that involve uncovering a gap in SUR and recovering from this gap. The context of the case study, the research approach and the data collection and analyses, are discussed in the next section.

4   The Research Approach

The high-level aim of this study is to gain an understanding of how shared requirements understanding emerges, develops and is maintained in the context of a team undertaking collaborative software development, with a view to suggesting strategies for supporting its development. The research approach is to develop a detailed local account of the phenomenon by observing a team as they collaboratively develop software. This is achieved by analyzing step-by-step how such shared understanding develops from an initial lack of shared understanding to successively clearer shared understanding, as well as how misunderstandings are collaboratively uncovered and recovered from. The level of analysis is the team, as part of a distributed cognitive system. This is grounded in the TMM conceptualization as well as arguments put forward in [13] for a new science of Group Cognition, in the notion of a functional system as the computational engine of Distributed Cognition described in [14], and in the emergence of collective intelligence presented in [15]. The development of the cognitive model presented is based on thematic content [16] and interaction analyses [17] of the data. This approach is similar to that taken by Stahl ([18]) in his analyses of online data of teams solving mathematics problems where he emphasizes the centrality of team members' interactions to the development of group cognition.

4.1 The Case Study Organisation

A non-participative in-depth case study methodology was adopted [19] with data collected by the author over a 5-month period in a single case organization. The single case study research methodology is appropriate to the research aim of developing an in-depth understanding of the collaborative work of practitioners in their place of work, and all the complexity this involves [20]. The organization is in the Financial/Insurance sector and of the five organizations invited to participate, they were selected based on their large in-house software development program, their use of Agile methods, and their willingness to participate. The study involved observation of an in-house development team collaboratively developing software for both in-house and external clients using a customized Agile process. The project involved the improvement of existing systems and the implementation in sites geographically spread throughout New Zealand. Ethics approval for the research was granted and participants voluntarily signed consents to participate and be recorded, prior to the start of the study. Participants had the option of opting out of the study at any time during the study, although this situation did not arise.

The core team consisted of three business analysts (BA), two legacy system developers, a Java developer, two testers, a project manager (PM), and two Product Owners (PO). The POs had their own managerial jobs in addition to being POs for this project and did not sit in the team's work area. They were generally available for relevant meetings, however. The PM acted as a team mentor and liaised with higher management and other development teams doing related work, as well as doing some long-term resource and roadmap planning. Two subject matter experts (SMEs) from customer services and an architect were closely associated with the project, but not full-time, and did not sit in the team's work area. The SMEs were a source of requirements (from customers) and elaborated stories, described process constraints and argued for prioritization of certain requirements. The architect was often consulted (or stepped in) to provide advice regarding system and design constraints, business processes and explain historical decisions related to these. The architect had the authority to veto a user story or and its proposed implementation design. Other SMEs and managers were involved regularly (for example the National Sales manager, the Communications manager,) and others as-needed. There was no Scrum Master role identified, although one of the BAs had the role of Sprint Coordinator and often acted as Scrum Master. The experience level of the team members in using Agile practices varied from novice to expert, and some training in the implementation of Agile ideas was provided during the period of observation. In addition while I was there, the team had three afternoons set aside to discuss how to make Agile work for them in this project.

The development process followed a customized Agile process using a Scrum framework with 4-week sprints, daily stand-up Scrum meetings, sprint planning meetings, sprint reviews and retrospectives. Before each Sprint there were sprint planning meetings to elaborate, prioritize and estimate requirements. Planning poker was used to negotiate effort estimations of user stories. Scrum meetings were typically between 5 and 10 minutes and anyone could attend them, although only the core team and project stakeholders could speak. They kept track of who is talking by passing a ball around and generally postponed any lengthy discussions of problems identified until after the Scrum meeting.

User stories were the main representation of requirements and these were generally written on physical cards in the common "As a…I want…so that…" structure. The user stories were duplicated on an Excel spreadsheet, although included more detail than on the cards. Some team members also duplicated the user story cards in Jira. A story board was at the front of the work area, visible to the core development team members at all times. Scrum meetings took place in front of this board. The board had columns representing the development workflow during a sprint. Other information on the story board included: the sprint goal, a delivery roadmap, a vision statement, the definition of "done", and a sprint burn-down chart. The story board was personalized with a theme selected by the team and on the board team members were represented by pictorial avatars related to that theme. Acceptance tests were designed and run by the two testers who worked closely with the developers and BAs. Maintenance and support of implemented features were handed over to a separate department.

4.2   Data Collection

During the field work the author was stationed at a desk in the team's main work area and attended many of the team meetings, but did not participate in discussions. Fieldwork was interleaved with some data analysis and other academic duties outside the organization. Typically the fieldwork was between 10 and 30 hours per week depending on the researcher's other duties. The software development lifecycle observed in the study included pre-project work with some team members still involved in an earlier project, pre-sprint activities, and three full sprints of four weeks each. The data were collected in the form of extensive field notes (meeting details, observations and ideas), as well as photographs and electronic recordings (audio and some video) of many of the formal and informal meetings and the work area. The field notes, media files, and documents were cross-indexed so that all the data related to any specific meeting, meeting type, date, team role, or location could easily be identified. The audio and video recording were kept unobtrusive by discreetly using an iPad as the recording device. Important artifacts were collected or photographed. Around 100 hours of audio and video were collected and a subset of these was transcribed for further analysis. Meetings observed and recorded included meetings for story prioritization, story elaboration, story estimation, management updates, inter-team updates, sprint planning, roadmap planning, organizational strategic planning, retrospectives, process understanding, team problem solving, as well as daily standup meetings, retrospectives and informal ad hoc meetings. Occasionally participants were interviewed briefly after a meeting to clarify observed behavior, provide background information or clarify the meaning of unfamiliar language. The results of the interviews were generally noted in the field notes and occasionally recorded, typically for longer interviews.

4.3 Data Selection and Analysis

During the fieldwork episodes observed that were significant with respect to the development of shared requirements understanding were noted in the field notes. This typically included episodes in meetings where collaborative sense-making of requirements was significant: the collaborative understanding of a requirement was the focus of sustained effort; a gap in the shared understanding of a requirement was uncovered; the shared understanding of a requirement changed significantly; the shared understanding of a requirement was socialized to a wider group; the interactions with each other and artifacts were particularly rich. The media data (audio and in some cases video) associated with the meetings containing these significant episodes were then selected for further analysis based on a judgment of their significance. Other meetings and episodes were also selected for further analysis based on the aims of: good coverage of meeting types, temporal coverage of the full lifecycle of specific user stories, coverage of phases of sprints (e.g. start and end) and coverage of role involvement.

A selection of recorded audio and video episodes (16 hours of audio and 1 hour of videos) was selected for transcription and these transcriptions were imported in to an analytical tool, NVivo. Their inclusion for transcription and subsequent analysis was based on the high-level framework of analysis in Figure 1, with the aim of including examples of uncovering different types of gaps in shared understanding of requirements and addressing these gaps, in a variety of collaborative contexts. For a specific identified episode the entire meeting containing the episode was transcribed to ensure sufficient context for interpreting interactions and content meaning. For example, a user story related to providing a feature to synchronize the billing cycles of a customer for different products purchased at staggered times was particularly challenging, and all meetings in which the shared understanding of this user story gained the team's attention were transcribed. Studying the changes to the shared understanding of this user story and the interactions involved in these changes provided a rich dataset on a micro- and macro-level involving many team roles, artifacts, meeting types and types of collaborative cognition. The transcriptions of meetings involved transcribing dialog, identifying speakers consistently (from 2 to 12 speakers in any one meeting) and time-stamping significant episodes.

In order to understand the "content" property of a state of SUR and changes to this SUR content, a content analysis of the relevant data was performed, based on the inductive approach described in [16]. The data used includes the transcription of the episode dialog, as well as any related artifacts (e.g. story cards, spreadsheets, photographs of material developed on a white board, photographs of the story board, or videos of the episode). The aim of the content analysis was to develop a representation of the team's shared knowledge structure about a requirement (the SUR content) at that point in time. A concept map [21] was selected as a suitable representation since it depicts significant concepts and their relationships in a network structure. Following the method described in [16] the transcripts of the episodes were coded and categorized (using NVivo) to identify significant concepts and their relationships related to a requirement. This content analysis has a quite a restricted aim and inclusion of the "latent content" (e.g. silence, laughing, body language, tone) was considered unnecessary. The concept map was constructed with the aid of a software tool CMapTools [22]. The concept map developed was crosschecked against other shared artifacts representing shared understanding of that requirement at that time, and any appropriate additions or modifications to the knowledge structure represented in the concept map were made. The same exercise was repeated using data from an episode at a later time and the differences in the concept maps analyzed to identify the changes in content of the two states of SUR. Lack of space precludes presenting examples of the concept maps and their analysis. The technique shows good promise as a method of depicting a snapshot of the content of a state of SUR. The concept map also proved useful as a (dynamic) representation of the application domain knowledge relevant to a specific requirement. It is also interesting to note that the knowledge structure representing a state of SUR includes technical and process knowledge as well as application domain knowledge.

In order to develop the collaborative cognitive model of the development of SUR principles from interaction analysis [17] and content analysis [16] were used. Analysis of the data followed paths of both inductive and deductive reasoning as described in [16]. The framework presented in Figure 1 was used as a starting point to provide two general categories of cognitive activity, namely uncovering a gap (in SUR) and addressing that gap. This was used deductively to gather and code content according to these high-level categories. An inductive approach was taken with the interaction analysis. The interaction analysis is concerned with both the enactment and the content of the interactive dialog and how development of SUR is achieved through this participant interaction. The interactions, as sequences of actions and speech, were coded, grouped, categorized and abstracted to develop the cognitive model depicted in Figure 2. Twenty-nine types of cognitive interaction were initially identified and coded using NVivo, grouped into the two general categories of uncovering and addressing a gap in SUR, as previously discussed. (These include, for example, proposing, questioning, persuading, reinforcing, explaining, describing, comparing, abstracting, testing and deciding). These interaction code were grouped and categorized to provide a smaller subset of key categories that were then abstracted to the key cognitive tasks and decisions presented in Figure 2 and described in section 5. Another researcher crosschecked parts of this coding and abstraction process from the data. The empirical cognitive model of the development of SUR is presented in the next section, and a brief overview is given.

5   An Empirical Cognitive Model of SUR Development

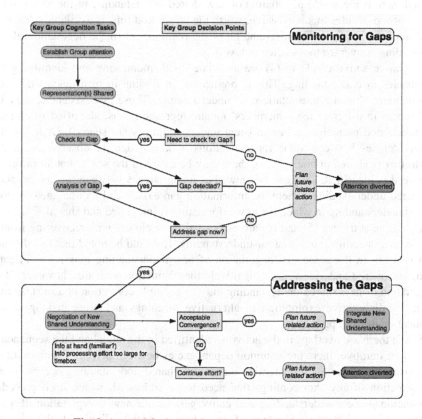

Fig. 2. An empirical cognitive model of SUR development

The model depicted in Figure 2 presents a high-level conceptual model of the group-level cognitive tasks involved in refining SUR. It is based on patterns of interaction identified from analysis of the collected data across many collaborative episodes and RE activities. It follows the form of the state-change model in Figure 1 in terms of describing the cognitive tasks involved in monitoring for gaps in SUR and addressing any uncovered gaps.

5.1   Collaborative Cognitive Tasks

The significant high-level cognitive tasks identified are: (1) establishment of the team's attention on some aspect of the shared understanding of a requirement; (2) the presentation (oral or visual) of some representation of the requirement within the horizon of observation of the group; (3) the group checking for some shortcomings in the current shared understanding of a requirement (a gap) (if the need for a check is agreed on); (4) deeper analysis of the nature of the gap and how to address it (if it is agreed there is a gap) (5) negotiation of new shared understanding of the requirement (if the group decides this is possible, worth the effort, and time is available); (6) integration of the new shared understanding of the requirement (if the negotiation of understanding converges to a sufficient level).

Cognitive activities (1) to (4) are associated with monitoring and identifying inadequacies in understanding. This is predicated on finding inconsistencies between two or more shared representations of understanding. These inconsistencies may be differences in different team members' mental representations, identified when they are articulated publicly (i.e. a consistent understanding is not shared). Or it may be inconsistencies between some representations of knowledge, or observation of the world that is shared publicly. Also, there may be a gap in the sense that an information need is identified. This can be viewed as inconsistency between the current state of shared understanding (where the information gap exists) and an imagined state of shared understanding in which the new information is integrated and shared.

Cognitive activities (5) and (6) are associated more closely with recovering from a gap in understanding, such as a misunderstanding. It should be noted that this distinction is fuzzy in the sense that negotiation of new understanding may result in gaps being uncovered and vice versa. Cognitively the distinction is clearer, however. The negotiation of new shared understanding may be a simple correction of a mistake to a lengthy collaborative exploration of alternative meanings and sense-making of the application domain problem.

While there are overlaps in the activities identified in the model and the sequencing was often iterative, there are common dependencies between activities. For example establishment of the team's attention on current shared understanding occurs before the detection of any shortcomings that need to be addressed, which itself precedes negotiation of new understanding and convergence on a new interpretation of a requirement. In addition, integration of new shared understanding with the existing shared understanding in the wider project context is generally dependent on sharing and agreement on some new or deeper understanding of a requirement. If the team decides (rightly or wrongly) that a requirement is not worth attention at that moment, then the other cognitive activities shown in Figure 2 will not occur. Similarly a shortcoming in shared understanding may NOT be detected (rightly or not), halting further consideration of that requirement. If, during exploration of alternative interpretations, an information need is detected that is not immediately available, then further exploration, negotiation and integration may be postponed until this new information is obtained and shared.

Each aspect of the depicted model may have varying levels of effort and formalism during different episodes of shared understanding refinement. For example, it may be a very quick and "intuitive" decision that a specific requirement needs attention (or not) or has a deficiency (or not). Or it may be the result of considerable cognitive effort and extended interaction. Exploration of alternative interpretations and sense-making may be rapid, based on the accepted intuition of experts in the team at the time, or it may involve extensive modelling and analysis, possibly with information sought from outside the immediate group at a later time. It may be that coordinated attention is established quickly because it expected by the group in a particular meeting, or that it takes considerable cognitive effort to coordinate attention because the participants have separate agendas.

5.2   Group Decision Points

There are a number of decision points throughout this model where continued effort on sharing understanding of a particular requirement may be diverted, perhaps with an agreed plan to come back to it in the future.

The model captures the observed situations where:

(1) The team does not detect a gap in shared understanding during the collaborative episode, even though there is a gap. This may be because the specific aspect of the requirement that has a gap is not given attention, or that the deficiency in shared understanding is not uncovered even after some effort checking for a gap.

(2) The team recognises a gap in shared understanding of a requirement, but defers effort in closing this gap to the future. This may be because the gap is out of scope, unimportant at this point in time, or they have run out of time in the meeting.

(3) A gap is detected and effort is made to close the gap by negotiating a new shared interpretation, however agreement cannot be reached during the collaborative episode. This may be due to non-convergence of views and unwillingness to compromise, or it is recognised that it will require an effort too long for the time available in the meeting and so it is postponed.

(4) A gap is detected and effort is made to close the gap by negotiating a new shared interpretation, however information needed to interpret the requirement at the level of detail is not at hand

The model in Figure 2 provides a framework to analyze the potential barriers and enablers of the development of shared understanding from a cognitive perspective. For example, what are the barriers and enabler of establishing the group's attention? With the assumption that attention is a limited cognitive resource and so attention to the shared understanding of a particular requirement is competing with other stimuli, it is important to understand how to minimize the effects of stimuli other than those directing attention related to the requirement in question. Principles from cognition theory also provide explanations for the coordination and propagation of attention in a group that could be useful [15].

This brief explanation and discussion of the empirical cognitive model developed shows its potential for further analysis using principles from cognition theory.

6   Conclusion and Future Work

This paper proposes a novel framework for studying the development of shared understanding of requirements as state changes in requirements-focused Team Mental Models. This, together with ideas from other related cognitive theories, is then used to inform the analysis of field data gathered from an extended, non-participatory observational case study of a team developing software in a commercial setting. This thematic interaction analysis results in a new model of the group-level cognitive tasks that contribute to the collaborative development of shared understanding of requirements. The model is discussed briefly and some new insights into the development of SUR are touched on. A more detailed description of the tasks depicted in the model and their implications for practitioners and researchers will be the subject of a follow-up paper. This will include identifying barriers and enablers of shared understanding of requirements development in light of this mode.

The next stage in the research is to analyze the cognitive model of Figure 2 using Hutchins' Distributed Cognition framework [14] to understand the "how and why" of the framework. Building on the work of [23] this will involve the application of cognitive principles to the model using a modified DiCoT framework as described in [24]. The results of this will then be used to explain the barriers and enablers of SUR development and suggest strategies for better supporting it.

References

1. Kamata, M.I., Tamai, T.: How Does Requirements Quality Relate to Project Success or Failure? Presented at the 15th IEEE International Requirements Engineering Conference RE 2007 (2007)
2. Sutcliffe, A.: User-Centred Requirements Engineering. Springer, London (2002)
3. Bubenko, J.A.: Challenges in requirements engineering. In: Proceedings of the Second IEEE International Symposium on Presented at the Requirements Engineering (1995)
4. Sadraei, E., Aurum, A., Beydoun, G., Paech, B.: A field study of the requirements engineering practice in Australian software industry. Requirements Eng. (2007)
5. Buchan, J., Ekadharmawan, C.H., MacDonell, S.G.: Insights into Domain Knowledge Sharing in Software Development Practice in SMEs. Presented at the APSEC 2009: Proceedings of the 2009 16th Asia-Pacific Software Engineering Conference (December 2009)
6. Hansen, S., Berente, N., Lyytinen, K.: Requirements in the 21st Century: Current Practice and Emerging Trends, 1–44 (2008)
7. Cannon-Bowers, J.A., Salas, E.: Reflection on shared cognition. Journal of Organizational Behavior 22, 195–202 (2007)
8. Mohammed, S., Ferzandi, L., Hamilton, K.: Metaphor No More: A 15-Year Review of the Team Mental Model Construct. Journal of Management 36, 876–910 (2010)
9. Rouse, W.B., Cannon-Bowers, J.A., Salas, E.: The role of mental models in team performance in complex systems. IEEE Transactions on Systems, Man and Cybernetics 22, 1296–1308 (1992)
10. Klimoski, R., Mohammed, S.: Team Mental Model: Construct or Metaphor? Journal of Management 20, 403–437 (1994)

11. Cannon-Bowers, J.A., Salas, E., Converse, S.A.: Shared mental models in expert team decision making. In: Castellan, J. (ed.) Current Issues in Individual and Group Decision Making (1993)
12. Edwards, B.D., Day, E.A., Arthur, W.J., Bell, S.T.: Relationships Among Team Ability Composition, Team Mental Models, and Team Performance. Journal of Applied Psychology 91, 727–736 (2006)
13. Stahl, G.: Group cognition. The MIT Press, Cambridge (2006)
14. Hutchins, E.: Cognition in the Wild. MIT Press, Cambridge (1995)
15. Heylighen, F., Heath, M., Van, F.: The Emergence of Distributed Cognition: A conceptual framework. Presented at the Collective Intentionality IV (2004)
16. Elo, S., Kyngäs, H.: The qualitative content analysis process. Journal of Advanced Nursing 62, 107–115 (2008)
17. Jordan, B., Henderson, A.: Interaction analysis: Foundations and practice. The Journal of the Learning Sciences 4, 39–103 (1995)
18. Stahl, G.: How to Study Group Cognition. In: Puntambekar, S., Erkens, G., Hmelo-Silver, C. (eds.) Computer-Supported Collaborative Learning Series, pp. 107–130. Springer (2011)
19. Runeson, P., Höst, M.: Guidelines for conducting and reporting case study research in software engineering. Empirical Software Engineering 14, 131–164 (2008)
20. Yin, R.K.: Case Study Research: Design and Methods. Sage Publications, Thousand Oaks (2003)
21. Cañas, A.J., Carff, R., Hill, G., Carvalho, M., Arguedas, M., Eskridge, T.C., et al.: Concept Maps: Integrating Knowledge and Information Visualization. Knowledge and Information Visualization, 205-219 (2005)
22. Cañas, A.J., Hill, G., Carff, R., Suri, N., Lott, J., Gómez, G., et al.: Cmaptools: A Knowledge Modeling and Sharing Environment. Paper presented at the First International. Conference on Concept Mapping Pamplona, Spain (2004)
23. Sharp, H., Robinson, H.: A Distributed Cognition Account of Mature XP Teams. In: Abrahamsson, P., Marchesi, M., Succi, G. (eds.) XP 2006. LNCS, vol. 4044, pp. 1–10. Springer, Heidelberg (2006)
24. Blandford, A., Furniss, D.: DiCoT: A Methodology for Applying Distributed Cognition to the Design of Teamworking Systems. In: Gilroy, S.W., Harrison, M.D. (eds.) DSV-IS 2005. LNCS, vol. 3941, pp. 26–38. Springer, Heidelberg (2006)

Evaluating the Cognitive Effectiveness of the Visual Syntax of Feature Diagrams

Mazin Saeed, Faisal Saleh, Sadiq Al-Insaif, and Mohamed El-Attar

King Fahd University of Petroleum and Minerals,
P.O. Box 5066, Dhahran 31261, Kingdom of Saudi Arabia
{Mazin,melattar}@kfupm.edu.sa, faisal86@me.com,
sadiq.alinsaif@gmail.com

Abstract. **[Context and Motivation]** Feature models are widely used in the Software Product Line (SPL) domain to capture and communicate the commonality and variability of features in a product line. Feature models contain feature diagrams that graphically depict features in a hierarchical form. **[Problem/Question]** Many research works have been devoted to enriching the visual syntax of feature diagrams to extend its expressiveness to capture additional types of semantics, however, there is a lack of research that evaluates the visual perception of feature models by its readers. Models serve a dual purpose: to brainstorm and communicate. A very sophisticated yet unreadable model is arguably useless. To date, there has not been a scientific evaluation of the cognitive effectiveness of the visual syntax of feature diagrams. **[Principle Ideas]** This paper presents a scientific evaluation of the cognitive effectiveness of feature diagrams. The evaluation approach is based on theory and empirical evidence mainly from the cognitive science field. **[Contribution]** The evaluation reveals drawbacks in the visual notation of feature diagrams. The paper concludes with some recommendations for improvement to remedy the identified flaws.

Keywords: Feature Models, Visual Syntax Evaluation, Software Product Lines.

1 Introduction

Software product line engineering is concerned with all development aspects for producing a set of related products that share more commonalities than variations [1]. Software product lines are emerging as an effective development paradigm that enables flexible response and mass customization [22]. Mass customization is about *"producing goods and services to meet individual customer's needs with near mass production efficiency"*, according to [26]. Mass customization is a critical factor for development success as traditional mass production lines no longer suffice market needs [22]. Software product line engineering enables mass customization in mass production development environments [1].

D. Zowghi and Z. Jin (Eds.): APRES 2014, CCIS 432, pp. 180–194, 2014.

Feature models are commonly used to document features in a software product line at different levels of abstractions. A feature model consists of one or more feature diagrams, composition rules, issues and decisions, and a system feature catalogue [11]. Features in a feature diagram are represented hierarchically with different relationships amongst features. Feature diagrams provide a visual summary of the features in a software product line. The visual language of feature diagrams was first introduced by Kang et al. in 1990 [11]. Similar to other diagrams, the core purpose of a feature diagram is to convey the mental model of a modeler to a reader of the model. If the reader of a model misreads or misinterprets it, then the intrinsic goal of the modeling exercise has failed. A misread or misinterpreted feature diagram can lead to the development of end products that do not possess the correct set of features as intended by its stakeholders. Since the introduction of feature diagrams in 1990, many research works have been devoted to enriching the visual syntax of feature models to extend its expressiveness to capture additional semantics and operations. While such stream of research provides valuable contributions to the field of software product line modeling, it is arguably equally as important to investigate the visual perception of the visual syntax by its readers. However, there lacks research that evaluate the cognitive effectiveness of feature diagrams. Cognitive effectiveness for software engineering notations is defined as *"the speed, ease and accuracy with which a representation can be processed by the human mind"* [15]. The most outstanding reason for neglecting this stream of research is the lack of a theoretical basis to conduct notation evaluations scientifically [14].

In 2009, Moody [14] documented nine principles for evaluating and designing cognitively effective notations in what is considered the seminal paper in the area of cognitive effectiveness evaluation in the software engineering field. The nine principles were compiled and collated from theory and empirical evidence mainly from the cognitive science field, amongst other fields. The nine principles focus on the visual perception of notations rather than their coverage of semantic constructs. In this paper, we introduce a new stream of research in the area of feature modeling by presenting the evaluation results of feature diagrams using the nine principles of cognitively effective notations as defined in [14]; a critical aspect of feature diagram modeling that has thus far been overlooked.

The remainder of this paper is organized as follows: Section 2 presents a brief background on feature diagrams. Section 3 provides the theoretical basis for evaluating the visual syntax of feature diagrams. Section 3 also presents the evaluation results of the feature diagram notation. Suggestions for improvements to the feature diagrams notation are presented in Section 4. A discussion of related works is presented in Section 5. Finally, Section 6 concludes and suggests future work.

2   Feature Diagrams Background

This section provides a brief background on feature diagrams. Due to the absence of a formal standard for feature diagrams, a review of the literature was required to identify the most state-of-the-art and canonical notational constructs. The evaluation presented in this paper is based on this derived set of notational constructs.

Feature diagrams made its first appearance in the literature as part of the Feature Oriented Domain Analysis (FODA) [11]. The original form of feature diagrams is shown in Figure 1.

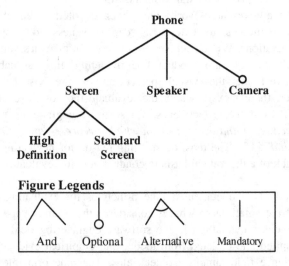

Fig. 1. The original FODA Feature Diagram

The notational set for feature diagrams has since been extended in many research works [1, 2, 4, 5, 6, 10, 12, 24] with the intention to increase the semantics covered by feature diagrams. Table 1 presents the notational set of feature diagrams and a brief definition of each symbol's semantics. Table 1 also shows the literature references where each symbol was first introduced. An example feature diagram that shows the entire notational set considered in this paper is shown in Figure 2. To the best of the authors' knowledge, the notational set described below is the most state-of-the-art and canonical notational constructs for feature diagrams.

Table 1. Feature diagrams semantics and symbols legend

Semantic	Symbol	Explanation	Ref.
Root or Concept		Symbolizes the software product line.	[12]
Feature		Descendent / child node of the root.	[12]
Mandatory		Feature should be implemented whenever its parent is selected in the product	[4]
Optional		Feature could be optionally implemented whenever its parent is selected in the product.	[11]
And		Children feature could be selected when its parent feature is selected in the product.	[11]
alternative		Exactly only one of the children could be selected when parent feature is selected in the product.	[11]
Or		One or more of the children could be selected when parent feature is selected in the product.	[4]
Require		If feature A requires feature B, the inclusion of A implies the inclusion of B.	[10]
Exclude		If feature A excludes feature B, both features cannot be part of the same product.	[10]
Feature cardinality	[n,m]	Defines number of instances of features that could be part of the product.	[6]
Group cardinality	<n,m>	Limiting the number of child features which could be part of the product when their parent is selected.	[6]
Attribute		An extension to a features to accommodate extra information	[2]
Dead Feature		Feature which can't be part of the product due to modeling anomaly.	[1]
Refer feature	▶	Special symbol for decomposing feature to sub-tree of features.	[5]
Generalization		Relationship between two features in which one of them is a generalization for the other.	[12]
Implementation		Relationship between two features in which one of them is an implementation for the other.	[12]

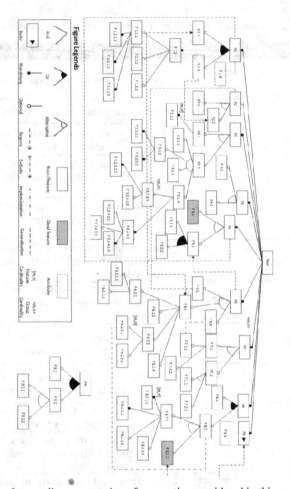

Fig. 2. The feature diagram notations & semantics considered in this paper

3   Evaluation of Feature Diagrams using the Principles for Cognitively Effective Visual Notations

This section provides the theoretical basis for evaluating the visual syntax of feature diagrams. Also in this section we present the results of evaluating the cognitive effectiveness of the visual syntax of feature diagrams. The evaluation is based on nine evidence-based principles that provide a theoretical basis for designing and evaluating a visual syntax. The nine principles defined in "Physics of Notation" [14] are: Semiotic Clarity, Perceptual Discriminability, Semantic Transparency, Complexity Management, Cognitive Integration, Visual Expressiveness, Dual Coding, Graphic Economy and Cognitive Fit (see Figure 3). Each subsection begins by explaining the principles (outlined in Figure 3) followed by the analysis of Feature Diagram using the specified principle.

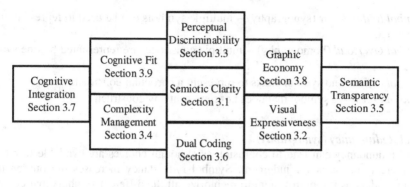

Fig. 3. The nine principles for cognitively effective visual notations

Evaluating the cognitive effectiveness of a visual notation requires the consideration of two "spaces": the problem space and the graphic space. The problem space is defined as the semantics that is supposed to be represented by a notation. This paper focuses on the cognitive effectiveness of feature diagrams. Formal semantics of a visual language is typically defined in its metamodel or a standardization document. However, for feature diagrams, no such metamodel or standardization document is available. Therefore, determining the problem space for feature diagrams can only be achieved by conducting a literature survey of feature diagrams in order to determine the relative semantics. For this task, we consulted a recently published comprehensive literature review (in 2010) on the analysis of feature models 20 years after their invention [1]. To the best knowledge of the authors, there are no newer publications in the literature that present new and canonical notations for feature diagrams. The graphic space or the "The Visual Alphabet" is the set of all potential graphical encodings (visual variables). According to [14, 15, 16], there are eight fundamental visual variables that can be used to encode semantics graphically. The eight visual variables are: shape, brightness, size, orientation, color, texture, horizontal and vertical positions. Notation designers can use combinations of these variables to create an infinite number of graphical symbols. As a prelude to evaluating the symbols, it is required to determine the visual variables used by each symbol and the values of each visual variable used. The third space that is conceptualized by the "Physics of Notations" [14] is the *Solution Space*. The solution space is concerned with choosing the most cognitively effective set of symbols produced out of the endless combinations from the graphic space. The solution space is considered for suggesting improvements to the suboptimal design aspects of feature diagrams (Section 4).

3.1   Semiotic Clarity

As shown in Figure 1, the principle of Semiotic Clarity is at the center of the nine principles for cognitively effective notations, which is an indication of its primacy. The principle states that a visual language should have a one-to-one mapping between its symbols and the constructs they represent. One or more of the following anomalies are possible if a notation does not have the desired a one-to-one mapping:

- *Symbol Redundancy* (synography) – multiple symbols can be used to represent one construct.
- *Symbol Overload* (homography) – multiple constructs are represented by one symbol.
- *Symbol deficit* – no symbol exists to represent a particular construct.
- *Symbol excess* – a symbol that does not represent any construct.

Symbol Redundancy (synography)

Symbol redundancy can lead to confusion as although choices are available to modelers, there is no basis for judgment. Symbol redundancy increases the burden on diagram readers as it requires them to memorize all the different symbols that can be used to represent one construct. Consequently, symbol redundancy increases the learning curve required to effectively use feature diagrams. However, feature diagrams do not contain such anomaly.

Symbol Overload (homography)

Only one case of symbol overload exists in feature diagrams. The box symbol is used to represent 2 different constructs: *root* and *feature*. However, the same shape is used in *dead feature*, *attribute* and *referring feature* with slight differences which can negatively affect Perceptual Discriminability (see section 3.3). Symbol overload is perhaps the most dangerous of the four anomalies as it directly leads to confusion since there is no means to visually determine the semantic that is conveyed by a particular symbol [14].

Symbol Deficit and Symbol Excess

No symbol excess has been identified in the notational set of feature diagrams as each symbol represents at most one semantic construct. The only case of symbol deficit is concerned with the specification of feature and group cardinalities. Cardinality is only conveyed via textual annotation. Which is discouraged by principle of Dual Coding (see section 3.6).

3.2   Visual Expressiveness

The principle of Visual Expressiveness for a notation is concerned with the number of visual variables used and the ranges of values used in each variable. The larger the number of visual variables a notation uses and the wider the ranges of values used in each variable, the more visually expressive the notation becomes. Feature diagrams only use two visual variables: *shape* and *brightness* (see Table 2). With respect to the shape variable, feature diagrams use three values; rectangles, tree-tops and lines. With respect to brightness, feature diagrams use three levels: white, black and grey for shape fills. For edges, there is solid and two types of dotted lines. Further details of feature diagrams' use of the graphic space is presented in Table 2. Overall, the visual syntax of feature diagrams makes very limited use of the graphic space and hence cannot be considered visually expressive.

Table 2. Visual expressiveness of the feature diagrams notation

Alphabet	Usage
Shape	3 levels which are 5 rectangles (boxes), 3 for tree-tops (and/or/alternative), 7 lines (mandatory, optional, generalization, implementation, require, exclude and attribute line).
Brightness	Low, high and medium, also dashed edges with two levels of dashes.

3.3   Perceptual Discriminability

The principle of Perceptual Discriminability refers to the ease by which symbols from one notational set can be differentiated from each other. This principle requires the language designers to increase the **visual distance** [14] between symbols within a notational set. Visual distance is increased by utilizing a large number of visual variables and utilizing a wider range of values for each variable. Larger visual distance between symbols allows them to be easily differentiated from each other. In this analysis we highlight symbols that are similar and thus have low levels of perceptual discriminability. Here similarity is determined by the *shape* variable since it has the greatest influence on cognition by humans [14]. Based on the findings from Section 3.2, three shape categories are identified: boxes, tree-tops and lines. A discussion of the perceptual discriminability of symbols within each shape category is presented below:

Boxes

This shape includes the *Root, feature, dead feature, refer feature* and *attribute* constructs. The brightness visual variable is the predominant variable used to distinguish symbols that use box shapes. The *root* and *feature* constructs are visually identical. *Dead features* are distinguishable by a grey color filling, while the *attribute* can be differentiated by a dotted border. The *refer feature* is distinguishable by a small "play-button" symbol inside the rectangle.

Tree-tops

This shape includes the *and*, *or*, and *alternative* decompositions. The *or* and *alternative decomposition* symbols can be differentiated by their brightness. The *or* and *alternative decomposition* symbols have black and white fillings, respectively. The *and decomposition* symbol can be differentiated by the absence of an upwards arc.

Lines

This shape includes the *mandatory, optional, generalization, implementation, require, exclude* and *attribute* line edges. The *generalization* and *attribute* symbols are identical while the *implementation* symbol is differentiated by coarse line brightness. The *require* and *exclude* symbols are very similar. The *require* symbol has one arrowhead at one end, while the *exclude* symbol has two arrow heads at both its ends. The *mandatory* and *optional* edges can be distinguished from each by their brightness. The *mandatory* and *optional* edges have black and white fillings, respectively.

It can be concluded that the visual syntax of feature diagrams overall suffers from low levels of perceptual discriminability.

3.4 Complexity Management

The principle of Complexity Management is described as *"the ability of a visual notation to represent information without overloading the human mind"* [14]. The presence of mechanisms that support the handling of complexity is essential for visual notations. High levels of complexity can severely limit model comprehension especially amongst novices. Complexity can be dealt with through modularization and hierarchical structuring. Modularity is a common practice to break down complexity by dividing large components into smaller ones. The notation of feature diagrams offers no mechanisms for complexity management via modularization. Hierarchal structuring manages complexity by providing representations of different levels of details and abstraction. Feature diagrams manage complexity by decomposing features into sub-features using the *refers* notation (hierarchal structuring).

3.5 Semantic Transparency

The principle of Semantic Transparency suggests the use of visual representations whose appearance is highly suggestive of their meaning. Using semantically transparent symbols reduces the cognitive load because they have built-in mnemonics: their meaning can be either perceived directly or easily learnt [9]. The visual syntax of feature diagrams cannot be considered as semantically transparent. Users of feature diagrams are required to memorize the semantics of the symbols prior to reading or creating feature diagrams as they cannot infer the meanings of symbols simply by viewing them.

3.6 Dual Coding

According to Dual Coding theory [20], using a combination of text and graphics together makes information presentation more obvious than using either on their own. Graphical and textual information are encoded in separate systems in working memory. Consequently, referential connections between the two systems in working memory are strengthened. It needs to be emphasized that text should not replace graphics and it certainly should not be used as the only means to differentiate between graphical symbols (textual differentiation). Text should be used to complement graphics as a form of redundant encoding [9, 21].

Feature diagrams make no use of text as a form of redundant encoding. However, text has been combined with symbols in [1] for the *require, exclude* and *extend* edges. While [24] showed the same dual coding for the *require* and *extend* edges. This use of dual coding however is not consistent amongst the feature diagram modeling literature and hence were not considered in this evaluation.

3.7   Cognitive Integration

The principle of Cognitive Integration refers to the ease of which a notation allows its reader to integrate different information from different diagrams. This is especially important when different diagrams are used to represent a system, which is often the case. There are two aspects of cognitive integration: conceptual and perceptual integration. Conceptual integration allows a reader to assemble a coherent mental representation of the system as a whole from separate diagrams. Perceptual integration is concerned with features in a notation that allow its reader to effectively navigate from one diagram to the next. Navigation in this sense requires a notation to have features that provide information about orientation, route choice, route monitoring and destination recognition.

Feature diagrams do not offer any such mechanisms that support either type of cognitive integration. In [23], the authors presented a mechanism that allows the integration of feature diagrams with other UML diagrams. However, the approach is based on a model transformation technique that maps metaclasses of a *proposed* metamodel for feature diagrams with metaclasses of UML diagrams. This means that the approach is based on the metaclasses (semantics) of feature diagrams rather than directly based on its visual notation.

3.8   Graphic Economy

The Graphic Economy principle refers the number of graphical symbols in a notation. A large number of symbols in a notation reduce its cognitive effectiveness. The literature has identified an upper limit of around six categories for the human ability to discriminate between perceptually distinct categories [13]. Although the number of symbols in feature diagrams is far greater than six, the number of perceptually distinct symbols was determined to be only 3: boxes, tree-tops and lines (see Section 3.3). It is advised to leverage the extra room identified from the assessment based on the Graphic Economy principle to resolve other issues in the notation, such as symbol overload (see Section 3.1). However, caution needs to be exercised when introducing new perceptually distinct symbols by utilizing the shape variable. As mentioned before, shape is the most influential visual variable. Studies have shown that humans recognize different shapes as constructs that have categorically different meanings [15]. For feature diagrams, the semantic constructs of a *root*, *feature*, *dead feature*, *attribute* and *referring feature*, are not categorically different. They are all types of features. Therefore, it will be ill advised to use different shapes to represent these different semantics. Not to be deterred by this limitation, perceptual discriminability can be increased via using additional visual variables, such as color, texture and size, and textual encoding as a form of redundant encoding.

3.9   Cognitive Fit

The principle of Cognitive Fit suggests the use different visual dialects for different tasks and audiences. Some dialects can be made complex and suitable for advanced users while other dialects can be simplified and made suitable for novices. However, feature diagrams have only one dialect, which is the case with most Software Engineering notations. Such drawback is referred to as "monolingualism" [14].

4   Recommendations and Suggestions

The results of the notation evaluation indicate a number of suboptimal design aspects in the visual syntax of feature diagrams, thus reducing its cognitive effectiveness. In this section we suggest some enhancements based on deficiencies identified in Section 3. A summary of the suggested improvements is presented in Table 3.

Symbol overload and perceptual discriminability are an outstanding issue in the notation of feature diagrams. Visual distance is increased in similar notations that categorized under boxes, tree-tops and edges. We suggest a new symbol for feature and group cardinality instead of only using textual annotation, these symbols will remove ambiguity and increase the cognitive effectiveness.

Table 3. Suggestions made to feature diagram notations

Semantic	Symbol.	Suggested	Justification
Root			Slightly changing the shape to increase the visual distance between the root and features
Feature			Change the color of the box according to its status if it's either mandatory or optional
Mandatory			Distance is increased by making mandatory colored red and optional with dark yellow. Mandatory is further distinguished by its strict symbols filled inside the circle
Optional			
And			Edges are colored to match the feature "mandatory – optional" status
alternative			Arc is colored dark yellow to match the "optionality" behavior. Edges are colored to match feature status (not necessary dark yellow)
Or			Arc sector is filled with dark yellow to indicate its optionality behavior found in optional and alternative. Edges are colored to match feature status (not necessary dark yellow)

Table 3. (*Continued*)

Semantic	Symbol.	Suggested	Justification
Require			Visual distance between require and exclude is increased by making require colored green and exclude blue, colors varies to avoid possible confusion with others edges of mandatory, optional, etc.
Exclude			
Feature cardinality	[n,m]	[m,n] [m,n]	Feature cardinality symbol, colors and shape are made to match feature mandatory or optional status introduced earlier
Group cardinality	<n,m>	<m,n> <m,n>	Group cardinality is differentiated by adding darker background on the effected features
Attribute of feature		Att.	Attribute is changed to note symbol
Dead Feature		Dead	Dead feature brightness now is low, additionally the skull symbol is introduced
Refer feature		Refer	Blue color of refer, underlined text and symbols are inspired by hyperlinks vogue
Generalization			End arrow is changed by increasing the arrowhead to increase the visual distance between the generalization and implementation
Implementation			End arrow is changed, by decreasing the arrowhead to increase visual distance between generalization and implementations. Also the dash line is changed to increase visual distance

5   Related Work

Shortly after the publication of Moody's seminal paper [14], the area of visual notation evaluation has been increasingly gaining attention in the research community. In this exertion; an initial evaluation of visual syntax of the goal-oriented modeling language i* has been presented in [16]. Based on the principles defined in [14], the authors of [16] highlighted a number of shortcomings in the visual syntax of i*. In their ensuing work, the authors suggested various improvements to improve the semantic transparency of the i* visual syntax. John Thomas et al. also used the principles to design and improve cognitively effective business decision models [25]. A general evaluation of the UML (Unified Modeling Language) [19] suite of diagrams was presented in [17]. The study reveals that the design of the visual syntax of UML diagrams is not cognitively effective due to a lack of attention to visual aspects. Class diagrams in particular have been singled out as having the worst visual representation amongst UML diagrams [17]. The authors suggested general improvements that are applicable to all diagrams in UML. An evaluation of the visual syntax of the BPMN (Business Process Modeling Notation) [18] modeling language is presented in [8]. The notation of BPMN is expected to be understood by all stakeholders, however, the results of the evaluation revealed several shortcomings that hamper its comprehension by a subset of its stakeholders. The authors provided suggestions to improve the cognitive effectiveness of BPMN. In [7], the visual notation of use case maps [3] was evaluated. The evaluation shed light on several common weaknesses. The authors provided suggestions for improvements [7]. To the best of the authors' knowledge, no evaluation of the visual syntax of feature diagrams based on Moody's principles was presented.

6   Conclusion and Future Work

The cognitive effectiveness of Software Engineering notations has long been a neglected area of research. The notation of feature diagrams is no exception. This paper presented a scientific evaluation of the visual syntax of feature diagrams. The evaluation revealed a number of suboptimal design aspects in the visual syntax of feature diagrams. A set of improvements were suggested that can potentially overcome these design drawbacks and improve the overall cognitive effectiveness of feature diagrams. The improvements were conjured based on the same principles used to assess the visual syntax.

The effectiveness of the improvements suggested in Section 4 is highly subjective unless empirical evidence can be provided. Therefore, future work can be directed towards conducting an empirical evaluation of the new notation to validate its cognitive effectiveness. In the experiment, the current notation will be used as a benchmark to compare against the new notation. Once empirical evidence becomes available, future work can be directed towards providing automation support for the new notation. Automation support will greatly aid its adoption by potential users. Many necessary research works have been conducted that evaluates visual notations in Software Engineering. However, many more notations remain to be assessed. The improvements suggested in the literature with respect to various Software Engineering notations lack empirical evidence. Empirical validation of these improvements will increase the confidence to apply and standardize changes to existing notations.

Acknowledgements. The authors would like to thank the Deanship of Scientific Research (DSR) at King Fahd University of Petroleum and Minerals (KFUPM) for funding this research.

References

1. Benavides, D., Segura, S., Ruiz-Cortés, A.: Automated Analysis of Feature Models 20 Years Later: A Literature Review. Information Systems 35(6), 615–636 (2010)
2. Benavides, D., Trinidad, P., Ruiz-Cortés, A.: Automated Reasoning on Feature Models. In: Pastor, Ó., Falcão e Cunha, J. (eds.) CAiSE 2005. LNCS, vol. 3520, pp. 491–503. Springer, Heidelberg (2005)
3. Buhr, R.J.A., Casselman, R.S.O.: Use Case Maps for Object-Oriented Systems. Prentice Hall, Upper Saddle River (1996)
4. Czarnecki, K., Eisenecker, U.W.: Components and Generative Programming. In: Nierstrasz, O., Lemoine, M. (eds.) ESEC/FSE 1999. LNCS, vol. 1687, pp. 2–19. Springer, Heidelberg (1999)
5. Czarnecki, K., Helsen, S.: Feature-Based Survey of Model Transformation Approaches. IBM 45(3), 621–645 (2006)
6. Czarnecki, K., Helsen, S., Eisenecker, U.: Formalizing Cardinality-Based Feature Models and their Specialization. Software Process: Improvement and Practice 10(1), 7–29 (2005)
7. Genon, N., Amyot, D., Heymans, P.: Analysing the Cognitive Effectiveness of the UCM Visual Notation. In: Kraemer, F.A., Herrmann, P. (eds.) SAM 2010. LNCS, vol. 6598, pp. 221–240. Springer, Heidelberg (2011)
8. Genon, N., Heymans, P., Amyot, D.: Analysing the Cognitive Effectiveness of the BPMN 2.0 Visual Notation. In: Malloy, B., Staab, S., van den Brand, M. (eds.) SLE 2010. LNCS, vol. 6563, pp. 377–396. Springer, Heidelberg (2011)
9. Goonetilleke, R.S., Shih, H.M., On, H.K., Fritsch, J.: Effects of Training and Representational Characteristics in Icon Design. International Journal of Human-Computer Studies 55(5), 741–760 (2001)
10. Griss, M.L., Favaro, J., d'Alessandro, M.: Integrating Feature Modeling with the RSEB. In: Proceedings of the Fifth International Conference on Software Reuse, pp. 76–85. IEEE (1998)
11. Kang, K.C., Cohen, S.G., Hess, J.A., Novak, W.E., Peterson, A.S.: Feature-Oriented Domain Analysis (FODA) Feasibility Study (1990)
12. Kang, K.C., Lee, J., Donohoe, P.: Feature-Oriented Product Line Engineering. IEEE Software 19(4), 58–65 (2002)
13. Miller, G.A.: The Magical Number Seven, plus or Minus Two: Some Limits on Our Capacity for Processing Information. Psychological Review 63(2), 81–97 (1956)
14. Moody, D.: The 'Physics' of Notations: Toward a Scientific Basis for Constructing Visual Notations in Software Engineering. IEEE Transactions on Software Engineering 35(6), 756–779 (2009)
15. Moody, D.L., Heymans, P., Matulevičius, R.: Visual Syntax Does Matter: Improving the Cognitive Effectiveness of the I* Visual Notation. Requirements Engineering 15(2), 141–75 (2010)
16. Moody, D.L., Heymans, P., Matulevičius, R.: Improving the Effectiveness of Visual Representations in Requirements Engineering: An Evaluation of I* Visual Syntax. IEEE, 171–180 (2009)
17. Moody, D., van Hillegersberg, J.: Evaluating the Visual Syntax of UML: An Analysis of the Cognitive Effectiveness of the UML Family of Diagrams. In: Gašević, D., Lämmel, R., Van Wyk, E. (eds.) SLE 2008. LNCS, vol. 5452, pp. 16–34. Springer, Heidelberg (2009)
18. OMG. Business Process Model and Notation (BPMN) Specification 2.0 V0.9.15. Object Management Group, Inc. (2009)
19. OMG. Unified Modeling Language, Version 2.4.1. Object Management Group, Inc. (2012)

20. Paivio, A.: Mental Representations: A Dual Coding Approach. Oxford University Press (1990)
21. Petre, M.: Why Looking Isn't Always Seeing: Readership Skills and Graphical Programming. Communications of the ACM 38(6), 33–44 (1995)
22. Pohl, K., Böckle, G., van der Linden, F.: Software Product Line Engineering Foundations, Principles, and Techniques. Springer, New York (2005)
23. Possompès, T., Dony, C., Huchard, M., Tibermacine, C.: Design of a UML profile for feature diagrams and its tooling implementation. In: Proceedings of the 23 International Conference on Software Engineering & Knowledge Engineering, pp. 693–698 (2011)
24. Schobbens, P., Heymans, P., Trigaux, J.-C.: Feature Diagrams: A Survey and a Formal Semantics. In: 14th IEEE International Conference on Requirements Engineering, pp. 139–148. IEEE (2006)
25. Thomas, J.C., Diament, J., Martino, J., Bellamy, R.K.E.: Using the 'Physics' of Notations to Analyze a Visual Representation of Business Decision Modeling. In: 2012 IEEE Symposium on Visual Languages and Human-Centric Computing (VL/HCC), pp. 41–44. IEEE (2012)
26. Tseng, M.M., Jiao, J.: Mass Customization. In: Handbook of Industrial Engineering. John Wiley & Sons, Inc. (2001)

The Role of Requirements Engineering Practices in Agile Development: An Empirical Study

Xinyu Wang[1], Liping Zhao[2], Ye Wang[3], and Jie Sun[4]

[1] College of Computer Science, Zhejiang University, China
wangxinyu@zju.edu.cn
[2] School of Computer Science, The University of Manchester, Manchester, U.K.
liping.zhao@manchester.ac.uk
[3] School of Computer Science and Information Engineering, Zhejiang Gongshang University, China
yewang@zjgsu.edu.cn
[4] Ningbo Institute of Technology, Zhejiang University, China
jiangbin@zju.edu.cn

Abstract. Requirements Engineering (RE) plays a fundamental role in all sorts of software development processes. Recently, agile software development has been growing in popularity. However, in contrast to the extensive research of RE in traditional software development, the role of RE in agile development has not yet been studied in depth. In this paper, we present a survey with three research questions to explore the treatment of RE in the practical agile development by investigating eight agile groups from four software development organizations. To answer the three research questions, we targeted at 108 participants with rich agile experiences and designed a questionnaire to collect their answers. Our survey shows that agile RE practices play a crucial role in agile development and they are an important prerequisite for projects' success though many agile methods advocate coding without waiting for formal requirements and design specifications.

Keywords: requirements engineering, agile software development, scrum, survey, requirements analysis.

1   Introduction

In recent years, agile software development grows in popularity as it tackles a lot of software development problems in dynamic contexts, such as Scrum [1], XP [2] and so on. The RE process runs through the whole agile development process [3]. Many RE practices have been proposed particularly for agile development [4][5]; however, little literature studies the role of agile RE practices and the attention paid to agile RE in practice from the empirical perspective.

In order to move a step towards understanding the role of RE practices in agile development, we conducted an empirical study to explore and explicate the RE process during a project in the context of agile software development. To ensure rigor, we designed this study by strictly following the survey process proposed in [6]. We have

D. Zowghi and Z. Jin (Eds.): APRES 2014, CCIS 432, pp. 195–209, 2014.

set out to answer the following research questions (RQs) through the survey in eight agile groups.

RQ1: Is agile RE performed as important as what agile practitioners thought?

RQ2: Which type of requirements (i.e. FRs and NFRs) are agile practitioners more concerned with?

RQ3: At each RE stage, what methods and tools do agile practitioners often use?

For RQ1, we attempt to investigate whether agile RE is performed different from what agile practitioners expected and what consequences it brings. RQ2 investigates if non-functional requirements (NFRs) are treated as important as functional requirements (FRs) in agile development. Finally, RQ3 aims to investigate what methods and tools agile practitioners usually use for requirements elicitation, requirements representation and documentation, and requirement management. In a word, RQ1 studies the overall role of agile RE played in agile development. RQ2 studies agile RE from the problem aspect whereas RQ3 studies agile RE practices from the solution aspect.

In the following sections, we will present the whole process of the survey and the conclusion we have obtained.

2   Research Method

2.1   Survey Design

Sampling. Before conducting a survey, we need to choose a relevant survey population. According to [7], "a prerequisite to sample selection is to define the target population as narrowly as possible". In this survey, therefore, the target population should be those who have participated or are participating in agile projects. In order to make the survey results as precise as possible, we selected agile practitioners from four different kinds of software development organizations which have established collaborations with the authors.

The four organizations that we chose have their own typical characteristics. The first company (C1) is the worldwide leader in networking that transforms how people connect, communicate and collaborate. It provides various kinds of products and services such as borderless networks, data center and virtualization, VOIP phones and gate-way systems, video conferencing and so on. The second company (C2) is a software development firm that specializes in information processing and management. It provides services to financial and health organizations worldwide. The third company (C3) is a multinational corporation that designs, develops and manufactures flash memory storage solutions and software. The fourth company (C4) is a software outsourcing company in China. It develops a large amount of services systems and provides different kinds of services for its customers around the world. We selected the survey sample from the software developers who either have been involved or are involved in agile projects.

According to the ability of the interviewer to gain access to the study subjects, we chose four agile groups (G1, G2, G3, G4) from C1, one group (G5) from C2, two groups (G6&G7) from C3 and one group (G8) from C4. The total number of participants from these groups is 108. Table 1 presents the detailed information of these eight groups is listed in whereas table 2 explains the primary role that the survey participants had in the studied projects.

Table 1. Participant and project details. Project duration is in week

Group ID	Group Members	Agile Method	Project Description	Domain	Project Duration	No. of Iteration
G1	Master x 1 BA x 1 Dev x 2 QA x 1	Scrum	Web Conference System Development	Network	40	20
G2	Master x 1 BA x 1 Dev x 3 QA x 2	Scrum	Online Training System Development	Network	28	14
G3	PO x 1 Designer x 1 Dev x 3 QA x 2	Scrum	Survey Report System development	Network	36	12
G4	PO x 1 Dev x 3 QA x 2	Scrum	Integration of Client Support Systems	Network	26	13
G5	Master x 1 BA x 2 Designer x 1 Dev x 6 QA x 4	Scrum	Fund management system reengineering	Finance	96	24
G6	Coach x 1 Designer x 1 Dev x 8 QA x 5	XP	SQL Database Development	Database	24	12
G7	Coach x 1 BA x 1 Designer x 2 Dev x 14 QA x 9	XP	Flash Optimization	Memory Storage	24	8
G8	Master x 1 BA x 3 Designer x 1 Dev x 13 QA x 9	Scrum	Barreled Water Ordering Management System Development	E-commerce	15	5

Survey Types Selection. There are many types of surveys, such as written survey, face-to-face survey, phone survey and mixed mode survey. Our survey is a mixed mode survey, which consists of two parts, including both face-to-face survey and written survey.

First, we had a face-to-face interview with agile coaches (Scrum Masters or XP Coaches), POs and BAs of each agile project on the development process of each project, specifically on the RE process. Then we sent our electronic questionnaire to all participants for their responses. The reason why we chose these two survey modes is that it would take a lot of time to face-to-face interview and impossible to let all group members involve in the interview. Another reason is that not all group members know well about the RE process. Therefore, it is not necessary to let all of them involve in the first-part interview.

Table 2. Participants summary in the survey

Participants' primary role	No. of participants
Agile Coach	6
Designer	6
BA	8
PO	2
Developer	52
QA	34
Total Number of Participants	108

2.2 Survey Instrument Development

At a fundamental level, one challenge in developing survey instrument is to design a coherent set of questions. As said by Fowler [8], "a good question is one that produces answers that are reliable and valid measures of something we want to describe".

In order to design an applicable questionnaire, we followed a set of three steps as proposed in [9]:

1) Compose a preliminary questionnaire which is relevant to the aforementioned three RQs,
2) Do a pilot interview to agile coaches, POs and BAs of each group and ask them to validate the questionnaire,
3) Implement changes in the questionnaire based on their feedback.

The questionnaire consists of both open-ended questions and close-ended questions. Open-ended questions allows the participants to freely present what they think about the RE practices in agile development, whereas close-ended questions require the respondent to choose from among a given set of responses, such as those provided by Likert scales. Compared to open-ended questions, close-ended questions are easiest for participants to answer and for researchers to analyze the data. Therefore, in order to save participants' time, close-ended questions account for more than 50% in our questionnaire.

2.3   Survey Execution

Face-to-Face Interview. We conducted open interviews with agile coaches, POs and BAs from the eight groups.

First, we asked agile coaches to give us a general introduction to their development process and then directly asked them what kind of problems they have encountered in their projects. Each interview session was between 1 hour and 2 hours. This interview provided an overview for us to understand how each project executed and what kind of role agile RE played at each stage.

Second, we asked BAs to describe agile RE process in their projects and what kind of problems they have encountered during agile RE. As some POs were also responsible for requirements analysis, we also interview POs in this round interview. We use an umbrella name "Requirements Analyst (RA)" for both BAs and POs. The interview questions focused on the participants' experiences of working with agile RE practices and in particular around their roles on agile projects. For example, we asked about the challenges RAs faced in projects and the strategies they used to overcome them. The answers varied with the individual participants. This process usually took 30 to 60 minutes.

Throughout each interview session, the interviewer took handwritten notes. These notes helped us to discover questions from what interviewees stated.

Finally, the interviewer and the interviewee walked through the questionnaire which served to guide the second-part survey.

Written Survey. The questionnaire was composed of four parts, each of which corresponds to a research question except the first part. The first part aims to investigate the background of the participant including his/her role in the agile project, project size, agile method and so on. Answers in this part have been summarized in Table 1 and Table 2.

The second part, corresponding to RQ1, consists of four questions: the first question discussed the importance of agile RE that each participant considered whereas the second question discussed the actual effort paid by the participants with respect to the RE practices of agile projects. The third and fourth question investigated the problems or difficulties that different groups have encountered. The third part corresponds to RQ2 and discusses the degree of participants' concern on different types of requirements in different agile development phases. The last part corresponds to RQ3 and includes questions related to the agile RE methods and tools. Questions in the last part can be categorized into four classes: requirements elicitation, requirements representation and documentation, requirements analysis and requirements management. The final questionnaire is shown in Table 3. Some questions have multiple options.

3   Results

Table 3. Questions in the survey. Questions specific for RAs are marked as *

Questions
RQ1: Is agile RE performed as important as what agile practitioners thought?
Q1: How important do you think agile RE is?
Q2: How many RAs are there in your project?
Q3: What's the percentage of delayed iterations in your project?
Q4: Which development activity(s) usually causes difficulties in your project?
RQ2: Which type of requirements (i.e. FRs and NFRs) are agile practitioners more concerned with?
Q5: Which type of requirement costs more effort in your project?
Q6: How much attention is paid to FRs in the following development activities – project planning, requirements analysis, design, coding, and testing? Please sort the five activities from the most to the least.
Q7: How much attention is paid to NFRs (e.g. performance, security, reliability, etc) in the following development activities – project planning, requirements analysis, design, coding, and testing? Please sort the five activities from the most to the least.
Q8: Are customers satisfied with the quality of the system your group developed?
RQ3: At each RE stage, what methods and tools do agile practitioners often use?
Q9: How often do you communicate with customers to discuss requirements?*
Q10: What type of method do you use to elicit requirements? *
Q11: Why do you choose the above method(s) to elicit requirements?*
Q12: Do you use any tools to elicit requirements? What are they?*
Q13: What type of methods do you use to describe requirements? *
Q14: Do you use any tools to document requirements? What are they? *
Q15: What method do you use to find any inconsistency, incorrectness or incompleteness in the requirements you captured from the customer? *
Q16: Do you pay a lot of attention to the dependency among requirements, such as the dependency between two FRs or between NFRs? If yes, how do you maintain these dependencies? *
Q17: What method do you use to manage requirements changes? *
Q18: Why do you choose the above method to manage requirements changes? *
Q19: Do you use any tools to manage requirements? What are they? *

3.1   RQ1: Is Agile RE Performed as Important as What Agile Practitioners Thought?

According to the 108 responses, we obtained the answer for Q1 as shown in Figure 1. More than 90% participants considered RE important, amongst which 85.19% considered it very important. None of the participants denied its importance. Therefore in most agile practitioners' minds, agile RE is undoubtedly crucial for the success of their projects despite their role.

To investigate how many efforts have been devoted in agile RE practices, we designed Q2 and Figure 2 shows the result of this question in groups. All of G1, G2, G3, G4, G6 and G7 had one RA, whereas G5 assigned two RAs and G8 assigned three. Noted that for G3, G4, G6 and G7, they didn't particularly assign one person to do the

RA job; instead, their coach plays the role of RA. The percentage of RAs in total number was from 3.7% to 20%. Most groups severely cut the resources for agile RE for the purpose of cost saving. In the face-to-face interview, we learned that all agile coaches preferred to assign more resources to coding and testing though they have encountered many problems during requirements analysis. We can see that most agile RE does not get due attention as it was thought before.

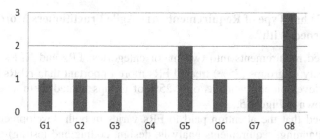

Fig. 1. The importance of RE in agile practitioners' minds

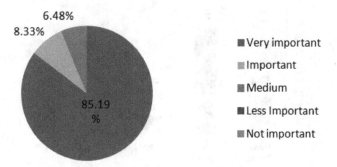

Fig. 2. The number of people assigned to RE in agile projects

In order to obtain the delay rate of each group, we designed Q3 and the results are shown as Fig. 3. Of all the eight groups, G6, G7 and G8 have much higher delay rates which respectively are 50%, 41.67% and 40%, follow by G3, G4 and G5 whose delay rates respectively are 19.44%, 21.43% and 25%. G1 and G2 have the lowest delay rates which respectively are 5% and 7.69%.

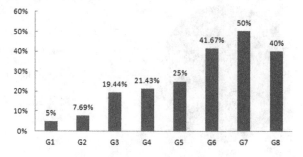

Fig. 3. The delay rate of each group

Figure 4 shows the reasons that cause delays in the previous question. In all the five development activities, requirements analysis is considered by 78 participants as the most crucial factor that causes delays, followed by the factor of project planning as preferred by 42 participates. The other three development activities only receive small amounts of blame: 16 participants ascribe delays to the testing stags; 13 participants ascribe delays to design; 7 participants ascribe delays to coding.

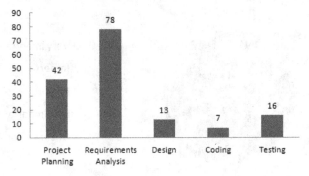

Fig. 4. The delay rate of each group

3.2   RQ2: What Type of Requirements Are Agile Practitioners More Concerned With?

We categorized requirements into two major categories: FRs and NFRs. We found that the majority of groups (75%) treated FRs more important than NFRs in the context of agile development, whereas only 25% of groups treated them as equally important, as shown in Figure 5.

We observed that the attention paid to FRs varies in both development activities (i.e. project planning, requirements analysis, design, coding and testing) and groups. The participants listed five activities in an order of most to least attention that have been paid to FRs, which is shown in Table 4. Most groups assessed efforts in terms of function points (FPs) of system requirements; as a result, they paid most attention to FRs at the beginning of the project, i.e. at the stage of project planning. There is no doubt that almost all groups put "Requirements Analysis" in the first or second place as the aim of this activity is to analyze FRs. Table 4 tells us that every group paid less attention to FRs when coding and testing.

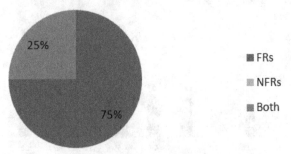

Fig. 5. NFRs compared to FRs

Table 4. The degree of attention paid to FRs in terms of development phases and groups

Group ID	Attention paid to FRs in the order of development phases
G1	Project Planning, Requirements Analysis, Testing, Design, Coding
G2	Requirements analysis, Design, Project Planning, Coding & Testing
G3	Requirements Analysis, Testing, Design, Project Planning, Coding
G4	Project Planning, Requirements Analysis, Testing, Design, Coding
G5	Requirements analysis, Project Planning, Design, Testing, Coding
G6	Project Planning, Requirements Analysis, Design, Testing, Coding
G7	Project Planning, Requirements Analysis, Design, Coding, Testing
G8	Project Planning, Requirements Analysis, Design, Coding, Testing

For NFRs, the degree of attention is significantly different from what was obtained for FRs. Table 5 shows the result. For example, they paid more attention to NFRs when designing and testing than that they paid to FRs. Most groups didn't consider NFRs at the beginning of their projects as their customers only concerned FRs; instead, these groups started to deal with NFRs from the stage of design. Testing is the only way to evaluate whether the system meets NFRs, therefore, it is also necessary to pay a lot of attention to NFRs during testing.

Table 5. The degree of attention paid to NFRs in terms of development phases and groups

Group ID	Attention paid to NFRs in the order of development phases
G1	Requirements Analysis, Testing, Design, Coding, Project Planning
G2	Project Planning, Design, Testing, Requirements analysis, Coding
G3	Requirements Analysis, Testing, Design, Coding, Project Planning
G4	Project Planning, Requirements Analysis, Design, Coding, Testing
G5	Design, Requirements analysis, Project Planning, Coding, Testing
G6	Design, Requirements Analysis, Testing, Coding, Project Planning
G7	Testing, Requirements Analysis, Project Planning, Design, Coding
G8	Design, Coding, Testing, Project Planning, Requirements Analysis

To obtain the customer satisfaction of system quality, we designed Q8. The results are as follows: Customers of G1, G3 and G4 are highly satisfied with their system quality; Customers of G5, G6 and G7 are satisfied with their system quality; finally customers of G2 and G8 are dissatisfied with their system quality.

3.3 RQ3: What Methods and Tools Do Agile Practitioners Often Use?

Questions for RQ3 are only left particularly for RAs to answer, so as to conduct an in-depth investigation on RE practices including both methods and tools.

Requirements Elicitation. In agile groups, 45.45% of RAs discussed requirements with customers once a week, 20.37% twice a week, 16.67% communicated with customers once they needed (more frequent than once a week) and only 9.09% communicated with their customers every day (see Figure 6).

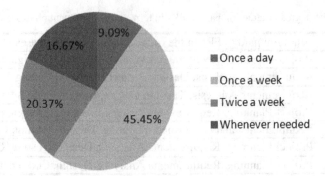

Fig. 6. The frequency of requirements elicitation from customers

We also investigated the common methods that were used by RAs to elicit requirements and the reason why RAs preferred those methods. From Figure 7, interview and user story were the most frequently used methods (More than 90% RAs used them). As interview is as means of face-to-face communication with customers, RAs found it *"quite simple and efficient to capture requirements from customers"*. Compared to other methods, interview is more efficient and direct; moreover, it is easy to use for most RAs. Since most customers cannot define their requirements correctly, RAs adopted user story to *"refine vague requirements into more precise and detailed ones"*.

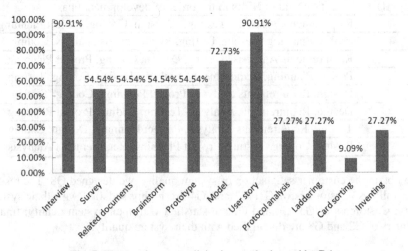

Fig. 7. The requirements elicitation methods used by RAs

In many RE surveys, modeling was usually mentioned by RE practitioners to elicit requirements, such as business process modeling [10], goal modeling [11]. In our survey, modeling was the second frequently used method for requirements elicitation. 72.73% of RAs preferred to use models as *"models can show their ideas easily and quickly"*.

Face-to-face survey [12] and prototyping [13] were also preferred by a lot of RAs due to the ability that they can "*enable in-depth understanding between stakeholders*". Brainstorming was popular in agile groups as it can "*involve as many stakeholders as possible to participate in the requirements discussion and clarification*". As G5 aimed to reengineer a legacy system, analyzing existing documents was the most important way to retrieve requirements.

Compared to the aforementioned approaches, knowledge acquisition methods [14] such as protocol analysis, laddering, card sorting and inventing requirements were less often used by RAs. The reason is that only a few RAs are familiar with these methods.

Based on the above methods, three types of tools were often used by RAs: 1) Microsoft Word and Excel were used for interviewing, user story authoring and survey; 2) Visual [15], Enterprise Architect [16] and other UML modeling tools were used when RAs wanted to build models; 3) Balsamiq Mockup [17] and Photoshop [18] were used for prototyping.

Requirements Representation and Documentation. According to our interview to the RAs, we summarized six frequently used methods for representing and documenting requirements. The usage percentage of each method is shown in Figure 8.

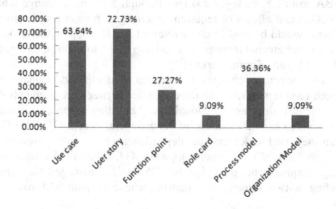

Fig. 8. The requirements representation methods used by RAs

This figure reveals that both use case and user story are the most preferred methods. This is not surprising because these two methods are very well known due to their prominent comprehensibility, decomposability and interactivity. Additionally, function point and process model are also frequently used for specific intensions. For example, function point is capable of expressing system internal functions; process model is a necessity for describing the requirements of process-intensive systems. Sometimes, role card and organization model are also used as the peripheral support for requirements representation and documentation.

To facilitate the representation and documentation of requirements, tools are commonly leveraged. The most popular ones are Microsoft Word and ScrumWorks [19]. Others such as Wikipage [20], Testlink [21], Microsoft Excel and Microsoft Visio are also utilized by some QAs as auxiliary tools.

Requirements Analysis. Another responsibility of RAs is to discover and handle inconsistent, incorrect and incomplete requirements (i.e. requirements defects) captured from customers. According to the responses from RAs, there are several ways helping them to discover requirements defects.

For example, the common method they used is comparison. They designed a set of scenarios and then compared the process flows of these scenarios to check the inconsistency and incompleteness between requirements. Another way is to confirm the existing requirements with customers and experts. Generally, customers are more sensitive to requirements incorrectness than BAs as they are more familiar with the business. However, some requirements defects cannot be discovered at the stage of requirements analysis. In some cases, RAs asked developers and QAs for their helps to find out these defects.

Requirements Management. In agile software development, the changes of requirements and the dependencies between requirements are so frequent that they need to be maintained and managed.

Requirement changes are usually managed by several ways in agile groups. For example, BAs from G5 managed changes through highlighting them in the requirement documentations and also maintained documentation versions through SVN [22]. In doing so, they make requirements easy to trace and the whole process more time-saving. The BA from G8 managed changes through building a change table, which consisted of details and effects of requirement changes, project risks, solution plans. All of these items would be confirmed by relevant stakeholders. Other project groups employed some requirements management tools to assist to manage changes, such as JIRA [23], Rally [24] and ScrumWorks [19].

In addition to requirement changes, it is crucial to identify and manage the dependencies between requirements, as the dependencies between requirements determine the order to implement different functionalities. According to the questionnaire, most groups take actions to handle requirement dependencies except G2. Both G1 and G8 mentioned that they tried to decrease the dependencies between requirements through coupling business-relevant requirements together. G3, G4 and G5 marked the dependencies through requirements prioritization. G6 and G7 managed the dependencies through building a two dimensional matrix, whose column and row were both requirements.

4   Discussion and Threats

4.1   Discussion of Results

Little literature studies agile RE practices. Our study looked at agile RE practitioners from three different aspects and revealed a few findings as below:

1. With respect to the overall project management aspect, we observed that the importance of agile RE practices deviated from what agile practitioners thought in their minds. Although the majority of agile groups acknowledged the importance of RE in agile development, very few resources were allocated to capture and analyze customers' requirements, which results in constant requirement changes from

customers. Correlating to the interview with agile coaches from each group, we found that project delays usually occurred in G6, G7 and G8 and their agile coaches admitted that the vague, incomplete and ambiguous requirements were the major reason for the project delays, whereas in other groups, project delays were less common. It is interesting to find that the proportion of the number of RAs in these groups was between 14% and 20% while the proportion in G6, G7 and G8 was under 10%. This study suggests that agile practitioners should carefully leverage the time cost and labor cost of RE in their projects.

2. With respect to the problem aspect, the study found that most agile practitioners were more concerned with FRs than NFRs. Only a few part of them treated FRs and NFRs equally. The major reason was that customers usually cannot give an accurate definition of NFRs. They didn't know how they expected the system to be performed. They cannot tell agile developers where they did not satisfied until they started to use the system. As a result, agile practitioners didn't treat NFRs seriously in the first couples of iterations. It is interesting to notice that FRs got more attention at the stage of project planning and requirements analysis whereas NFRs were just the opposite, i.e. at the stage of design and testing. However, the quality of systems developed by those groups that didn't pay much attention to NFRs at the stage of requirements analysis was not satisfying. The quality issues were hurriedly fixed in the last several iterations according to the feedback from customers. This finding suggests that agile practitioners should not ignore NFRs analysis at the beginning of their projects.

3. With respect to the solution aspect, we observed that in agile practices, most RAs discussed requirements with customers very often, about 80% of RAs got in touch with their customers at least once a week, 100% at least twice a week. Two reasons led to this situation: 1) In each iteration, new requirements need to be implemented and it is necessary to confirm new requirements with customers before implementation; 2) RAs wanted to capture requirement changes as early as possible in order to reduce the total cost brought by project changes. Interview, user story, modeling and prototyping are the most widely used requirements elicitation methods, whereas user story and use cases are the most widely used requirements representation methods. We also observed that both customers and RAs preferred to use natural-language-based methods to describe requirements due to the fact that such methods are simple and intuitive. Yet, these methods will generate a large number of documents which make them difficult to manage. This finding suggests that agile RE practices should promote requirements management tools in order to manage a large set of requirements, prioritizations and the dependencies between requirements.

4.2   Threats to Validity

We evaluated the possible threats to validity of the results we have obtained from the empirical study.

First, the level of agile practitioners' experience is one possible threat which may affect the results. We believe this threat to validity is small as we selected experienced agile practitioners from different agile groups. All these agile practitioners have participated in at least one agile project. Second, we acknowledge the possible risks that answering all questions may be time-consuming for the participants. In order to save their time, we substituted a lot of close-ended questions for open-ended questions. However, we admit that there is another threat as we were noticed that close-ended questions may restrict the scope of answers to those questions. Besides, the list of questions we present is not comprehensive, which needs improvement in the future.

5   Conclusions

Our study reveals that RE practices play a crucial role in agile development. Although many agile methods advocate coding without waiting for formal requirements and design specifications, RE is still an important prerequisite for the success of projects. The value of the work presented in this paper is the identification of a set of following findings about RE practices for agile practitioners.

Lack of concern on RE in practice. Many project delays were caused by insufficient communication with customers or shortage of RE resources. The role of agile RE practices has been acknowledged by most agile practitioners, nevertheless, they didn't make an even resource allocation due to the project cost. Therefore, it is recommended that agile groups should carefully leverage the resources assigned to RE and the costs.

Lack of concern on NFRs. Agile practitioners should pay more attention to NFRs at the beginning of the project, rather than leave them to design or coding. We suggest them to adopt some methods such as NFR framework for NFRs analysis.

Preference for agile RE practices. In agile RE practices, the participants identified that interviewing and user story are the most important requirements elicitation practices whereas user story and use case are the most widely used requirements representation practices. In order to rapidly capture requirement changes from customers, it is important to intensively communicate with customers. Although agile RE differs from traditional RE in that it takes an iterative discovery approach, many traditional RE practices are still applicable in agile development such as use case, modeling and prototyping and so on.

Acknowledgements. This work has been supported by the National Natural Science Foundation of China under Grant No. 61103032. We also would like to thank those who participated in our study and gave us a lot of valuable feedbacks.

References

1. Schwaber, K., Beedle, M.: Agile Software Development with Scrum. Prentice Hall PTR (2001)
2. Beck, K.: Extreme Programming Explained: Embrace Change. Addison-Wesley (1999)

3. Paetsch, F., Eberlein, A., Maurer, F.: Requirements Engineering and Agile Software Development. In: 12th IEEE International Workshops on Enabling Technologies: Infrastructure for Collaborative Enterprises, pp. 308–313. IEEE Press, New York (2003)
4. Cao, L., Ramesh, B.: Agile Requirements Engineering Practices: An Empirical Study. IEEE Software, 60–67 (January/February 2008)
5. Ramesh, B., Cao, L.: Agile Requirements Engineering Practices and Challenges: An Empirical Study. Information Systems Journal 20, 449–480 (2010)
6. Glasow, P.: Fundamentals of Survey Research Methodology (2005), http://www33.homepage.villanova.edu/edward.fierros/pdf/Glasow.pdf
7. Salant, P., Dillman, D.A.: How to Conduct Your Own Survey. John Wiley and Sons (1994)
8. Fowler, J., Floyd, J.: Improving Survey Questions: Design and evaluation. Sage Publications (1995)
9. Racheva, Z., Daneva, M., Sikkel, K., Wieringa, R., Herrmann, A.: Do we Know Enough about Requirements Prioritization in Agile Projects: Insights from a Case Study. In: 18th International Requirements Engineering Conferences, pp. 147–156. ACM Press, New York (2010)
10. Becker, J., Rosemann, M., von Uthmann, C.: Guidelines of Business Process Modeling. In: van der Aalst, W.M.P., Desel, J., Oberweis, A. (eds.) Business Process Management. LNCS, vol. 1806, pp. 30–49. Springer, Heidelberg (2000)
11. Rolland, C., Souveyet, C., Achour, C.B.: Guiding Goal Modeling Using Scenarios. IEEE Transactions on Software Engineering 24, 1055–1071 (1998)
12. Nuseibeh, B., Easterbrook, S.: Requirements Engineering: A Roadmap. In: 4th International Conferences on Software Engineering, pp. 35–46. ACM Press, New York (2000)
13. Davis, A.: Operational Prototyping: A New Development Approach. IEEE Software 9, 70–78 (1992)
14. Shaw, M., Gaines, B.: Requirements Acquisition. Software Engineering Journal 11, 149–165 (1996)
15. Visual Paradigm: Visual Paradigm for UML (2013), http://www.visual-paradigm.com/
16. Sparx Systems: Enterprise Architects (2013), http://www.sparxsystems.cn/products/ea/
17. Balsamiq. Balsamiq Mockups (2013), http://balsamiq.com/products/mockups/
18. Adobe Systems: Adobe Photoshop (2013), http://www.adobe.com/cn/products/photoshop.html
19. CollabNet: ScrumWorks Pro (2013), http://www.collab.net/downloads/scrumworks
20. Wiki Books. Wiki Page (2013), http://en.wikibooks.org/wiki/Wikipage
21. Syncro Soft.: TestLink (2013), http://testlink.org/
22. Apache.: Subversion (2013), http://subversion.apache.org/
23. Atlassian.: Jira (2013), https://www.atlassian.com/zh/software/jira
24. Rally Software: Rally (2013), http://www.rallydev.com/

Support Method to Elicit Accessibility Requirements

Junko Shirogane

Tokyo Woman's Christian University, Japan
junko@lab.twcu.ac.jp

Abstract. Various accessibility guidelines have been developed to meet the increased demand for accessible software, but due to the numerous elements within these guidelines, applying all elements to target software is burdensome and expensive. Additionally, whether all the elements should be applied depends on the software's purpose and target end users, who do not often clearly recognize difficulties. Moreover, accessibility requirements elicited in the late software development phase cannot always be applied. To ensure that these requirements are implemented properly, they must be elicited in the early software development phase by considering end users' conscious and unconscious characteristics. Here a method to elicit accessibility requirements in the early software development phase is proposed. Specifically, end users complete checklists, which are designed to determine disabilities with respect to guidelines. Then guideline elements are prioritized and applied to the target software as specified by the accessibility requirements.

Keywords: requirements elicitation, accessibility requirements, accessibility guideline.

1 Introduction

Accessibility requirements for software have been increasing. For examples, Section 508 [1] in the United States and JIS X 8341 [2] in Japan have been implemented. Accessibility means that various people, including the challenged and elderly people, can use software and websites easily. User interfaces are especially important because people directly interact with them. Most software uses GUIs (Graphical User Interfaces), which people operate visually, but people with visual limitations have difficulty and require specific support tools and devices. Thus, software must be developed considering the end users' characteristics (e.g., disabilities, age, etc.) to design accessible software and the proper support tools.

Many guidelines have been developed to realize accessibility (e.g., Web Content Accessibility Guidelines 2.0 (WCAG 2.0) [3] and JIS X 8341-3). In addition, companies and organizations have developed their own accessibility guidelines where problematic situations and their resolutions are described in detail. Consequently, the vast number of elements in guidelines is an issue. When guidelines are applied to software, the applicability of each element must be confirmed.

D. Zowghi and Z. Jin (Eds.): APRES 2014, CCIS 432, pp. 210–223, 2014.

This confirmation process is necessary for general use software, but not all software is intended for general use (e.g., for institutional use). In these cases, some elements are not required based on the software's purpose and the end users' characteristics.

In addition, some guideline elements can be applied in the late software development phase, whereas some cannot. To resolve these problems, it is necessary to elicit accessibility requirements in the early development phase and determine which elements within the guidelines to apply.

Moreover, it is possible that the accessibility requirements are not appropriately elicited. Because end users are often unable to recognize difficulties when using software, they cannot identify current disabilities. Hence, accessibility requirements should be elicited while considering these people.

In this research, we propose a method to analyze end users' characteristics and elicit accessibility requirements in the early development phase. Concretely, checklists are used to analyze the operational situations and problems of end users. Based on this analysis, guideline elements are elicited as accessibility requirements with priorities. The proposed method can elicit end users' accessibility requirements directly and appropriately, and implement the all required accessibility requirements while simultaneously reducing costs and burden on software developers.

This paper is organized as follows. Section 2 describes related works, while the features of the proposed method is described in section 3. Section 4 shows the support strategies to challenged users. Section 5 provides a detailed description of this proposed method. Section 6 describes the simulation of this proposed method, and section 7 concludes our paper.

2 Related Works

Requirements can be classified into functional and non-functional requirements. Functional requirements describe how to process inputs, while non-functional requirements define attributes that software should satisfy (e.g., security, reliability, usability, etc.). There are various types of non-functional requirements, and accessibility requirements are non-functional requirements. Strategies of eliciting non-functional requirements differ from the types. Although many studies have examined security requirements (a type of non-functional requirements) [4][5], few have focused on accessibility requirements.

Baguma et al. have proposed a method to integrate accessibility requirements with functional requirements [6]. Functional requirements and non-functional requirements, including accessibility requirements, have been analyzed by User Centered Design (UCD) techniques [7]. In this analysis, user group profiles, personas, and scenarios are documented. User group profiles are characteristics of users. Personas are concrete examples of typical users, while scenarios describe how personas use the products. Then, accessibility requirements (AR) graphs are described using the Non-Functional Requirements (NFR) goal graphs approach [8]. Finally, use case diagrams, including accessibility requirements, are described. Because this method describes accessibility requirements and functional requirements in the same diagrams, their relationships can be clarified. However, this approach does not consider the priorities of accessibility requirements.

AccessOnto is an ontology-based tool kit for accessibility requirements [9] that provides a repository of accessibility guidelines and a specification language to describe accessibility requirements in user requirements documents. Items related to user interfaces, such as user agents, languages, guidelines, checkpoints, and user characteristics, are defined. Although AccessOnto easily describes requirements specifications, including accessibility requirements, accessibility requirements are not elicited.

Minon et al. have proposed a method to integrate accessibility requirements into a user interface development method [10]. Accessibility requirements, which are elicited using accessibility guidelines and standards, such as WCAG [3] and ISO 9241-171:2008 [11], are described as task models of UsiXML (USer Interface eXtensible Markup Language) [12] of UIDL (User Interface Description Language) [13]. The task models are transformed into an Abstract User Interface (AUI) model of UsiXML that includes accessibility requirements. Because this method has high affinity with UIDL, accessibility requirements are easily integrated into user interface development methods. However, accessibility requirements are elicited using existing accessibility guidelines and standards. Because situations and levels of disabilities vary by end user, costs and burdens hinder software development. Thus, it is necessary to prioritize requirements after eliciting them from end users.

3   Features of the Proposed Method

Elicitation of Accessibility Requirements in the Early Software Development Phase

Regardless of their importance, some requirements elicited in the late software development phase cannot be realized. Although accessibility requirements to change color and font size using GUIs may be reasonable, preparing specific functions and support tools may not. Thus, it is necessary to elicit specific accessibility requirements in the early software development phase.

We assume that this proposed method is used in the requirements elicitation phase, which is part of the early software development phase. Hence, all requirements should be implementable.

Realization of Software Based on Detailed End Users' Characteristics

Because situations and levels of disabilities vary from person to person, the requirements differ. Software must be developed based on end users' situations and levels of disabilities.

In the proposed method, the situations and levels of disabilities are analyzed in detail. Then the accessibility requirements are prioritized, allowing software to be more appropriately developed for end users.

Reduction of Costs and Burdens

Eliciting requirements in the late software development phase causes iterations and the development returns to the early phase. In addition, applying accessibility guidelines requires software developers to confirm the numerous elements in the guidelines, which is expensive and burdensome.

In this proposed method, accessibility requirements can be elicited in the early software development phase. Because end users' characteristics are analyzed in detail, the scope of accessibility requirements can be tailored to the end users. These features can reduce the cost of burden on software developers.

4 Support Strategies to Challenged People

Many guidelines have been developed to make software accessible, but each person has a different level and situation of disability. When challenged people use software, they often use specific support tools, devices, and functions, which correspond to their situation. The availability of these tools and functions may be included in accessibility requirements.

4.1 Disabilities

Typical support strategies depend on the type of disability. Below are typical disabilities and their support strategies.

Blind Users. This is one kind of visual impairment in which people have completely lost their eyesight. Part of blind users can feel light, but cannot identify anything with their eyes.

Two types of basic support exist for blind users. One is that all contents should be described with text that is compatible with screen readers and braille displays. Screen readers are software to read texts on display, while braille displays convert texts into braille. Most blind people use screen readers. The other is that all contents should be operated with a keyboard. Blind users cannot identify where controls (e.g., links or buttons) are on display, so it is difficult to use a mouse.

Users with Weak Eyesight. Weak eyesight is another kind of visual impairment. In this disability, eyesight is barely corrected even if users wear glasses or contact lenses. Users can roughly identify things with their eyes, but their vision becomes inaccurate beyond a certain level.

There are two basic supports for users with weak eyesight. One is that small text and icons should not be used. These users can identify large texts and icons. The other is a function to adjust text size. Because the level of eyesight weakness varies by user, the text size must be adjustable to suit individual needs.

Users with Color-Vision Impairments. Color-vision is a third type of visual impairment. In this disability, users misidentify some colors (e.g., red, green, and blue). For example, users with this disability often have difficulty distinguishing between red and green.

There are two types of basic support. One is that contents should not be represented solely by color. For example, a description like "something is represented with red" should not be used. The other is a function to adjust the colors. Because color limitations differ according to the user, the color must be adjustable to suit individual needs.

Users with Hearing Impairments. In this disability, users have difficulty or cannot hear voices or sounds. For these users, the basic support is that all contents of software should be represented as text that they can read with their eyes.

Physically Disabled Users. In this disability, users have limited control of their hands, arms, and/or fingers. These users often use various support tools and devices, such as a software keyboard or a track ball. Basic support is that the software must be compatible with these support tools and devices.

Elderly Users. Although elderly users are not considered as challenged users, they have similar difficulties with challenged users by aging. Thus, it is possible to support elderly users with similar strategies for challenged users.

4.2   Accessibility Guidelines

Accessibility guidelines include detailed descriptions and resolutions of common difficulties of challenged users. In the guidelines, each element describes a specific issue or its resolution. Elements often include implementation. Because many guidelines have been developed (e.g., WCAG 2.0 [3] and JIS X 8341-3 [2]), elements must be prioritized.

5   Elicitation of Accessibility Requirements

In the proposed method, accessibility guidelines are prepared by initially employing checklists to analyze end users' characteristics. Associations between the questions in these checklists and elements in guidelines are specified. Then based on the end users' responses, the levels and situations of difficulties are analyzed, and the strength of relevance between difficulties of end users and guideline elements are calculated as numerical values. Finally, the necessary guideline elements are extracted and prioritized as accessibility requirements. Figure 1 shows the architecture of the proposed method.

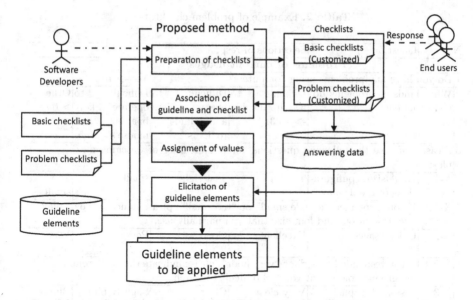

Fig. 1. Architecture of the proposed method

5.1   Preparation of Checklists and Accessibility Guidelines

Checklists. There are two types of checklists: basic and problem. Table 1 shows an example of a basic checklist.

Table 1. Example of basic checklists

No.	Question	Selections for response			
Situations of disabilities and abilities					
A-1	What is your eyesight?	Over 1.0	Over 0.3 and under 1.0	Under 0.3	None
A-2	Can you use braille?	No	Hardly	Almost can	Can
Usages of support tools and devices					
B-1	Do you use a screen reader?	No	Sometimes	Often	Always
B-2	Do you use a braille display?	No	Sometimes	Often	Always
B-3	Do you use a voice input system?	No	Sometimes	Often	Always
B-4	Do you use software to adjust view size?	No	Sometimes	Often	Always

Basic checklists include questions about the following:

− Situations of end users' disabilities
− Computer environments and configurations that end users use
− Support tools and devices that end users use, etc.

Table 2. Example of problem checklists

No.	Question	Selections of response			
		Problems of current usages			
1	Do you have any problems using computers?			Yes -> to 2.	No
2	What kinds of problems do you experience?	Difficult to watch display -> to 3.	Difficult to hear voices and sounds -> to 4.	Difficult to operate keyboards and mouse -> to 5.	Other -> 6.
3	Please response the following questions about difficulties of watching displays.				
	X-1	Font size configurations of the display	Too big	Just right	small	Too small
	X-1-1	If you responded "a little small" or "too small", please indicate the display size, resolution, and font size that you normally use.				
	X-2	Color usages	Excellent	Good	Poor	Very poor
	X-2-1	If you responded "poor" or "very poor", please indicate the background and foreground colors that you feel difficult to watch.				
	X-3	Vision of display	Very clear	Clear	Slightly blurry	Blurry

Problem checklists include questions about current usage problems. Table 2 shows an example of problem checklists.

Questions of checklists are associated to guideline elements, and there are various accessibility guidelines by governments, companies, and organizations. Additionally, important guideline elements may be different from software characteristics. Thus, templates for these checklists based on the policies of governments, companies, and organizations as well as currently realized support tools and devices were prepared. Because the actual templates can be customized, elements of various guidelines can be associated to checklist questions, and checklists can reflect the intended software characteristics.

Table 3. Examples of accessibility guideline elements

No.	Guideline element
	Usages of support tools and devices
1-1	All operations must performed by a keyboard.
1-2	All contents must be able to be read by a screen reader.
1-3	All contents must be able to be shown by a braille display.
1-4	Software to adjust view size must be available.
	Color usages
2-1	Contents must not be denoted solely by only colors.
2-2	Brightness contrasts of background and foreground colors must be sufficient.
2-3	System configurations must be applicable (e.g., color and font).

Accessibility Guidelines. In the proposed method, elements in the guidelines are elicited as accessibility requirements. Thus, the checklists and accessibility guidelines must be associated. We prepared our checklists based on the existing guidelines, such as WCAG 2.0 [3] and JIS X 8341-3 [2]. Table 3 shows examples of the guideline elements. If necessary, extra elements can be added.

5.2   Association of Guideline Elements and Checklist Questions

Questions in a checklist are associated with specific guideline elements. The association strength is identified as "Strong", "Medium", "Weak", and "None". The results indicate how each element should be realized during software development.

Table 4 shows an example of associations between checklist questions and guideline elements. Table 5 also shows an example of the association strengths.

The question numbers (e.g., "A-1" and "X-1") are from Tables 1 and 2, while the element numbers (e.g., "1-1" and "2-1") are from Table 3. Both the associations and association strengths can be customized.

Table 4. Example of associations between questions and elements

No.	Situations of disabilities
	Basic checklists
A-1	Determination of blind and levels of weak eyesight
A-2	Determination of braille display usages
B-1	Determination of blind, weak eyesight
B-2	Determination of blind, weak eyesight
	Problem checklists
X-1	Determination of levels of weak eyesight
X-2	Determination of types and levels of color-impairments
X-3	Determination of levels of weak eyesight

Table 5. An example of strength of associations

	A-1	A-2	B-1	B-2	B-3	B-4	X-1	X-2	X-3
1-1	Strong	Strong	Strong	Strong	Weak	Medium	Weak	Weak	Weak
1-2	Strong	Strong	Strong	Weak	Weak	Medium	Medium	Weak	Medium
1-3	Strong	Strong	Strong	Weak	Weak	Medium	Medium	Strong	Medium
1-4	Strong	Strong	Medium	Medium	Weak	Strong	Strong	Weak	Strong
2-1	Strong	Weak	Medium	Weak	Weak	Medium	Medium	Strong	Medium
2-2	Strong	Weak	Medium	Weak	Weak	Medium	Medium	Strong	Medium
2-3	Strong	Weak	Medium	Weak	Weak	Strong	Strong	Strong	Strong

5.3   Relevance of Assigned Values between Guideline Elements and Users' Responses

To analyze the situations and levels of users' difficulties, the strength between difficulties of end users and guideline elements must be calculated. Thus, the numerical values are assigned to the users' responses to checklists. Currently each response is assigned a value from 0 to 3, where 0 indicates that the support described by the question does not need to be considered, while 3 indicates that the support must be fully considered. Table 6 shows examples of assigned numerical values. The question numbers (e.g., "A-1" and "X-1") are from Tables 1 and 2.

Table 6. Example of numerical value assignments

Numerical values for responses	0	1	2	3
		Basic checklists		
A-1 What is your eyesight?	Over 1.0	Below 1.0 but above 0.3	Under 0.1	None
A-2 Can you use braille?	No	Hardly	Somewhat	Can
B-1 Do you use a screen reader?	No	Sometimes	Often	Always
B-2 Do you use a braille display?	No	Sometimes	Often	Always
B-3 Do you use a voice input system?	No	Sometimes	Often	Always
B-4 Do you use software of adjusting view size?	No	Sometimes	Often	Always
		Problem checklists		
X-1 Font size on display	Too big	Just right	Small	Too small
X-2 Color usages	Excellent	Good	Poor	Very poor
X-3 Vision of display	Very clear	Clear	Slightly Blurry	Blurry

In addition, numerical values are assigned to the levels of strength in Table 5. These values are used to calculate the necessity of applying guideline elements to the target software. Currently, 0, 1, 2, and 3 are assigned as "Strong", "Medium", "Weak", and "None", respectively. Table 7 shows the numerical value assignments to Table 5.

5.4   Elicitation of Guideline Elements as Accessibility Requirements

Based on the numerical values in Tables 6 and 7, guideline elements to be applied to the target software are specified and prioritized. The priorities are calculated in three steps.

Step 1. Based on the association strengths between basic checklists and guideline elements, the importance of each guideline element ($impB_{i-j,m-n}$) is calculated using the end users' responses via formula (1). $i - j$ indicates the number

Table 7. Example of association strenghs

	A-1	A-2	B-1	B-2	B-3	B-4	X-1	X-2	X-3
1-1	3	3	3	3	1	2	1	1	1
1-2	3	3	3	1	1	2	2	1	2
1-3	3	3	3	1	1	2	2	3	2
1-4	3	3	2	2	1	3	3	1	3
2-1	3	1	2	1	1	2	2	3	2
2-2	3	1	2	1	1	2	2	3	2
2-3	3	1	2	1	1	3	3	3	3

of a guideline element (e.g., "1-1" in Table 3), whereas $m - n$ indicates the number of a question (e.g., "A-1" in Table 1). $S_{i-j,m-n}$ indicates the value of association strength between guideline element $i - j$ and question $m - n$ in the basic checklists, and R_{m-n} indicates the value of users' responses to the question $m - n$.

$$impB_{i-j,m-n} = S_{i-j,m-n} \times R_{m-n} \tag{1}$$

Step 2. Similar to Step 1, the importance of each guideline element $(impP_{i-j,p-q})$ is calculated using the end users' responses via formula (2). $p - q$ indicates the number of a question (e.g., "X-1" in Table 2). $S_{i-j,p-q}$ indicates the value of association strength between guideline element $i - j$ and question $p - q$ in the problem checklists, while R_{p-q} indicates the value of users' responses to the question $p - q$.

$$impP_{i-j,p-q} = S_{i-j,p-q} \times R_{p-q} \tag{2}$$

Step 3. Finally, the priority of guideline elements is calculated by integrating the results of Step 1 and Step 2. Guideline elements with a higher priority can be specified as accessibility requirements of the target software. The priority is calculated using formula (3). $priority_{i-j}$ indicates the priority value of a guideline element $i - j$. $M - N$ and $P - Q$ indicate the maximum question numbers of basic and problem checklists, respectively.

$$priority_{i-j} = \sum_{m-n=A-1}^{M-N} impB_{i-j,m-n} + \sum_{p-q=X-1}^{P-Q} impP_{i-j,p-q} \tag{3}$$

After the priority values are calculated, the specified guideline elements are validated by generating prototypes. Previously, we have proposed methods to generate GUI prototypes from scenarios [14][15]. Then end users validate the methods to implement the guideline elements.

6 Simulation

A simulation was conducted to confirm whether the specified guideline elements are valid as accessibility requirements. Below is a summary of the simulated end user's situation. Table 8 shows select responses to the checklist where the question numbers (e.g., "A-1" and "X-1") are from Tables 1 and 2.

Basic checklist
- Have weak eyesight
- Use zoom software
- Sometimes use screen readers

Problem checklist
- Sometimes difficultly recognizing the display colors

Table 8. Select responses of the simulated end user

Basic checklists					
	A-1	A-2	B-1	B-2	B-3	B-4
Response	Under 0.3	No	Sometimes	No	Sometimes	Always
Value	2	0	1	0	1	3
problem checklists					
	X-1		X-2		X-3	
Response	Small		Poor		Slightly blurry	
Value	2		2		2	

Based on responses in Table 8, $impB_{i-j,m-n}$ and $impP_{i-j,p-q}$ are calculated using formulas (1) and (2). Tables 9 and 10 show the results.

Table 9. Calculation of $impB_{i-j,m-n}$

Guideline element No.	Question No.					
	A-1	A-2	B-1	B-2	B-3	B-4
1-1	6	0	3	0	1	6
1-2	6	0	3	0	1	6
1-3	6	0	3	0	1	6
1-4	6	0	2	0	2	9
2-1	6	0	2	0	1	6
2-2	6	0	2	0	1	6
2-3	6	0	2	0	1	9

Table 10. Calculation of $impP_{i-j,p-q}$

Guideline element No.	Question No.		
	X-1	X-2	X-3
1-1	2	2	2
1-2	4	2	4
1-3	4	2	4
1-4	6	2	6
2-1	4	6	4
2-2	4	6	4
2-3	6	6	6

Using the values in these tables, the priority values of the guideline elements are calculated by formula (3). Figure 2 shows the priority values of the guideline elements.

Using the values in these tables, the priority values of guideline elements were calculated by the formula (3) in 5.4. Figure 2 shows the priority values of guideline elements.

In this simulation, the average value of priority values of all guideline elements were calculated. The average value was 28.71 and shown in Fig. 2. Guideline elements were classified into two groups of higher and lower values than the average value. According to this classification, the following guideline elements have high priority values.

1-4: Software to adjust view size must be available.
2-1: Contents must not be denoted solely by colors.
2-2: Brightness contrasts of background and foreground colors must be sufficient.
2-3: System configurations must be applicable (e.g., color and font).

According to the checklist responses, the simulated end user has weak eyesight, uses zoom software, and occasionally experiences difficulty recognizing the display colors. Thus, the simulation specified appropriate guideline elements.

The following guideline elements have low priority values.

1-1: All operations must performed by a keyboard.
1-2: All contents must be able to be read by a screen reader.
1-3: All contents must be able to be shown by a braille display.

The simulated end user does not operate only by a keyboard and does not use braille displays. Thus, the priority values of guideline elements 1-1 and 1-3 are appropriately calculated. Although the simulated end user occasionally used a screen reader, the priority value of guideline element 1-2 is low due to the end user's response about the frequency of using a screen reader. The checklist questions result in a subjective gauge. However to specify appropriately guideline elements for the target software, the checklist questions must be improved so that

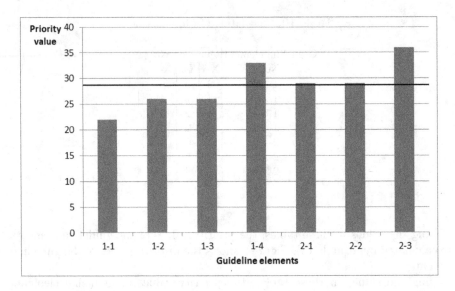

Fig. 2. Simulation results

end users' responses provide an objective gauge. In addition, the validity of the specified guidelines elements must be confirmed by end users.

However, according to this simulation results, almost all appropriate guideline elements are specified. Thus, this proposed method can appropriately specify the accessibility requirements.

7   Conclusion

In this paper, a method to elicit accessibility requirements is proposed by associating end users' disability situations and guideline elements. The calculated priority values are used to determine the priorities of the guideline elements. Although it is difficult to apply all guideline elements to the target software, the proposed method elicits the accessibility requirements in the early development phase and allows software to be appropriately developed based on end users' characteristics, reducing the cost and burden of software development. In addition, the appropriateness of the specified guideline elements is confirmed.

Future work includes:

- Confirming the numerical value appropriateness by simulating various end users' characteristics
- Designing checklist questions that objectively gauge end users' responses
- Evaluating the proposed method with actual challenged users
- Addressing challenges associated with the implemented guideline elements and automatically applying GUI prototypes

References

1. Section 508: http://www.section508.gov/u
2. Japanese Industrial Standards Committee: Guidelines for older persons and persons with disabilities-Information and communications equipment, software and services-Part 3: Web content, JIS X 8341-3 (2010)
3. Web Content Accessibility Guidelines (WCAG) 2.0: http://www.w3.org/TR/WCAG20/
4. Alexander, I.: Misuse Cases: Use Cases with Hostile Intent. IEEE Software 20(1) (2003)
5. Beckers, K., Heisel, M., Cote, I., Goeke, L., Guler, S.: Structured Pattern-Based Security Requirements Elicitation for Clouds. In: Proc. of 2013 Eighth International Conference on Availability, Reliability and Security, ARES (2013)
6. Baguma, R., Stone, R.G., Lubega, J.T., van der Weide, T.P.: Integrating Accessibility and Functional Requirements. In: Stephanidis, C. (ed.) UAHCI 2009, Part III. LNCS, vol. 5616, pp. 635–644. Springer, Heidelberg (2009)
7. Henry, S.L.: Just Ask: Integrating Accessibility Throughout Design, Lulu. Com (2007)
8. Cysneiros, L.M., Leite, J.C.S.P.: Nonfunctional Requirements: From Elicitation to Conceptual Models. IEEE Transactions on Software Engineering 30(5) (2004)
9. Masuwa-Morgan, K.R.: Introducing AccessOnto: Ontology for Accessibility Requirements Specification. In: Proc. of First International Workshop on using Ontologies in Interactive Systems, ONTORACT 2008 (2008)
10. Minona, R., Morenob, L., Martinezb, P., Abascal, J.: An approach to the integration of accessibility requirements into a user interface development method. Science of Computer Programming (April 29, 2013)
11. International Organization for Standardization: Ergonomics of human-system interaction – Part 171: Guidance on software accessibility (ISO 9241-171: 2008) (2008)
12. Limbourg, Q., Vanderdonckt, J., Michotte, B., Bouillon, L., Lopez-Jaquero, V.: USIXML: A language supporting multi-path development of user interfaces. In: Proc. of the 2004 International Conference on Engineering Human Computer Interaction and Interactive Systems (2004)
13. Guerrero-Garcia, J., Gonzalez-Calleros, J.M., Vanderdonckt, J., Muoz-Arteaga, J.: A Theoretical Survey of User Interface Description Languages: Preliminary Results. In: Proc. of Web Congress, LA-WEB 2009, Latin American (2009)
14. Shirogane, J., Fukazawa, Y.: A Method of Scenario-based GUI Prototype Generation and its Evaluation. ACIS International Journal of Computer & Information Science (IJCIS) 4(1) (2003)
15. Shirogane, J., Shibata, H., Iwata, H., Fukazawa, Y.: GUI Prototype Generation from Scenarios in the Requirements Elicitation Phase. In: Proc. of the 13th IASTED International Conference on Software Engineering, SE 2014 (2014)

Author Index